Memoirs of a Maverick Publisher

J. DAVID STERN

SIMON AND SCHUSTER · NEW YORK · 1962

LIBRARY OF CONGRESS CATALOG CARD NUMBER: 62-9610
MANUFACTURED IN THE UNITED STATES OF AMERICA

Sept 08 1992

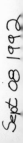

To Big Jill
for sixty years my sweetheart,
for fifty-three years my wife,
for thirty-five years
my fellow worker

Acknowledgments

I wish to thank my former associates for the considerable time they gave to jogging this old man's memory, which, at seventy-six, is as full of holes as a Swiss cheese.

Among many others who reminisced with me I am especially indebted to Harry T. Saylor, who joined me in 1915 to become my righthand man for thirty-two years; to Judge Harry E. Kalodner of the United States Court of Appeals, who played such a dramatic role in the development of the Philadelphia Record; to John A. Stevenson, now president of Greystone Press; to my nephew David S. Loeb, now publisher of Food Trade News; to my loyal secretaries for so many years, Edward G. Maguire and Frank M. Murphy; to my daughter, Mrs. Jill S. Capron, one-time reporter on the Record; to my wife, who worked so hard editing women's pages, church pages and book review sections on five newspapers; and, last but not least, to Maurice Mustin and Joseph McGoldrick, the Gold Dust Twins, who performed so valiantly during the last days of the Record.

Contents

I

From Fighting Cock to Capon

If all Printers were determined not to print anything till they were sure it would offend nobody, there would be very little printed.

—Benjamin Franklin

"As the only newspaper, we don't want to tread on anyone's toes."

Harry T. Saylor, managing editor, made this remark at our first editorial conference after the Camden (N.J.) Courier became a monopoly newspaper in 1926. I had just bought its competitor, the Post-Telegram.

Harry's words annoyed me. I had not foreseen this side effect of becoming a monopoly publisher.

"You mean we're to have no editorial policies?" I interrupted.

"Sure we have editorials," Harry reassured me. "But less noisy ones. Why make the opposition so furious they burn you in effigy as they did at last election?"

That hurried meeting was a turning point in my career. Crowded into my small office on the third floor of the ramshackle Courier Building were the key men in a hectic six-year newspaper war, an old-fashioned free-for-all with no holds barred. Besides Saylor, ex-professional ball player turned newspaperman, there was Al Haugh, assistant managing editor. Brilliant when sober, his weakness had cost him top positions on big-city papers. He was so able and likable we put up with his lapses, although they usually landed him in a police station at the end of a trail of property damage and mayhem. It was Al who offered my wife his sympathy: "I

9

know you never got a love letter from the boss because he can't write unless he's mad." Then there was Arthur Pierce, music lover, who, in return for complimentary tickets, wrote criticisms—and wrote them so well we had persuaded him to give up his job as civil engineer. He was to become chief editorial writer for all my newspapers. Youngest of the executives was Frank Ryan, city editor, who, against my advice, had transferred from composing to newsroom to prove he was a natural-born reporter and executive. A variegated crew, they were all excited and elated over our victory. The Courier had defeated the reputedly impregnable Baird machine, which had controlled South Jersey for twenty-five years. Now we could enjoy the rewards of monopoly: more profits and less work.

But Saylor's sound advice took the tang out of my triumph. Had I traded my fighting cock of a newspaper for a capon? Would dull routine replace the stimulation of competition? Just before it sold out, the Post-Telegram had bellowed across its front page, DAVE STERN IS A DIRTY DOG. The Courier did not refute the charge, but I enjoyed the last laugh. The night the headline appeared I met David Baird, Jr., publisher of the Post-Telegram, at a public dinner. I shouted across the room, "Dave, you know what a dirty dog does to a post." In those days of personal journalism, such exchanges between publishers were not unusual.

Now all contention was over. My capon newspaper waxed fat with higher earnings than anticipated, while my job as publisher grew tiresome. So I went hunting for trouble and found it. In 1928, I bought the Philadelphia Record, bottom of the heap of six keenly competing dailies and five Sundays. In 1933 I took on the New York Evening Post, low sheet on the totem pole of nine struggling for survival. I was pursuing the youthful dream which had lured me into journalism: that newspapers fought for causes, molded public opinion, determined government policies, constituted the fourth estate—with power equaling that of Lords, Commons and Clergy.

It was a vanishing dream. That type of newspaper, with editorial purpose and force, is fast becoming extinct in these United States. It has been replaced by today's monopoly newspaper, which serves a smooth mixture of many comic strips and syndicated features, with a minimum of wire stories and innocuous local news, as regularly and impersonally as other local monopolies supply gas. I use "monopoly" to designate a publisher without competition in his community, whether he issues one daily or a combination of morning, evening and Sunday editions.

The creeping blight of monopoly has engulfed the American press. Less than 10 per cent of our dailies are competitive. One publisher rules the roost in 1,417 of the 1,485 cities where daily newspapers are published. Of the 1,769 English language dailies in the United States (December 1, 1961) only 155 are in competition, and many of these 155 are losing money. Their publishers face the alternative of suspension or merging into a monopoly. At the present rate of consolidations, by 1970 competition will be reduced to a score of newspapers in our ten largest cities. The situation in New York is typical. Of its seven dailies, one is making a fair profit, two are breaking even, four are in the red.

In 1912, when I bought my first newspaper, the New Brunswick (N.J.) Times, there were nineteen cities in New Jersey with two or more competing dailies. Now monopoly newspapers serve all but two of these towns. It cost $50,000 a year to publish the Times. I paid compositors twenty dollars for a six-day week, and they never asked for overtime. Now compositors draw twenty-five dollars or more for a seven-and-a-half-hour day. Costs have increased twentyfold, which is faster than the dollar has gone down. But soaring costs are not the only cause of monopoly. Another is the growing importance of advertising in attracting readers. Half a century ago retail advertising was drab. It was poorly illustrated, if at all, with stock cuts, usually supplied by the newspaper. Food stores seldom advertised. As for national advertising, descriptions of patent medicines, often objectionable, predominated. In those days the man of the house chose his newspaper because of its editorials and news.

But as advertising developed bulk and attractiveness it became the dominant circulation factor. Women want the most complete catalogue of bargains and latest fashions. Realizing this, merchants tend to concentrate news of their stores in one newspaper. No longer does the man do the selecting. His wife demands the daily with the most advertising. Her appetite should be satisfied by some of our fat newspapers. The Los Angeles Times achieved a record in 1960 with eighty million lines of advertising, an average of ninety pages a day.

In 1940, American dailies averaged 24.15 pages a day, of which 10.4 were advertising, 13.75 news and features. In 1959 the figures were 37.5 pages a day, 23.11 advertising, 14.39 news and features. Advertising had increased 122 per cent, news and features five per cent. Capons have a tendency to put on fat faster than sinew.

The average reader cannot spare time to wade through all the ads in an oversize paper of sixty-four pages or more. It would be better for reader and advertiser, as well as for the publisher, if he charged more for advertising and limited the size of his paper. But such a policy would give his competition an advantage, and the slogan of newspaperdom these days is "Starve the opposition, make for monopoly."

Our system of piling personal on top of corporate income taxes is still another cause of newspaper mergers and monopolies. It makes it too difficult for a publisher to accumulate a nest egg to pay inheritance taxes and keep control of his newspaper in the family. After thirty-five years of fairly successful publishing, my safe-deposit box contained nothing but stock in my newspapers. Blame that on my appetite for more newspapers. But take the case of a man who stays put with one enterprise. He lives on his $50,000 salary, providently invests all dividends in sound securities, as a hedge against inheritance taxes and a protection for his family. But the government will take most of these dividends, 52 per cent in corporate income tax, and then two-thirds of the remainder for personal income tax. So he is allowed to retain less than $16 out of every $100 his company earns.

But he can sell his interest in the business for five million dollars, which, after capital-gains tax, will leave him with four million and a larger income than he had when he was working and taking risks. With such absurd tax laws it is a wonder there are not more mergers of newspapers and other businesses. Largely because of this double taxation, 560 American dailies, with 40 per cent of the national circulation, are owned by chains. Because chain managements vary so widely it is difficult to generalize on the effects of multiple control. Some chains maintain tight supervision of editorial policies. On the other hand, one of the most successful chain operators boasts that he pays no attention to news and editorial departments, only to the balance sheets of his many newspapers. The usual consequences of chain operation are much the same as those of monopoly. The hired manager hesitates to start a controversy which might get him in bad with the absentee owner. Most chain newspapers are robbed of initiative and enterprise.

Newspapermen blame the trend to monopoly and chain ownership on increasing competition from television, radio and magazines. In thirty years the newspapers' share of the advertising dollar has dropped from two-thirds to one-third. But whatever the causes, this change from a competitive to a monopoly press is unhealthy, sinister. It is making a travesty of our vaunted freedom of the press. For once established, the monopoly newspaper is impregnable.

What if the monopoly publisher is intensely partisan, unfair and unscrupulous? What if he opposes all public improvements and retards municipal development—or, just as bad, urges too many bond issues and bankrupts the town? Can public-spirited citizens establish another newspaper? Legally yes, practically no.

When I say a monopoly newspaper is impregnable I speak from experience. The citizens of Camden never tried to break my monopoly. But, because of a newspaper war across the river, the Philadelphia Inquirer twice attempted it with South Jersey editions. Both times they spent a lot of money but got nowhere. Camden merchants refused to advertise in the South Jersey Inquirer. Both Republican and Democratic officeholders tipped our city desk to news ahead of the intruder. It was the natural instinct of officials to keep in the good graces of the monopoly publisher.

Several times I was approached by disgruntled citizens of monopoly cities who offered to put up capital if I would establish a rival daily. While I never revealed their names, I did tip off the threatened publisher to watch his step. We monopolists stand by one another. Recently New England monopoly newspapers banded together to help a fellow monopolist, the Haverhill (Mass.) Gazette, drive out an intruder. In the course of litigation which grew out of this battle, the court found that "Haverhill is a one-paper area . . . what might be termed a natural monopoly . . . a city of that size [45,000] cannot support two good daily newspapers under present-day conditions." So now newspaper monopoly has the sanction of the law. To say that the judge was practically right, legally wrong, is to raise a fundamental philosophical question.

A newspaper monopoly is protected by many conditions of present-day publishing besides the high cost of competition. Even if they are furious at a vindictive publisher, the community's men of money are reluctant to invest in a second newspaper. The bank, the factory, the store, are vulnerable to attack by the established newspaper. They hesitate to stick their necks out in open revolt. Merchants generally are against a second newspaper. Even if they are paying high rates to the monopolist, they figure it would cost more to advertise in two newspapers.

Control of the circulation system gives monopoly a strangle hold. By its domination of newsstands, newsboys and suburban agents it can retard, if not prevent, the distribution of an intruder. It was such a conflict that Hearst encountered when he entered Chicago. Both sides employed strong-arm squads, and half a dozen men were killed in the gang warfare that ensued. When I sold the Springfield (Ill.) News-Record in 1919 I received a most attractive offer to take over the Kansas City (Mo.) Journal, which was withering under competition with the Kansas City Star. I was confident I could save the Journal until I looked into the circulation situation. The Star had such complete control I turned down the offer. Eventually the Journal died. When it was too late, the U.S. Department of Justice stepped in and convicted the Star of unfair competitive practices. A fine was paid but the Star still holds its monopoly in a city of half a million.

The habit-forming hold of syndicated comic strips and features gives the monopoly another advantage. Would newspaper readers welcome a change of entertainment in a new daily? They certainly

would not. Their appetite for features is similar to that of children
for bedtime stories. My children wanted the same tales repeated
over and over without change of a word. We grown-up children
crave the soothing repetition of the familiar rather than the stimulus of the new.

The high value publishers place on features in retaining or increasing circulation is illustrated by two incidents. In deference to
the government's request to conserve newsprint during World
War II, publishers of the four Philadelphia dailies met once a
month to devise ways and means to reduce paper consumption.
After polite greetings we sat around a table in silence. No one
wanted to risk an opening remark. A poker game of strangers,
holding their cards close to their vests, was a talkfest in comparison. After discussing such trivia as free papers to police and fire
stations we would adjourn with nothing accomplished. Once I
ventured a suggestion: "All of us are running two pages of comics.
Why not cut to one and save three thousand tons of newsprint?"
Dead silence was the only answer to my question. After a few
minutes one publisher looked at his watch and said, "I've got a
golf date." The meeting broke up and the embarrassing subject
was never mentioned again. During the greatest war in history
all four newspapers had cut news space to the bone but none of
my competitors dared to deprive his readers of their accustomed
escape "literature."

When the Philadelphia Evening Ledger suspended publication
in 1945, King Features Syndicate offered the Ledger's features,
Walter Winchell's column and three comic strips, to the highest
bidder. The Ledger had been paying $250 a week. I bid $600, the
Bulletin $650, the Inquirer $1,150. Figuring the worth of the
comic strips at $150, the Inquirer placed a value of $52,000 a
year on attracting Winchell fans. For half that amount it could
have hired a top-flight feature writer, but the present tendency is
to buy packaged features like brand-name goods in a supermarket.

The monopoly newspaper which runs popular features is insured
against competition. For it is an unwritten law of the trade that as
long as a publisher pays his bills he holds his features. A potential
competitor cannot bid them away from him. I know of only two in-

stances when this rule was broken. Just before Pearl Harbor I denounced William Randolph Hearst and Bertie (Robert Rutherford) McCormick, publisher of the Chicago Tribune, in such vitriolic terms that their syndicates cut off all services to my newspapers. I had persisted in personal journalism long after it had become outmoded. I survived the double assault, which inclines me to believe that syndicate features are overvalued and overplayed. But most dailies are more entertainment magazines than news journals. And the stronger the public addiction to syndicated features, the safer is the monopoly newspaper.

The lone newspaper is not only secure; it is also most profitable. Monopoly has lifted it from little to big business in its community and has correspondingly raised the status of the publisher. As owner of the Courier I associated with neighboring merchants, rarely met the heads of big industries. After I became a monopolist, and my gross soared well over a million a year, I drifted into the company of factory owners, bankers and utility tycoons. Instead of a quick lunch at the nearest grill, where I knocked elbows with the butcher and the baker, I was taking time out for a leisurely midday meal at the country club with the "gentry." Their company was pleasant but dull. They were so intent on their jobs they had little time for other interests. Every public question was weighed and measured by its immediate effect on each man's enterprise. "New water system? How much will it add to my taxes?" They were as shut off from the world as women in a harem. Secretaries substituted for eunuchs to guard their bosses from outside contacts. Occupied with technical reports and trade literature, they had little time for outside reading. I have a reporter's hunch that when Krupp and Thyssen were giving Hitler millions of marks they were too busy to read *Mein Kampf*.

Sometimes this detachment of big business was hard to believe. While thumbing through a magazine in 1928, I noticed an ad for the "largest table ever built, to seat 64." I sent it to the city desk with a note: "Might be for Pa. R.R. If so good story." I had forgotten it when Elisha Lee, executive vice president of the Pennsylvania Railroad, phoned me. "Dave, it's our table, but please no publicity—sounds too ostentatious."

"Why shouldn't the biggest railroad in the world sport the biggest table in the world?" I teased Lee, but agreed to kill the story. Having won his point, Lee said, "It's a remarkable piece of furniture. Come to lunch next Tuesday and I'll show it to you in our new board room." We lunched with General W. W. Atterbury, president of the railroad, and a half-dozen executives. Hothouse strawberries from the Atterbury "farm" were served for dessert.

"General, if you can grow strawberries like these you ought to give up railroading for farming," one guest remarked.

"Fine advice," Atterbury replied. "All I make as a railroader I lose as a farmer. These berries cost me a dollar apiece."

"You must be for the McNary-Haugen Bill," I said, referring to the controversial farm-relief bill twice passed by Congress and twice vetoed by President Coolidge.

"Perhaps I would be if I understood it," Atterbury said. "Can you explain how it works?"

"As head of the biggest grain-mover in America you know more about the bill than I do." I backed off. I thought he wanted to get me into an argument about the many editorials I had written in favor of the plan.

"Perhaps I should, but honestly I don't," Atterbury persisted. "And I don't think my associates are any better informed. Please give us a briefing."

"The General is trying to pull my leg," I said, turning to Elisha Lee. These top officials could not be ignorant of major legislation which so directly affected their railroad. Finally I was persuaded to give a short explanation. It was an hour before they ran out of questions.

＊　　　＊　　　＊　　　＊　　　＊

Of course there were exceptions to this single-purposed concentration among the business leaders I met. Wilfred W. Frye, president of N. W. Ayer & Son, a leading national advertising agency, was devoted to establishing Y.M.C.A. centers and similar recreational facilities throughout South Jersey. Eldridge R. Johnson, founder of the Victor Talking Machine Company, was interested in beautifying drab Camden with parks and works of art. But among half a hundred entrepreneurs with their noses to the grindstone I recall only these two men who had outside interests. And even a generous altruist like Johnson eventually became blinded by the big-money smog. Just after I bought the Philadelphia Record he complimented me on my campaign to clean up the Delaware River so that the people would not have to drink chlorinated sewage. "The pollution is terrible," Johnson said. "It's ruined the paint on my new yacht."

Most monopoly publishers are suffocating in this plutocratic atmosphere. They travel with big businessmen, think like big businessmen and talk like big businessmen. They may call themselves independent and claim to be impartial, but when the chips are down on any crucial issue, nearly all of them will be found in the big-business camp.

If newspaper publishers had not been so detached from their readers they would not have been so bitter and extreme in their denunciation of the New Deal in 1936. On the New Deal side were but a handful of metropolitan papers, the St. Louis Post-Dispatch, the Louisville Courier-Journal and my newspapers, the New York Post and the Philadelphia Record. Through a virulent verbal barrage by ninety per cent of the press, the voters marched to the polls to give President Roosevelt the largest majority in history. That election marked the end of American newspapers as a force in national politics.

Loss of influence is not the saddest catastrophe. Even worse, our newspapers are growing dull, and dullness to a newspaper is what loss of beauty is to a woman. By misconduct a beautiful woman may forfeit social standing, but wrinkles and fat mark the final tragedy. Few newspapers can withstand monopoly's enervating effect. Lack of competition lowers morale from editor to cub reporter. Much of newspaper work is routine. The same stories have a way of recurring. A common repeater is the recluse found dead in his room or shack. Rarely does such a tragedy prove newsworthy. But competitive reporters will dig for the one chance in ten of a story—the deceased was once a person of note or a miser who lived in penury to accumulate a fortune. The lone reporter for a monopoly newspaper accepts the police report. A buddy of the department, his tendency is not to discover additional facts which might embarrass his friends. This difference between competitive and monopoly reporting applies to stories of greater public importance. The capon is a lethargic and lazy bird.

Is dullness slowing the growth of our newspapers? Our population is increasing at the rate of 1.85 per cent per annum, newspaper circulation at the rate of less than one per cent. Net paid daily circulation in this country for 1961 was 60 million—333 per thousand population; in Great Britain it was 573 per thousand, in Sweden 464 per thousand. Newspapers blame their arrested growth on radio, television and neighborhood weeklies in metropolitan areas. An equally important factor is the lack of incentive for a monopoly newspaper to increase circulation. A five-cent monopoly newspaper, averaging thirty-two pages per edition, loses money on circulation, makes its profit from advertising. To justify higher advertising rates it must show a 10,000 increase in circulation. But this will cost $50,000 for promotion, plus high delivery expense to suburban areas. While making this drive for new readers, net profits will be reduced. A similar local monopoly situation kept farmers from obtaining electricity until President Roosevelt, in 1935, initiated rural electrification, financed by the government. Local electric monopolies did not want to cut present profits for future growth. The capon is an unambitious bird.

In a nation dedicated to free enterprise and a free press, the monopoly newspaper is a perplexing paradox which breaches both these fundamental principles. Where technology has made monopoly necessary it is either government-owned (water system, post office) or government-regulated (telephone, electricity, gas). But in the field where monopoly is most obnoxious, the press, it is unregulated.

The Department of Justice has brought a few actions against monopolistic press practices. I have already mentioned the suit against the Kansas City Star—where the government locked the barn door after the horse was stolen. In *United States v. Associated Press*, 1945, the Supreme Court ruled, five to four, that the First Amendment's freedom of the press does not include freedom to keep others from publishing newspapers. The Associated Press was ordered to discontinue exclusive memberships and sell its service to all newspapers which wanted it. In 1955 the government won a District Court conviction against the New Orleans Times-Picayune for monopolistic practices in restraint of trade. In another five-to-four decision the Supreme Court reversed the lower court on the ground that the government had not shown damage to the Times-Picayune's competitor, the Item, of which my son Tom (David Stern III) was publisher. During this litigation the Item had been barely breaking even. In the recession of 1958, the Item began to lose money. Tom sold to the Times-Picayune, and another great city became "blessed" with a newspaper monopoly. As A. J. Liebling's "Wayward Press" explained it, the Times-Picayune backed Tom "into a corner and shoved $3.5 million into his navel."

Uncle Sam is not to blame for the economic developments which have produced a monopoly press. His legal eagles are shackled not only by the First Amendment but also by the court ruling that a losing newspaper cannot be prevented from selling out to its competitor. If two publishers want to merge, it is not too difficult for one of them to go into the red.

✸   ✸   ✸   ✸   ✸

But for a shameful extension of local communication monopolies, blame rests on the government—and on President Franklin D. Roosevelt's first administration in particular.

"How do you feel about newspapers owning radio stations?" the President asked me in 1934, when the importance of this new method of mass communication was beginning to be recognized.

"It's against the public interest," was my answer. "And especially so in one-newspaper cities."

"That's the way I'm thinking," Roosevelt said. "And that's what I'm going to tell the FCC, but your fellow publishers are bringing a lot of pressure to get into the radio game."

As soon as I reached my home in New York that evening, Tom, then publisher of my Camden papers, had me on the phone. "Dad, I made a great deal with Mayor Brunner to buy the municipal radio station for ten thousand dollars. The city is losing twenty-five thousand a year. We'll make fifty thousand."

"Tom, we can't."

"Why not?"

"A few hours ago I told President Roosevelt he should not permit the sole publisher in a town to own a radio station."

Tom was fit to be tied. "Within the year they'll be dishing out radio franchises to newspapers," he predicted. He was so right. When I confronted the President with his shift in policy he was frank: "I've more important fish to fry on the Hill." At the time I did not blame him for his expediency. I knew how publishers were putting the heat on their Senators and Congressmen, who, in turn, were ganging up on the White House to grant radio licenses. A score of newspaper-owned radio stations seemed a small price to pay for New Deal legislation. Thus died the obviously sound policy against newspaper-radio, and later -television, monopolies. Between my first and second conversations with the President, Camden sold its radio station. It was not until 1946 that I acquired a radio subsidiary.

Today more than 750 radio and television stations are owned by newspapers. In 76 cities a monopoly daily owns the only radio station. Railroads must not control paralleling bus or truck lines. Steamship companies may not have interests in airlines. Suppliers of electricity and gas must be kept competitive. But, all hail consistency, the monopolistic combine of printing and broadcasting news is sanctioned.

The fat's in the fire. This unhealthy piling of monopoly on monopoly will never be corrected. Legislation to compel newspapers to divest themselves of radio and television subsidiaries has as much chance of success as a law making them pay the cost of second-class mail. Politicians are gun-shy of publishers, who are allergic to regulation. Any act which even remotely affects the newspaper business is denounced as an invasion of that holy of holies, freedom of the press. On this ground the American Newspaper Publishers Association opposed the National Recovery Act in 1934. I was the only publisher Old Iron Pants (General Hugh S.) Johnson, Director of NRA, could persuade to appear in his behalf at a U.S. Senate committee hearing. I testified that government regulations which applied to the manufacturing part of my business had no bearing on my freedom as an editor. I said in part: "If the board of health ordered me to clean up my toilets and I claimed that it was interfering with freedom of the press, I would be as great a hypocrite and villain as the man who falsely cries 'fire' in a crowded theater."

My fellow publishers berated me for advocating what they termed "an entering wedge to control of the press." So many newspapers were being run from their business offices they could not see the distinction between the two functions of publishing. In 1936 I resigned from the A.N.P.A. when it passed a resolution recommending that its members neither recognize nor even bargain with the Newspaper Guild. This was illegal defiance of the Wagner Act, an important New Deal measure, passed in 1935, which required employers to deal with the elected representatives of their employees.

✿   ✿   ✿   ✿   ✿

I had plenty of warning that the role of the newspaper was changing and that the daily journal of opinion was becoming obsolete. Adolph S. Ochs, most able publisher of The New York Times, kept cautioning me not to be so controversial and abrasive. "Just present the news fairly, and as fully as you can afford," he counseled. "Let your readers draw their own conclusions. Take sides and you make more enemies than friends." In his early days E. W. Scripps, the newspaper genius who founded the Scripps-Howard chain and the globe-encircling United Press International, wrote: "A good newspaper comforts the afflicted and afflicts the comfortable." But in old age he warned fellow publishers never to support a candidate who had any chance of winning an election, lest the newspaper be saddled with responsibility for the man when he took office.

Perhaps I am merely expressing the nostalgia of a retired publisher for the glamorous days of old when Greeley and Pulitzer never hesitated to call a spade a goddam shovel. The press of yesteryear was far from perfect. Partisanship was often distorting, crude and cruel. From the earliest days of the republic, its record is unsavory. Our first President was doused with vitriol. One newspaper even rejoiced at the death of the Father of his Country. Our

greatest President was called an ape and a gorilla. When Lincoln
delivered the most perfect prose poem in our literature, most of
the "gentlemen of the press" disgraced their profession by dis-
paraging the Gettysburg Address with such profundities as "We
pass over the silly remarks of the President" (Harrisburg Patriot
& Union) and "The cheeks of every American must tingle with
shame as he reads the silly, flat and dish-watery utterances of the
man who has to be pointed out to intelligent foreigners as the
President of the United States" (Chicago Tribune). As there was
only one foreign correspondent present at the dedication of the
battlefield, this Chicago reporter was "pointing out" Lincoln to the
London Times man who wrote: "The ceremony was rendered
ludicrous by some of the sallies of that poor President Lincoln.
Anything more dull and ludicrous it would not be easy to produce."
That "intelligent foreigner" was reflecting resentment of the
North's blockade of cotton shipments from Southern ports, which
had idled British textile mills.

Granted our old-fashioned partisan press smelled to high heaven,
it was the stimulating stench of human emotion. It roused the
nation to brave deeds and great accomplishment. A newspaper
was established to express a point of view. Publishers of the nineteenth century were concerned with public problems and they
made their readers share this concern. Political zeal frequently
exceeded the bounds of reason and decency, but it was an antidote
to complacency, which is the Achilles heel of a nation grown rich
and prosperous.

Today most newspapers—especially monopoly and chain newspapers—follow Saylor's formula and avoid treading on toes. But
there never was a worthwhile reform which did not bruise someone's pedal extremities. Propose stopping stream pollution and the
chemical plant threatens to close, which will throw a thousand
employees out of work. Demand that school teachers be paid as
much as truck drivers and overtaxed home owners cry out in an-
guish. When the monopoly newspaper cannot avoid such a controversy it tries to be impartial.

"Impartial" is a tricky word. It is humanly impossible to be completely objective in thinking and writing. The publisher can be

sure a dispute is being handled fairly only when both sides complain that he is unfair. A letter from a student at the Columbia School of Journalism posed a question: "Does the New York Post permit editorial policy to influence its news reporting?" Harry Saylor, by that time editor of all my newspapers, wrote our answer. I liked it so well I used it as an editorial. An excerpt:

A proposed constitutional amendment comes up for consideration at Albany. The Post headlines "Child Labor Amendment up for Vote." The Herald-Tribune headlines "Youth Control Amendment up for Vote." Both papers are reporting the news. Or are they? The theory that news columns are reserved solely for facts, and editorial columns held sacred for opinion, is one of the hoariest pieces of bunk ever peddled to a class in journalism. We think it good for our readers to know the facts of life. We do our best to print both sides. But we are only human. So, thank God, are our competitors.

Child Labor or Youth Control Amendment? It is such conflict in news and editorials which stimulates public interest and thinking. Two points of view give perspective on public problems. This insight is denied communities served by monopoly newspapers. The spirited arguments of yesteryear have been replaced by polite conversation which avoids subjects that might give offense. "I can take anything but an evening of polite conversation," my friend Arthur Garfield Hays used to say.

The monopoly newspaper's tact and restraint generate apathy, which reveals itself in the small percentage of citizens who take the trouble to go to the polls. Our nation's voting record is much below that of other democracies. How little grit the capon has in its gizzard.

But, looking back, I see two sides to the question. With old age comes double vision and the frustration of recognizing more than one solution to a quadratic equation. For thirty-five years, as publisher of seven dailies, I was so busy telling my readers what to think I had no time to think. As a fighting liberal I wrote thousands of editorials, always on the side of the angels. In a perpetual lather of altruistic zeal and righteous indignation, how certain I was as to the precise position of the heavenly host on the political horizon! Now, in retirement, I have time to think. No longer am I so certain or concerned as to just where the angels stand. No longer have I the urge to expound my views, political or otherwise.

But I do wish to record the significant change in newspaper making through which I lived and worked. Because at one time or another I was both a monopoly and a chain publisher, because, as cub reporter, I faked and distorted stories, I feel competent to recount the ills of the press. At a revival meeting the reformed bum rises to testify, "I drank and I whored and I rolled in the gutter. The wages of sin are death." The theory is that he who transgresseth is best qualified to warn of the consequences. And, at seventy-six, I still retain enough sense of humor to appreciate the serio-comic aspects of my publishing adventures. Ability to laugh at ourselves, according to Kipling, is the one faculty which separates man from beast.

In those publishing days there stood on my desk a small Buddha-like image of the great god Tell'em. To him the more superstitious members of my staff and I made obeisance before undertaking difficult assignments. Moistening a finger and rubbing saliva on Tell'em's bald head was the prescribed ritual. On that tense night in 1920, when we decided to raise the price of the Camden Courier from one to two cents, all my executives anointed Tell'em—all except one narrow-minded freethinker who disdained such pagan practices. In the early nip-and-tuck days, when I had to forage for cash to meet the payroll, I invoked the aid of the talisman before setting out on my unpleasant missions. It was often a close shave, but, thanks to Tell'em, I always managed to make the ghost walk. In retrospect, always meeting those payrolls was the most difficult achievement of my career—and the least appreciated.

Bewitchment by Tell'em is not confined to newspapermen. Politicians, preachers, hucksters, are intent on telling the world how to get rid of war or dandruff. Robert Frost says that the ruling passion in man is not sex but "minding each other's business." And the public is always ready to swallow the new recipe concocted by Tell'em's articulate spokesmen. In a fairytale world we grown-up children are eager for an open sesame, the magic words which will unlock the door to our heart's desires. Nor is faith and credulity shattered when the formulas fail, when the United Nations does not achieve world peace or when prohibition does not prove a panacea. An undiminished audience still watches the door to see if the next cure-all slogan will make magic.

Tell'em claimed me at the age of nine, when I was given a mimeograph machine and published a family weekly. From the thrill of telling uncles, aunts and cousins developed an appetite for a wider forum. To own a daily in which I could guide my readers to the millennium became my youthful obsession.

I could not foresee that the American press would trade its political power for profit and that the editorial page would deteriorate into a journalistic vermiform appendix, vestige of a forgotten function, to which publishers pay little attention and the public even less. I did not notice that in the newspaper-trade symbol, the proud rooster atop the N E W S weather vane, was turning into a capon.

But that is what happened between my start as a cub reporter in 1908 and my retirement in 1947. And that is what this book is about.

II

Cub Reporter

"And you!"

Assistant city editor Weber, confronted by the new cub, did not conceal his annoyance.

That Weber used the same words as Caesar, when Brutus stabbed him, sticks in my memory. It was an important occasion, my first chance as reporter on a big city newspaper. Weber had just finished handing out all the assignments in his day book to the other reporters, who had left. He had overlooked the most recent addition to his staff. Because I was "on space," paid only for what I was fortunate enough to have printed, he felt obligated to give me a chance to earn carfare. The two of us were alone in the cavernous newsroom of the Philadelphia Public Ledger on that very hot and very dull Sunday of June, 1908. Weber sat scratching his ear with a pencil. I stood waiting before the city desk while my self-importance shriveled and shrank. Finally he clipped a corner from the church page and handed it to me.

"You might pick up a few shorts at meetings of spiritualists and other strange cults listed here." Then with a slow, kindly smile, "But youngster, don't be disappointed if you can't hit pay dirt this slowest of all Sundays." Although he called me "youngster" Herb (Herbert S.) Weber could claim only a few years more than my twenty-two. He was an unusually handsome man. My appraisal of his good looks was endorsed by Sarah Stilwell, the artist, who painted many covers for the Saturday Evening Post. Herb's slow smile had charmed her into marrying him. It spurred me to resolve I would bring back a story if I had to provoke a riot at a spiritualist meeting.

Among the notices Herb handed me was one of a Mazdaznanist

meeting, scheduled for 3 P.M. It looked like my best bet. In the Ledger library I found "Mazda, god of light, worshiped by Zoroastrians, oldest of Persian religions." When I rang the bell of a small row house in West Philadelphia a little old lady gingerly opened the door. I told her I was from the Ledger. She tried to slam the door but I had my foot in the jamb.

"Sister, I'm a devout follower of Zarathustra," I pleaded. "Just because I'm a reporter, would you shut me into outer darkness?" She let me in. Members began to arrive, a sorry lot of frustrated faddists. They practiced a form of yoga. To breathe correctly was to attain superhuman strength and wisdom. "If you breathe right, can you lift that piano?" I asked the frail old lady. "Of course," she answered. She refused to demonstrate. But let my first reporting speak for itself:

Fifteen followers of Mazdaznan philosophy were gathered yesterday afternoon in an attempt to gain Heaven through a proper use of their lungs. Slow, harmonic breathing is all that is necessary to attain this great end. Air is the link between man and God, the finite and the infinite, and once right breathing is accomplished, religion, law, ethics, morals, may be dispensed with.

The little parlor at 50 North Douglas Street became close and stuffy during the discussion of the principles, but the right-breathers never swerved from their rhythmic breathing or their attempt to reach the "Heights" through proper inhalation and exhalation.

The leader, Arthur Smith, was formerly a German university student. He is now in business in New York. Four years ago he was so stout from wrong breathing that he laced his shoes with difficulty. He became a Mazdaznanist, and is now the picture of health. Together with the ability to lace his boots Mr. Smith has attained a deeper insight into the meaning and mystery of life. All was accomplished by proper harmonic breathing—seven seconds for inhalation, eight seconds for exhalation, and keep your body relaxed and your mind concentrated. Now, together, please—

And so on for a column.

Because, as Weber had said, it was the dullest of Sundays, my copy was used in full on the front page. Of course it broke one of the basic rules of decent editing. The cub should have been told "Never make fun of a religious meeting," as his copy was thrown into the wastebasket.

Henry Wills, my senior on the staff by a week, came over to my desk to congratulate me on hitting the front page "first crack out of the box." He invited me for a nightcap at Green's Hotel across the street. Reporters, copyreaders, editors were lined up at the long bar. Everyone was there but the star reporter whom Henry had pointed out to me earlier in the evening.

Then the star made his entrance, tripped, sprawled on the floor and writhed in delirium tremens. An ambulance carted him off and we went back to the bar. A few rounds loosened tongues. I was told not "to get a swelled head because, on the dullest Sunday since Christ was born, my trivial tripe had been used to plug a hole in the front page." At three in the morning Henry suggested we join a crap game at the Pen and Pencil Club. It was a thrilling first day as a reporter. "This is the life for me," I thought, as I turned in at five.

Bleary-eyed, I reported for work at 1 P.M. Monday. Hank (Henry M.) Eaton, the city editor who had hired me, was back at his desk. A large, heavy-set man with shaggy sheep-dog hair, bushy eyebrows and clothes unpressed, an unlighted cigar stub in one corner of his mouth, he growled orders out of the other. An able newsroom executive, he did not overedit. "Don't pick fly dirt out of pepper," was the way he put it. "You have to sense how much correction a man can take without losing his zip, and usually your best men can take the least." A tough taskmaster, but his staff would have gone to hell for him.

I had obtained my job through a combination of brass and blunder. Armed with a letter of introduction I had gone to see the publisher, George Washington Ochs, younger brother of The New York Times' Adolph S. Ochs. I was ushered into an imposing office decorated with busts and pictures of Napoleon, to whom George Ochs bore a striking resemblance. As I recited my experience in amateur and college journalism, Ochs, a small, nervous man, kept fumbling papers on his desk. He cut me short with an abrupt,

"When we have an opening I will let you know." He rose, grasped my hand and led me to the door.

I took a seat in his outer office. I explained to his secretary, an elderly spinster, "I'm waiting for instructions from Mr. Ochs." When Ochs came out he stared as though trying to place me. "Stern is the name," I reminded him. "You promised me the next opening as a reporter."

"You don't have to wait here," Ochs barked. "I'll let you know."

"I prefer to wait here, Mr. Ochs," I mustered the nerve to reply.

The letter of introduction had come from my Aunt Fannie Muhr, an old friend of his family, so he hesitated to order me out of his office. He glanced at his watch and muttered, "I'm late for lunch. Haven't time to argue with you, young man, but it won't do any good to hang around here." During the rest of the day when Ochs went in and out of his office he looked the other way.

The next morning I was waiting for his secretary to unlock the office door. On the third day Ochs capitulated. He continued to ignore me when he said, "Miss Brown, ask Mr. Eaton to see the young man. He wants to be a reporter." My hunch is I had Miss Brown to thank for this surrender. We had become friends during my occupation of her office.

"So you're the young fellow who has been laying siege to the boss," Hank Eaton said and chuckled. "You look as though butter wouldn't melt in your mouth. If you've got that much brass, you're entitled to a try. You're on space, five dollars a column for what we print. Report here next Sunday at one."

Years later, when we had become close friends, Hank told me that a few minutes after he had given me the job, Ochs phoned him to say, "Don't hire that Stern boy."

"But I've already hired him. Why did you send him to me?"

"To get him out of my office," Ochs replied.

"If you know anything wrong, it won't take long to be rid of him. Have you some reason you don't want him here?"

"Not exactly, but he's that pushing type," Ochs explained. "Next thing he'll want to own the Ledger."

I have always questioned that last flourish to Hank's tale but he swore it was true. When I became publisher of the Philadelphia

Record George Oakes (he followed the example of Britain's royal family and anglicized his name during World War I) was most friendly and helpful. Through him I met his brother Adolph and both of them gave considerable time and attention to advising me. I have always felt that George's scholarly ability was overshadowed and thwarted by his dominating older brother. George Oakes' son, John B. Oakes, is now head of the editorial board of The New York Times.

My Monday assignment was to interview Dr. Charles L. Doolittle, Professor of Astronomy at the University of Pennsylvania, about an eclipse of the moon. In the Ledger library, I found an article by Doolittle on the eclipse. He was pleased that I had read it. He gave me additional data and a chart. Result: a column-long story.

On Tuesday I was sent to ask Rear Admiral George W. Melville, naval architect and Arctic explorer, why Philadelphia shipyards had lost a $50,000,000 contract to build warships for Brazil. Admiral Melville was a close friend of my Uncle Simon Muhr. As a youngster, I had sat on his knee while he told me horrendous tales of his Polar explorations. Melville Land, a large Arctic peninsula, commemorates his heroism as leader of expeditions. He had served as engineer on the *Monitor* in its battle with the *Merrimac*. Bald as a billiard ball, from his shining dome descended copious cascades of white hair, both front and back, a full beard halfway down his chest and long locks over his shoulders. When my sister Agnes said he wore his hair that way because he never changed his shirt, I was able to refute this insult to my hero. From the vantage point of his lap, I could peek behind his beard and see that he was wearing a clean shirt.

"Davy, we've got to concoct an interview which will compel attention," said the old Admiral, stroking his beard. "A new bearing on a grave danger to our nation."

"Because labor unions will not let a skilled workman teach his trade to his own son! That is the reason the United States lost the $50,000,000 contract for ships for the Brazilian Navy" was the lead we worked out together. "One apprentice to every four workmen is what the unions are pleased to allow in the shipbuilding trades."

Then he went on to tell of his apprenticeship in the East Brooklyn Engine Works. "Of every five boys who entered that shop with me, only one remained the full time . . . Only a small percentage of those who sign on as apprentices stick to the trade." The interview ran on the editorial page next to an editorial on the subject.

On Wednesday I was sent to interview Leonard White, a public school janitor. In a letter to the Mayor, D. Clarence Gibboney, secretary of the Law and Order Society, had accused the Board of Education of employing criminals who endangered the morals of school children. He cited White's long police record as one instance. Gibboney's letter, obviously politically inspired, was given front-page play by all the Philadelphia newspapers. Hank Eaton was the only city editor who assigned a reporter to find out what White had to say.

He had nothing to say. A punch-drunk former strong-arm man for the numbers racket, he was inarticulate. But I persuaded his wife to let me write a piece which might be helpful. With this leeway, I composed what the lawyers call a plea of confession and avoidance which delighted all the enemies of the strait-laced reformers. The story in part:

There was no lamp in the room, but near the window the bowed head of the wife, buried in her hands, was silhouetted against the light from the street, and the breathing of the big man in the shadow came brokenly.

"Why does Gibboney want to break me?" he said at last. "Why don't he think of robbing a man of his last chance to make good? Why don't he think of my wife, here, who never did a wrong thing in her life, except stick by me? Why don't Gibboney think of those things when he sets out reforming?

"Why do they begrudge me this work? Surely it's no cinch! From 6 in the morning till 7 at night I must be working and the wife here helping me a good part of the time. In winter I have to go to work at 5 or earlier to get the furnaces going and the place heated up for the kiddies. And what do I get for it? Fifty-eight a month; just an honest

living. I ain't walking around with a high hat and diamonds. I've just enough to live honestly and decently. Why do they want to ruin me?

"What's the use of asking? I'm not so young that I don't know what it means. I'm just a deuce spot in a political game. One of the big men wants to show up another big gun, and so he shows me up—ruins me and the little woman over there.

"Gibboney says I am liable to demoralize the children, does he? If he was out for the good of the kiddies he'd send word to me to resign. He'd give me a chance to lead an honorable life."

The next day Hank told me to get the reaction to my story. He gave me a list of civic leaders to interview. One of them was Judge Meyer Sulzberger, Philadelphia's most prominent and articulate Jew. At the end of the day I found the Judge sitting on the marble stoop of his home on Girard Avenue. He said that he was glad the story had appeared because it showed "Gibboney is a hypocrite." As I was leaving, he added, "Tell whoever wrote that story it was worthy of Dickens." The Judge's obiter dictum resolved any lingering doubts in my mind as to whether I should become a lawyer or a reporter.

A hole in one, a royal flush, throwing seven six times—it happens once in a lifetime. I had a column or more every day of that first week. Henry Wills helped me paste up my long "string" of eight columns, one hundred sixty inches, which came to forty dollars, a senior reporter's pay in those days. Looking back it was a most thrilling week. But I was too excited and eager to enjoy my happiness.

The following Monday Hank called me to his desk.

"Young Stern, you've made a good start." He removed the cigar butt for greater force and clarity. "You've done so well I'm making an exception. Instead of keeping you on space for the usual three months, I'm putting you on regular salary, fifteen dollars a week."

I was too stunned to protest. What a cockeyed system—my first raise was a cut from forty to fifteen dollars. When I became a publisher and checked cash vouchers myself, as Ochs did, I understood what had happened. Ochs had wanted to know why a cub reporter

made forty dollars. In those days we worked from one in the afternoon to one the next morning, six days a week, and no overtime
pay. The average reporter's salary was twenty-five dollars, thirty-
five cents an hour. When I retired in 1947, a reporter's pay for a
five-day, thirty-seven-and-a-half-hour week averaged three-fifty an
hour. After a month Hank did give me a five-dollar raise but,
though I covered important stories, twenty dollars was my top on
the Ledger.

One of these stories had to do with prostitution and gambling
in Atlantic City. Mid-Victorian Hank did not want a woman to
handle it. He sent me to replace Ruth Hale, the only woman reporter on the staff. During July and August Ruth always drew
the prize assignment of Atlantic City, which put her in a beach-
front hotel at the paper's expense. Ruth, a striking blonde, in evening clothes, met me in the hotel lobby. "What is your message,
young man?"

"Mr. Eaton sent me to take over the Kuehnle-Delaney fracas."
I could feel her fury as I hastened to add, "Mr. Eaton feels a lady
should not tangle with this story."

That did it. Ruth, later to become the wife of my friend, the
gifted columnist, Heywood Broun, thought she could cover any
story better than any man could. She was an ardent disciple of
Lucy Stone, pioneer feminist. Hank and the Ledger were cursed
so loudly the whole lobby came to attention. She had slaved for
that ungrateful blankety-blank Eaton and here was her reward.
Because she was a woman, he was taking her off the only important
story in Atlantic City. I was about to suggest we call Hank and
arrange to work together when she turned on me.

"And who does he send to take over? A little four-eyed shrimp
of a cub who isn't dry behind the ears."

My urge to be chivalrous evaporated. I told Ruth to take up her
troubles with Hank and left.

A college chum, Morgan Dewitt Blair, was in Atlantic City,
training racehorses for Samuel D. Riddle, later Mayor of Atlantic
City. Blair gave me the inside dope. While Atlantic City's summer
population swelled to a quarter of a million, more than half of the
25,000 permanent voting residents, in 1908, were Negro hotel em-

ployees. Whoever controlled this Negro vote controlled Atlantic City. Instead of paying cash for gambling and vice concessions, the underworld had worked out a barter system—so many votes per concession: fifty votes for a roulette wheel or crap game, ten votes for each woman in a house of prostitution, etc. By this arrangement the boss never touched vice money. His take was from municipal contracts and boardwalk concessions. Through Blair I got the first interview ever granted by Commodore Kuehnle, boss of Atlantic City. He explained that in the "Playground of America" there had to be some leeway. Soon after, Kuehnle went to the penitentiary.

My Atlantic City stories made a hit with Hank. They were given front-page play with art. That I had made good was indicated a few days later when I was assigned to a heavy story usually handled by a senior reporter.

The North American, the Ledger's most aggressive competitor, had been waging a crusade against railroad freight rates which diverted export shipments from the port of Philadelphia. The North American insinuated that the Pennsylvania Railroad had a secret agreement with the other big rail systems. If its competitors would stay out of Philadelphia, the Pennsylvania would join with them in developing New York as the chief port on the East Coast. The conservative Ledger, under New York ownership, had given little space to the controversy. Now it felt it had to get in on this civic movement.

Chairman of the Philadelphia Port Committee was Frank Neall, president of Peter Wright & Sons, established in 1818, Philadelphia's oldest and largest shipping agent. Neall had resigned as a director of the Pennsylvania because of what he contended was the railroad's discrimination against Philadelphia. During his unequal contest with the richest railroad in the world, he made a collection of freight-rate data which was the most complete in this country. Behind his office at Third and Spruce he had built a large library, its walls lined with books and pamphlets. Two librarians were required to keep this material in order.

Hank warned me Neall might be hard to handle. He was certain to be suspicious of a newspaper which had been taking the side of the Pennsylvania Railroad. After hastily wading through the clips in the Ledger morgue, I went to Neall's office. He kept me waiting from three-thirty to six-thirty. Finally, I was ushered into a room which seemed to whisper, "Please remember this firm is a century old"—dark paneling from floor to beamed ceiling, cannel coal burning in an old brick fireplace equipped with shining brass implements of pre-stove cooking. Behind a Washington desk sat Neall, the grim crusader, a replica of Don Quixote. He was thin almost to emaciation. The severity of his expression made me hasten to tell him that the Ledger was changing its policy.

Neall, wary of Greeks bearing gifts, was curt. He gave me a short statement that it was time Philadelphia awoke to the way its port was being ruined. It was cheaper to send a ton of cement or steel from Bethlehem, Pennsylvania, 150 miles to New York than sixty miles to Philadelphia. New York and Jersey City piers were crowded while Philadelphia's were idle.

"The Ledger has not been fair to the Port Committee," said Neall. "I will hold you personally responsible that I am correctly quoted. Write your name on this pad."

"What was your father's name?" he asked after glancing at the pad.

"David Stern."

"Was he in business at Twelfth and Cherry? Did he serve in the Civil War? Did he die last year?"

I answered yes to all three questions.

Neall came from behind his desk, put his hands on my shoulders, and said, "So you're the son of my friend Dave Stern. He was a gentleman in the true sense of the word. I found that out when we first met. Sit down again. I must tell you about it. I was a sergeant, your father a new recruit in my squad. He was built like you but better looking. We had run out of rations and were foraging near Carlisle. While my boys searched a deserted farmhouse, I kept guard outside. They found plenty and ate it without saving a scrap for me. But when your father came out he handed me a loaf of bread and a jar of jam. I must have been terribly hungry from the way that sticks in my mind. We became friends, met frequently after the war, but drifted apart when your father moved to New York. I saw him for the last time, the year before he died, at a G.A.R. reunion.

"So now I have a chance to get even for that loaf of bread. You must handle this important story better than any other reporter. I can help you with material no one else has or can get. Come back into the library."

Neall gave me an intense briefing, loaded me down with reports, invited me to dine with him. I could not accept because I had to get back to the office.

Under his guidance, I ran away with the story, much to the annoyance of the North American, which had initiated it. The copy desk dubbed me "Statistical Stern." Hank unbent to say, "Young Stern, you're certainly a shark at figures." I did not tell him that the credit really belonged to my father, who had cast a loaf of bread on the right sergeant.

Frank Neall's long fight finally bore fruit. The Pennsylvania Railroad took cognizance of the public clamor and invited the Port Committee to a conference. General John B. Thayer, its executive vice president, a distinguished-looking and rather pompous individual, opened the meeting with an account of Philadelphia's development during the past fifty years in which the Pennsylvania Railroad had played such an important part. It grieved him to hear the canard that this great railroad system had ever been unmindful of the best interests of its home city.

After the usual shadowboxing, E. A. van Valkenburg, publisher of the North American, asked: "General, is it true that the Pennsylvania Railroad entered into an informal arrangement with competing transcontinental lines to develop the port of New York instead of the port of Philadelphia, in return for assurance that the other roads would not interfere with your virtual monopoly here?"

"That's a long question," parried General Thayer, "and it deserves a full answer. Before I reply, I'm going to excuse myself for a moment to go to the washroom." When he returned, he made a detailed denial of the charge. I did not include this denial in my story. I ended with van Valkenburg's question and a closing sen-

tence, "General Thayer left the room." The story read as though
Thayer had failed to answer. What possessed me to play this silly
trick? I was battling on the side of the angels, and my friend, Frank
Neall, against the big bad railroad. This crusading spirit was to
get me into plenty of trouble in future years.

If Hank had been on duty that night he would have caught the
hoax. Because I had been handling the story capably for two
weeks, the copy desk accepted it without question. The headline
played up the dramatic climax.

When I came in the next day, Hank was waiting for me.

"Young Stern, what have you gone and done?" The Pennsylvania's public relations people must have been giving him a rough
morning. One look at his grim face was enough.

"I guess I had better resign," I said in a weak voice.

"You sure had and right away," was Hank's verdict.

"I resign to take effect immediately."

"Accepted. You're off the Ledger staff as of now."

At that moment, George Ochs stuck his head through the door
and asked, "Where's that Stern?" in a loud shrill voice. When he
caught sight of me, he said, "Stern, you're fired."

"You can't fire me, Mr. Ochs," I declared with what was left of
my dignity.

"Why can't I fire you?" This time his voice was higher than Lily
Pons' but not so melodious.

"Because I resigned before you came in."

Ochs slammed the door.

"You beat him to it by thirty seconds," said Eaton. "So now that
you have resigned instead of being fired, your reputation as a
reporter is unblemished." He turned his back on me. I picked up
my belongings from my desk and left.

I began to realize what an awful breach of trust I had committed. I had betrayed my friend and hero, Hank Eaton. My reporting career was over.

Still I had the nerve to walk into the North American office and
send my name to van Valkenburg. Although three generations removed from his Holland ancestors, he had a long Dutch face end-
ing in a jutting chin which seemed not to fit his quick abrupt

speech and nervous mannerism. He had been publisher of an up-state daily when he managed John Wanamaker's campaign for the United States Senate. Tom Wanamaker, John's son, was so impressed with his father's campaign manager that he bought the North American to provide Van with a vehicle for cleaning up Philadelphia.

Van welcomed me in great good humor.

"That was a fine story in the Ledger this morning. How did you manage to slip it over on the old lady of Chestnut Street (nickname for the Ledger)?" Then, without waiting for an answer, "I've been watching your work, young man. You've the makings of a reporter. If you're free, we might find a place for you."

"I've resigned from the Ledger, Mr. van Valkenburg. If I hadn't resigned, I would have been fired. I'm ashamed of that story. My only excuse is that your editorials had me so worked up I blew my top."

"How would forty dollars do as a starter?" van Valkenburg asked.

"That would be fair."

He picked up the phone. "Mr. Benn, I'm sending Stern to you—the young fellow we talked about. Put him on at forty dollars—yes, today." Van Valkenburg held out his hand. "Good luck, and glad to see you any time."

How come? One hour after I resigned from the Ledger in disgrace, I was on the North American at double my former pay.

To add to my confusion Henry Wills phoned me the next day to say that just because I was working at the North, I didn't have to drink with those bums and I should show up at Green's bar "as per usual."

When I rejoined the Ledger boys, they ribbed me plenty. Dave Smiley, the slot man (head of copy desk, so-called because he sits in a slot in the copy table), had been held responsible for passing my story. He told me it was a disgraceful trick for which, in any decent society, I should have been shot at sunrise. Then he destroyed the effect of his reprimand by inviting me to have another drink. Ben K. Raleigh insisted I had sold out the Ledger to butter up Van and get myself a bigger salary.

A few weeks later, when I ran into Hank, he wished me well in my new job. Frank Neall said he regretted my story but gave no indication that it had impaired his friendly interest. I did not see Ochs again until years later in New York. If he remembered trying to fire me, he was too polite to refer to the incident. Why was I treated with such leniency—my first story, lampooning a religion, played on the front page, my salary doubled as the result of a slick half-truth? During my four years' apprenticeship on seven newspapers, no one, editor or fellow reporter, ever mentioned ethics of reporting. At the time this silence on the subject appealed to me. I was surfeited by overemphasis on legal ethics at the Law School of the University of Pennsylvania, which I had attended in 1907, and another dose of the same in the office of Fox & Rothschild, where I had served as clerk for three months.

Charlie (Charles E.) Fox, senior partner of that firm, was head of the Big Brothers, an organization devoted to reclaiming delinquent youths. I was Charlie's favorite delinquent. After my father's death in 1907, he gave me special attention, coming out to the U.P. dorms to plead with me to reform.

"I see Save-your-soul Charlie crossing the triangle," my roommate, David J. Loeb, would warn me. I would duck out the back way to give Dave a chance to regale Charlie with my iniquities. After a few quick drinks at the nearest bar, I would return to complain, "Charlie, why didn't you let me know you were coming so I could sober up?" Charlie would set to work on me, sometimes spend the night, sleeping on the uncomfortable couch in our study. I could sense how much he was enjoying his most difficult case, and I never let him down. When I came to work for him he gave me extra-heavy treatment on "the high standards of the noble profession you are about to enter."

Over the years my attitude has changed. I see indifference to a formal code of ethics as a great weakness in our national press. While editorial associations and schools of journalism are making some endeavor and progress toward rules of moral responsibility, the profession of journalism, if it be a profession, remains singularly free from self-restraint. As the first publisher to sign a contract with the American Newspaper Guild, it was my hope it would develop a code similar to those of doctors and lawyers. But that hope was shattered when the Guild changed from a craft to an industrial union which represented all nonmechanical departments of a newspaper.

❊   ❊   ❊   ❊   ❊

My career on the North American was short and undistinguished. I went there in September and left at the end of November to get married and return to law school. Van advised me to complete my law course. He promised me my job back any time I wanted it.

I bungled the one important story to which I was assigned. William Randolph Hearst was raising political hell with letters stolen from the private file of John D. Archbold, president of the Standard Oil Company of America. One letter indicated trafficking with the Superior Court of Pennsylvania. That bombshell exploded on a Saturday night. The Superior Court happened to be sitting in Philadelphia. The judges agreed to meet the press Sunday afternoon at the Aldine Hotel. Instead of a conference with all the reporters, the judges elected to see one of us at a time. The seven members of the court were seated around a table in a private dining room. A shaft of light from a single window illuminated the white hair of the dignified jurists. The scene reminded me of Rembrandt's *The Anatomy Lesson of Dr. Tulp*. My usual brashness deserted me. I had to ask these distinguished old gentlemen whether they were crooks. My imminent return to law school may have added to my embarrassment. I managed to enunciate, "The North American wants to know if Mr. Hearst's accusations are true."

One judge rose from the table and walked over to me. I noticed his left sleeve was empty.

"Young man." He held me with piercing, scornful eyes as he raised his one arm above his head. "I gave one arm in the Civil War to preserve this nation. Little did I think I would ever have to raise the other to Almighty God to swear that I did not use it to destroy that for which its fellow member was sacrificed." After a pause he continued, "I am authorized by my colleagues of the

Superior Court of the Commonwealth of Pennsylvania to state that not one of us ever received money from John D. Archbold. There is not a word of truth in the blasphemous accusations of that yellow kid of journalism, William Randolph Hearst."

As I left I met Ben Raleigh of the Ledger waiting for his turn with the judges.

"What did the bastards hand you?" he asked.

"A complete denial," I replied. "Not a word of truth in Hearst's charges."

"And the child reporter swallowed it whole." Ben's growl expressed his disgust with the world in general and my naïveté in particular.

My colorless story ran on an inside page. The early edition of the Ledger carried nothing about the judges, but its late and main edition gave full play to the partial admission which Ben had obtained—while none of them had received any gift from Archbold they would not deny that their former law partners might have received fees from Standard Oil. At Green's bar Ben handed me a copy of the Ledger and proceeded to soliloquize so all could hear.

"Little Dave isn't as dumb as he looks. He's going to be a lawyer, so he has to be nice to the judges. He sold out the Ledger to get a job from van Valkenburg and now he sells out the North American. Leave it to Dave always to do the wrong thing at the right time."

"I'm not going to be a lawyer," I protested. "I'm coming back on the job next June." But I felt thoroughly deflated. Fortunately I was off duty the next day so I did not have to face Jim Benn, the city editor. For sympathy and comfort I went to see my bride-to-be, Jill (Juliet E.) Lit. I ended my tale of woe to her with, "Perhaps your father is right. I should stick to the law. It's safer and surer for a married man."

We were walking through the woods that autumn day. Jill stopped, turned to face me, stamped her foot. "Don't let that miserable Ben Raleigh or anyone else keep you from what you have set your heart on doing. Where the heart is there lies the treasure." We were a pair of sentimental youngsters. I have my wife to thank for making up my mind when I was on the point of deserting journalism.

That walk in the woods changed other lives. Whenever I encountered a young man wavering between law and newspaper work I felt it my duty to win him over to my camp. Two of my converts were Leonard Lyons and Samuel Grafton.

Sam, just graduated from the University of Pennsylvania College in 1929, was awarded a prize by Henry L. Mencken's Mercury for the best essay on "What's Wrong with American Colleges?" His cynical impeachment of higher education had intrigued Mencken as it did me. I sent for the young man. When he told me he was about to enter law school I went to work on him.

"You have a rare gift for writing. Why throw it away to become another member of an overcrowded, stuffy profession? You'll be lucky if you earn a decent living after ten years. I'll pay you more now than you'll get from a law office when you graduate in three years."

I won the decision. I did not know it at the time but I had an ally in Edith Kingstone, whom Sam married two years later. After a year's training in the newsroom Sam became a brilliant member of our editorial board, later associate editor of the New York Post, columnist, author and magazine writer.

"I hate the law," Leonard Lyons, a young lawyer, wrote in 1934 when he submitted samples of the column he wanted to write for the New York Post. The material was good. "But we don't need another local column," Saylor objected. Nevertheless I felt I had to rescue Len from the law. And I am glad I did. He has become one of the most successful syndicated columnists in America. Again I must acknowledge an assist from the distaff side. Sylvia (Mrs. Leonard) Lyons, in a magazine article, tells about Len getting his job on the Post and adds, "A few days later we were married."

III

Skeleton in My Uncle's Closet

Interruption of my newspaper apprenticeship by marriage affords a "break for station identification"—vital statistics and family background.

I was born in Philadelphia on the most disgraceful day of 1886. On my fourth birthday, eager to see my presents, I opened the breakfast room door, to be drenched with water from a paper bag skillfully planted by my sister Agnes, aged fourteen. Father took me on his lap to dry my tears and clothes.

"You needn't be ashamed of your birthday," he assured me. "Prince Bismarck, smartest man in Europe, was born on April Fool's Day." Father neglected to tell me that, a few weeks before, Bismarck had been the victim of a grim joke when he was ousted by Kaiser Wilhelm II, new head of the empire Bismarck had created.

Don't get me wrong. I do not believe in the significance of birth dates or astrology. But I am curious as to why so many other people do. It always annoyed me that astrology columns in my newspapers drew more mail than editorials. I once planned a scientific test of astrology. A committee of astrologers would prepare horoscopes of twenty prominent men and women. At the end of a year investigators, under supervision of a committee of university professors, would check what percentage of the predictions had come true. I outlined this project to the New York Post's astrologer, a pompous little man who took himself and his work most seriously.

"Talk it over with your associates," I said to the astrologer. "If they'll co-operate, I'll recruit a committee of professors, and then we'll work out the details."

In a few days he was back. My secretary, Frank M. Murphy, told him I was tied up and suggested he come the next day. "The stars say I must see Mr. Stern today," he explained. Frank was so impressed he squeezed him in between other appointments.

"Mr. Stern, it's a great idea." The astrologer came right to the point. "I've had my lawyer apply for a copyright."

"Copyright?" I asked. "In whose name?"

"In my name."

"My idea in your name!" I exploded. "Get out of my office before I throw you out." As the astrologer made a hasty exit, Frank shouted after him, "You certainly misread the stars."

I dropped the plan. As far as I know astrology has never been scientifically tested and probably never will be. Disbelievers are convinced that it is nonsense. Believers feel no test is necessary. Astrology is big business in this country. More than 500 newspapers, with 20 million circulation, carry astrology features. Astrological magazines and services flourish.

No, I do not believe in the stars, but I am careful to avoid 13, walking under a ladder, placing a hat on a bed, and a score of other potent taboos, while I share with other Occidentals a feeling of superiority over superstitious Orientals.

✿   ✿   ✿   ✿   ✿

My father was a garment manufacturer. He retired in 1905 with $500,000, a fortune in those days. He lost most of it in the market crash of 1907. He died that year, brokenhearted that his carefully laid plans for his two children had been wrecked. I inherited $60,000 from what was left of the estate. This gave me an income of sixty dollars a week, not enough to enable me to live in the way to which I had been accustomed. If I had inherited $250,000, as my father had intended, I would not have had to work. As Winston Churchill says, "You never can tell whether bad luck may not, after all, turn out to be good luck."

Father overlooked the real legacy he left me—love and respect for the kindest and most unselfish of fathers. His eight brothers and sisters used to tell me, "Your father is rightly named David, which, in Hebrew, means 'best beloved,' for that's what he is in this family." When I returned to Philadelphia, in 1928—twenty-one years after his death—his memory was still warm in the hearts of old-timers. They would stop me on the street to recall his consideration and thoughtfulness.

Father was an ardent abolitionist. As a small boy, it embarrassed me when he would offer his seat in a streetcar to a colored woman, with a bow and tip of his hat as though she were a dowager duchess. By the 1890's Civil War idealism had become a bit tarnished in the City of Brotherly Love.

When old soldiers visited us they regaled me with tall tales of the war. "Don't glamorize," Father would interrupt. "Tell the boy about the dirt and disease and boredom." The few times he talked of the war it was to make fun of it: "When I was on night sentry duty I was more afraid of dogs than of Rebs." . . . "Those of us who had dysentery wished we had been shot, but I never met a wounded man who wished he had dysentery." The only serious war story I remember him telling me was in connection with the Battle of Gettysburg. His regiment, in reserve, was drawn up on a street in Carlisle. Shells were cutting furrows through its formation. Green officers did not have the sense to order their men to break ranks and seek shelter. Finally, a company of country boys ran for cover.

"We city boys stood like cattle waiting to be slaughtered," Father said. "It wasn't bravery. We were more afraid of what our neighbor would say than of cannon balls." Father was always the iconoclast. He loathed pretense—a reaction to his father's extreme ritualism.

My grandfather, Julius Stern, from whom I derive my first name, was born at Miltenberg, Bavaria, in 1804. He was the son of Simon ben Levi, who operated canal boats on the Main. When Napoleon conquered Bavaria his tax officials found it difficult to collect from Jews who used the Biblical "ben" (Hebrew for "son of"). There might be a dozen Simon ben Levis in one village. Jews were ordered to register surnames with the town clerk. Great-grandmother Reiz begged Simon to slip the clerk ten marks for a *grossartige* name. Great-grandfather Simon insisted he would leave it in the hands of God and take his name from the first letter he opened in the next day's mail. It was from a merchant named Stern. Reiz wept at this calamity, another instance of bad luck turning out to be good. So abrupt was this edict that brothers living in different villages did not have time to agree on a common name. Simon's brother Isaac, living in another village, paid for a fancy name. So I have distant cousins named Rosenheim.

Julius Stern landed in Philadelphia in 1830. He was a fencing instructor and, according to family tradition, the strongest man in Philadelphia. He could bend a silver dollar with his fingers; in a fist fight on Second Street he hit his opponent so hard the man rolled into the Delaware River a quarter of a mile away; on his deathbed, he gripped his sons' hands with such force they winced with pain.

Grandfather found pupils among the prosperous Portuguese Jewish families who had settled in Philadelphia before the Revolution. When he eloped with the sister of one of his students, he was ostracized and lost his clientele. His bride was a member of the Gratz family, noted for its beautiful women, one of whom Scott immortalized as Rebecca in *Ivanhoe*. After six weeks his bride left my grandfather. Under family pressure she declared him too crude to live with and divorced him.

At this time the long-established Jewish community was becoming embarrassed by the influx of "uncouth" German Jews. Grandfather's elopement added fuel to the flame of social cleavage. The newcomers so annoyed the old families that many of them crossed over to the Episcopal and Friends churches—the Madeiras, Belmonts, Rosengartens, *et al.*

His career as a fencing master ruined, Grandfather became a pack-on-back peddler. He must have been a good one. Within five years he had a peddlers' supply business and became a leader in the growing German Jewish community. In 1845 he organized Keneseth Israel, the first Reform synagogue in Philadelphia, and one of the first in the United States. Sermons were preached in German, later in English, instead of in Hebrew which most of the

German Jews did not understand. Men and women sat together in the synagogue, and there were many other reforms.

The Orthodox Portuguese declared that "Reform" was not Judaism. To refute the *verdammte Portuguesim* the president of the new synagogue prayed longer than any other Jew in Philadelphia, and he made his six sons pray with him, morning and evening. After Grandfather died, so bitter was their reaction to this overdose of ritual, his sons never again entered a synagogue or observed religious ceremonies at home.

It worried Father that he was depriving his children of religious education. When I was thirteen he engaged private tutors. Grandfather must have turned in his grave when Father selected Miss Charity Solis-Cohen, a relict of one of the oldest Portuguese families in Philadelphia, to teach me Hebrew. She was a capable instructor and I made good progress.

The Bible lessons did not go so well. Dr. Cyrus Adler, later to become director of Dropsie Institute, center of advanced studies in Hebrew lore, was a small man with a big forehead. A profound and serious scholar, he was doubly serious in the difficult task of snatching a child from the influence of an agnostic father. In mental equipment he had everything except a sense of humor. My ignorance and irreverence kept him in perpetual shock. We made slow progress because I argued about every verse in the Bible. It took three months to reach Chapter XII of Genesis. I voiced disgust with Abraham for telling his wife to pass herself off as his sister in case Pharaoh wanted to sleep with her. "Sarah was Abraham's half sister as well as his wife," Dr. Adler explained. "Such marriages were customary in those days." Dr. Adler closed the lesson with, "I must tell your father I cannot continue if you waste time in silly arguments based on ignorance."

When Father came home I reported Dr. Adler's ultimatum. After Father heard a detailed account of the lesson, he sat silent for a time. I wondered what my punishment would be.

"Better if you were out playing these spring days," he said. "No more Bible lessons. Tomorrow is Saturday. Come down to my office for lunch and we'll buy that baseball bat and glove you want."

Hallelujah! Reward instead of punishment—reward for not accepting the Bible. I sensed Father agreed with me that it wasn't cricket for a man to pass his wife off as his sister. Evidence has recently been discovered that some of the authors of the Bible felt the same way about Abraham's "diplomacy." Among the Dead Sea scrolls is an Aramaic version in which God instructs Abraham to tell Pharaoh that Sarah is his sister, thus transferring the onus from Abraham to God.

Bible lessons were never resumed. At that Saturday luncheon Father told me, "I do not want you to enter a synagogue until you are sixteen. Then you can decide for yourself what faith you want to adopt." He never again spoke to me of religion. But I overheard his conversation with others. He was convalescing from pneumonia when Sam Murray, commandant of the G.A.R. post to which Father belonged, was making a sick call.

"Dave, I prayed for you," said Murray.

"Thank you, Sam," said Father. "But why should you ask God Almighty to bother because I forgot my overshoes, was too lazy to change my wet shoes, and suffered what I deserved? Don't you think the good Lord is occupied with more important matters, such as running the universe?"

"Dave, you talk like a deist." Murray's tone showed his disapproval.

"Deist or theist, I've read all the arguments." My father's voice rose. "But what I can't understand is, if God is all-wise and all-powerful, why we should be forever telling him his business or asking him for special privileges. He punished me for forgetting my overshoes. You told this all-wise God not to make the punishment too severe. I know you meant well, Sam, but to me it sounds a bit impertinent, if not blasphemous."

The argument made a lasting impression on me. Did Father realize he was cutting me off from belief in any religion, from faith in a personal God? I have often wondered. I understand why he stopped the Bible lessons so abruptly. Victorian prudery had so inhibited him that he never was able to mention sex. He was shocked that Bible lessons involved discussions of incest and promiscuity. How could he provide his son with religious instruction, and at the same time protect him from such loathsome subjects? He never solved his dilemma.

❖   ❖   ❖   ❖   ❖

Grandfather had to live down the gossip that his first wife could not stomach his "German crudity." He went in for culture in his heavy-handed way. Literature and music were pounded into all of his nine children. They had a family orchestra. Uncle Simon, the oldest son, was an accomplished violinist. My father and Uncle Harry played the cello, Uncle Ed the zither, Uncle Aaron the cornet, Aunt Clara the piano; Aunt Rosie was an opera singer. Simon edited a literary magazine. He and Father translated Heine into English verse, published in 1875.

After Grandfather's death the family relaxed. By the time I became old enough to attend the Friday night family gatherings at Grandmother's home, music and literature had given way to cards, casual conversation and refreshments. Grandmother, a banquet cook before she married, held them together with her warmth, wisdom, and wonderful cooking. After her death in 1897, the tribe fell apart. Its war paint, a blend of devotion to religion and to the arts, put on to prove they were just as cultivated and devout as the Portuguese, had worn off. Grandfather's intense effort produced no musicians or scholars of note, with the single exception of one grandson, Dr. Walter S. Weyl, economist, author and editor of the New Republic. And the weight of evidence is that Walter inherited his brilliance from his father, Nathaniel Weyl, husband of Amelia Stern.

My mother, Sophia Muhr, born in Hurben, Bavaria, in 1851, was the daughter of Henry Muhr and Bepy (Rebecca) Friedberger from the neighboring village of Ichenhausen. I remember my maternal grandparents. Grandfather was a dignified old man who wore a skullcap and smoked a long porcelain pipe. To graduate as apprentice and become a licensed watchmaker, he had to complete a master work, the equivalent of a thesis for a Ph.D. An oversize pedestal clock which had to be wound only once a year, it stood in the lobby of the H. Muhr & Sons factory. His great-grandson, Phillip H. Muhr, writes me from California that the clock still keeps perfect time, but after one hundred and twenty-five years of ticking, age has taken its toll. It now requires re-winding every six months.

Grandmother Muhr was as volatile as her husband was phleg-matic. When she took me out she walked so fast my feet barely touched the ground. She would gather in a basket whatever was left over from the midday meal and race down the back street to distribute the food among less opulent neighbors—with me fly-ing along in the rear like the tail of a kite in a high wind. She was always in a hurry. Grandmother was the dominant force in the family and it was this dominance which brought it to America.

Grandfather Muhr, returning from a business trip, was sur-prised to find all the family belongings in his comfortable Hurben home packed. Grandmother had decided to move to America be-cause "I'm not going to have any more children where they do not treat Jews fairly." After a stormy passage which lasted a month, my grandparents arrived at Philadelphia in June, 1853, with their three children: Simon, eight; Fannie, six; and my mother, two. While Grandfather was going through customs, Grandmother asked a cousin to take her for a quick walk in the business district. On her return to the pier Grandmother an-nounced, "We're going to Cleveland where we have relatives."

"Why not settle here?" Grandfather asked.

"Too many watchmaker signs," Grandmother explained.

"You have dragged me so far. You will drag me no further." Grandfather finally rebelled.

At first the going was rough. The Muhrs lived in two rooms above a small watch-repair shop on Second Street. When a bur-glar smashed the shop window and stole all the watches hanging there, the family faced disaster. My Uncle Simon, aged thirteen, and my grandmother took control of the business. Within twenty-five years they developed one of the leading jewelry stores and watchmaking plants in the city.

Uncle Simon left school when he was thirteen. He spoke un-grammatically. But such was his charm that he became a favorite of Philadelphia society. He was a member of exclusive clubs and the friend of leading citizens. An elaborately engrossed and bound

In Memoriam on the Death of Simon Muhr (1896), from the Five o'Clock Club, is signed by one hundred and ten members, a Who's Who of financial, business and political leaders in Philadelphia of that day. The lengthy eulogy ends with, "No one joined more heartily than he in the discussions which were humorous, nor more seriously in those that were humane. His fellow members learned to admire him for the bigness of his heart and his splendid mental qualities."

One of his close friends was the financier George Earle II, father of George Earle III, whom I later helped to become Governor of Pennsylvania. My Uncle Simon Stern was manager of the Earle family bank, the Finance Company of Pennsylvania. The three families were intertwined for two generations.

Uncle Simon Muhr never married. When he died he left $10,000 to each of his five nephews and nieces. The bulk of his large fortune went to establish the Simon Muhr Scholarships. He wanted others to have the education he had missed. For many years he served on the Philadelphia Board of Education. A public school bears his name.

A portrait of Grandmother Muhr hangs in my New York home. We are spitting images of each other. I inherited her energy and intensity. As I contemplate her quizzical smile I understand the urge which drove her from Hurben to Philadelphia, and would have driven her on to Cleveland after a month at sea with three children. A similar urge drove me from one newspaper adventure to another.

When I was two my parents moved to Colorado Springs. It was hoped the high altitude would relieve my mother's asthma. She died when I was four and we returned to Philadelphia. While we were waiting for the train, my sister Agnes, then fourteen, showed me a big wooden box on the platform. She told me Mother was inside it. I did not believe her. I recall no emotion. Years after, I asked Agnes, "How is it I can remember you, Father, and my nurse, Sally, playing with me, kissing me? But as to Mother, it's a blank." "You were never allowed within ten feet of her because she had tuberculosis," my sister explained.

Sally, a short woman weighing two hundred pounds, was amply equipped to supply the fondling and caressing which Mother was forbidden to give me. Her naïve sayings have been preserved as family jokes. When she returned from a small circus at which the main feature had been an educated pig, she complained, "Mrs. Stern, that pig were no more educated than I am." The day after Harrison defeated Cleveland, I demanded an election badge. I came home proudly sporting an ornate Cleveland badge. "Why did you buy a badge of the losing side?" Mother asked. "I got it half-priced," said Sally. "Got it half-priced" is still family vernacular for a blunder.

Agnes was prematurely aged by Mother's death. My earliest recollection is of her riding at a full gallop through the Garden of the Gods, with long hair streaming out. After Mother's death, I do not remember her playing a game. She took upon herself the role of housekeeper to her widowed father and foster mother to her baby brother. She was a wonderful woman, patient and wise and understanding. As an adolescent what a time I gave her, resenting her discipline, protesting, "You're my sister, not my mother." She never appealed to Father to uphold her authority. But when my naughtiness made her cry, I gave in because I loved her very dearly. She was as conservative as I was the opposite. But this never diminished her faith in me. Against the advice of our uncles and aunts she lent me the money to buy my first newspaper.

After my mother's death we returned to Philadelphia to live with the Muhrs in their recently acquired mansion at Twentieth and Arch Streets, a sprawling mid-Victorian monstrosity with large gardens and stables. Grandfather, smoking his pipe, was the only peaceful element in that hectic household. Aunt Fannie, my mother's older sister, a divorcee, ran the home for her parents and three bachelor brothers: Simon, head of the family business; Jacob, a partner in the firm; and Phiz (Phillip), an artist who had just returned from the Sorbonne. They all had horses and rigs in the large stable, where I spent most of my time when I could give Sally the slip. My uncles and aunt made a great fuss over their dead sister's child. My special chum was Uncle Phiz, who let me paint in his studio on the fourth floor. He made a miniature easel and small palette. He taught me how to use "grownup" oils instead of "baby" water colors. It was in that studio that I met Jack Bones.

I was not allowed in the studio unless Uncle Phiz was there. But, of course, I kept sneaking into this wonderland to explore. One day I opened a closet door and a skeleton fell on me. I can still feel his long arms embracing me. It took all my strength to stuff those rattling swaying bones back into the closet and slam the door. Up to that moment I was more startled than afraid. Once the door was closed terror gripped me. Agnes found me guarding the closet door. "You were armed with one of Uncle Phiz's Indian clubs. Your long curls stood straight out as though you were charged with electricity. But you would not tell me what had scared you."

I have never recovered from that meeting with Jack Bones. I still pull the sheet over my head when I go to sleep. I used to test myself to see how far I could go in defying Jack Bones, how long I could stay in a dark room or in the woods at night. It was a slow struggle with many setbacks. The family doctor decided I was too nervous to go to school. A private tutor tried to teach me my ABC's but got nowhere with her skeleton-shocked pupil. It was two years before I came out of my daze, ten years before I told Father and Agnes about the skeleton in the closet. Getting the better of Jack Bones was my first achievement. Others stemmed from it. According to Toynbee, primitive people develop a civilization when they stand up to a challenge by nature or by foe.

I was so occupied with Jack Bones that I did not sense the family feud which was disrupting the household. Aunt Fannie wanted to marry Father. Grandmother, Uncle Simon and Uncle Jake were on her side. Uncle Phiz and Agnes backed Father. Grandfather was neutral. Aunt Fannie insisted that even if Father did not love her, it was the only sensible arrangement for his children's sake. Father declared that, out of respect for Mother, he would never marry again. The bitter family fight never was healed. Father resigned the presidency of the Keystone Watch

Company, manufacturing branch of H. Muhr & Sons, and moved to New York, where he rejoined his former partner in the clothing business. Except for Uncle Phiz, I never saw my Muhr relatives again until after Father died.

IV

Education

When the family moved to New York I was seven, a lethargic, backward child, still under the spell of Jack Bones. Father engaged Miss Emma P. Wride, a New England spinster, as governess. Thin pointed features, strong chin, long nose, snow-white hair, gave her the appearance of a strict disciplinarian. But back of this outward austerity were kindliness and understanding. An experienced teacher, with patient persistence, she pulled me out of my torpor. We covered six years of school work in two and my rating changed from backward to precocious. The family's pride was exceeded only by my own conceit.

In 1895 Father took his business and family back to Philadelphia. The New York move had been largely to get away from the importunate Fanny Muhr who had wanted to marry my father. At nine I entered the William Penn Charter School, founded by William Penn in 1692. I was put in a class with boys of twelve. Although I was promoted, I was too small and underdeveloped to join my classmates in their games. I was taken out of school to build up my health: gymnasium, bicycle riding, swimming and horseback lessons. It sounded alluring, but I realized I had not made good with the boys. They set me apart as something cute. I would never belong to a street gang and be a "regular feller."

During this second period of depression, Uncle Ed (Edward) Stern gave me a toy mimeograph set, a pan of gelatine, a bottle of copying ink, and a roller. He suggested we use it to publish a weekly family newspaper. He wrote a few notes to give me a start and left me to fill out the rest of the page. The project fascinated me. It was thrilling to make copies of what I had written. Saturday, I peddled my newspaper to my many relatives. No publication has ever been received with more enthusiasm. Instead of the penny a copy I asked, quarters, halves, and dollars were showered upon me. Uncle Aaron Bamberger gave me a five-dollar gold piece. I came home with more than ten dollars. Then and there I made up my mind to be a newspaper publisher. This childish resolve might have faded, but that evening when Father came home he made it fade-proof. He forbade me to continue publication. "A small boy should not have so much money," was the reason he gave. But I suspect this was not the only cause for suppression of my first newspaper. Among Uncle Ed's contributions to the gossip column was a personal: "David (my father) added to the gaiety of the gathering by snoring during Aunt Clara's piano recital."

I had to wait two years for another chance to satisfy my journalistic urge. A friend, the late Maurice T. Fleisher, received as a birthday gift a mimeograph machine which could bring forth 100 copies in a jiffy. We organized the Emanon ("no name" spelled backward) Club and issued the Emanon Gazette for all of six months, a sixteen-page magazine of fiction, poetry and essays. At eighteen I became editor of the Young Men's Hebrew Association's Review, a four-page monthly bulletin. I gave up my vacation and worked through a hot summer to obtain five thousand dollars in advertising contracts, so I could expand the Review into a thirty-six-page magazine.

The lead editorial, my first in print, tackled the provocative question which has confused and divided Jews throughout the ages: Is a man a Jew by race or by religion? The Orthodox says by both; the Reform, by religion; the nonreligious Jew, by race. Anthropologists insist there is no such race, which leaves free-thinking Jews, like myself, out in no man's land. In this maiden editorial I explained that Jews were a cultural entity, bound together by tradition and habits of thought, whatever that may mean. I could not have chosen an introduction which was better calculated to irritate, if not offend. I was echoing Israel Zangwill, British playwright and novelist. He came to this country in 1903 to establish an American branch of the Jewish Territorial Organization. The British government had offered Uganda as a refuge for Jews fleeing the pogroms then raging in Eastern Europe. While this plan was favored by anti-Zionists, such as my father and Judge Sulzberger, it was so bitterly opposed by Zionists that prominent Jews hesitated to lend their names to such a controversial project. In this emergency I, aged seventeen, was elected national secretary of the organization.

Long, thin and swarthy, Zangwill was a homely man. But so great was his charm and wit, his looks were forgotten. When I went to see him, in Judge Sulzberger's home where he was living, I would usually find him in bed, worn out and unnerved by the strident Zionist opposition he had encountered.

"Why do I subject myself to such insults and humiliation?" he would complain. After a few months Zangwill returned to London and I dropped out of the movement. But though the Jewish Territorial Organization has never settled a single Jew in Uganda, its American branch still survives.

For 2,000 years devout Jews throughout the world have been asking God to lead them back to the Promised Land. My father told me that when, as a boy, he joined the family in prayers to be taken back to Jerusalem, he shook in his boots for fear the Lord would grant his request. American Zionists do not want to settle in Israel. But they make vicarious atonement for their reluctance to emigrate by donating liberally so Jews from other lands can fulfill the age-old dream. Zangwill flouted this dream when he suggested Uganda as a safer and more logical refuge for persecuted Jews. With his sensitivity and human understanding he should have known better than to pit logic against tradition.

Because of this early interest in the problem, at the suggestion of President Truman I went to London, in November 1945, with Senator Guy M. Gillette of Iowa, Professor Fowler Harper of Yale, and others, to ask the British Government to allow one hundred thousand Jewish refugees to enter Palestine. We made a futile round of officialdom. Because the Attlee cabinet was skating on thin ice between American and Arab public opinion, we were given the double-talk treatment at which the British are experts. Ernest Bevan, Secretary of Foreign Affairs, did say, "If you would just stop talking about a Jewish State you would make it easier for me with the Arabs." My confreres attributed this remark to anti-Semitism, of which Bevan had been accused, I think unjustly. The next day I repeated Bevan's remark to Anthony Eden, then second in command of the "Loyal Opposition." Eden said he agreed with Bevan.

On my return from London I reported to President Truman late on the afternoon of December 4, 1945. Earlier in the day he had received Dr. Chaim Weizmann, world leader of Zionism, and later in the morning Lessing Rosenwald, head of the anti-Zionist American Council for Judaism. The President was confused by their antithetical views. I reminded him that history was repeating itself. The Jews had lost Jerusalem to the Romans because they were so busy fighting one another they had no time to man the city walls. After I told the President of my talks with Bevan and Eden, he authorized me to make a statement to the press: "President Truman favors the creation of a truly democratic State of Israel. He is opposed to establishment of any sovereign nation based on religion, race or creed. He is opposed to creation of Israel as a state based on Judaism for the same reason that he would oppose basing it on the Moslem religion or the Baptist denomination."

Unfortunately this advice of Israel's great friend has been little heeded. Of all the peoples in the world, Jews should most cherish strict separation of state and church, with complete religious freedom. Instead, the Orthodox Rabbinate is in control and able to suppress other forms of Judaism, Conservative and Reform. But why look for logic in history? The Puritans fled to the New World to escape intolerance, only to become more intolerant than their former persecutors. The paradox of persecuted becoming persecutors the moment they get the opportunity is repeated throughout the history of the "advance" of civilization. As Georg Hegel said, "The one truth we learn from history is that man never learns from history."

In spite of my abrasive first editorial, the Review was a success, and I was persuaded to serve as editor a second year. By that time I was assistant managing editor of the Pennsylvanian, the University daily, as well as editor of the Zelosophic Magazine, journal of the college's oldest literary society. I was too busy to study, for there were other distractions besides newspapers and magazines —athletics and girls.

When I entered college at sixteen, I was an underdeveloped 95-pound shrimp. At a swimming meet, picking small pie plates from the bottom of the pool was one of the novelty stunts. An indifferent swimmer could retrieve half a dozen. When I surfaced with one, I was booed by the gallery. I slunk away resolved never to enter that pool again.

"Where you think you're going, Frosh?" A hulk of a man, built like a walrus, blocked the entrance to the locker room. A long, scraggly mustache added to the illusion. Although he stood only five feet nine, George Kistler, swimming coach, packed two hundred and forty pounds of muscle. As a youth in England, he had been a world champion swimmer. I did not look like promising material for his squad, but George, always for the underdog, had to counteract that booing.

"Going to get dressed, sir." Freshmen said "sir" to everybody, including a walrus.

"When you through classes tomorrow?"

"At four, sir."

"Report to me at four-fifteen," the walrus commanded.

Thanks to George's hard but skillful training, within two years I made the swimming and water-polo teams. I tipped the scales at a hundred and sixty-five, all the muscle my five feet six could carry. While it looks very fierce, water polo is really a harmless game. In four years of intercollegiate play I never saw anyone seriously injured. Overcoming the instinctive fear of being held under water is the key to the game, and George was a wizard at curing this initial panic.

On the many trips I made with the team, conversation was strictly limited to athletics, women, booze and barroom jokes. College work and serious subjects were taboo. By the mask of The Great God Brown we played our roles as tough athletes. Ed Hopkinson, captain of the team, a long lanky sprinter nicknamed "Beanpole," is now the head of Philadelphia's leading investment banking house, Drexel & Company, parent of J. P. Morgan & Company. We went to school together for twelve years, five at Penn Charter, four at college, and three at law school, but never got to know each other until twenty-five years later, when I bought the Philadelphia Record. Then in opposite camps, the conservative Republican banker and the liberal Democratic publisher, we no longer wore adolescent masks. I blocked the plan to refinance the Philadelphia transit system for two hundred fifty million dollars, a deal on which Ed's underwriting syndicate would have received a five-million-dollar fee. Ed did not let a small incident like that mar our friendship. He went out of his way to do many personal and business favors for me. In 1945 I outlined to him an industrial page to improve labor relations, to be financed by the big corporations. I asked him to call some business leaders and prepare them for my visit. "Why should you go to see them?" Ed asked. "I'll have them come to you." Within the next few days the heads of Philadelphia Electric, Bell Telephone of Pennsylvania, and other similar corporations came to my office to sign contracts.

Another member of the team was Bob (Robert E.) Lamberton, who later became Mayor of Philadelphia. He was our giant goalie, a position which required a combination of wrestler, boxer, and swimmer. Bob, son of the head of our Greek Department, planned to follow in his father's footsteps. The half-dozen students majoring in Greek studied together in an alcove of the college library. I was the laggard who held the others back. My stupidity exasperated Bob and Chad (Congressman E. Wallace Chadwick), who were the brains of our group. When I would interrupt to ask a question, Bob would say to Chad, "Phenomenal that anyone could know so little after four years." To get back at Bob, I remarked one day that Greek culture was phony and that present civilization owed more to the Babylonians, Persians, and Arabs.

Bob turned white. I had found his Achilles heel. I made it a practice to prick it each time we met to study. To provide plenty of needles, I read up on the subject, the only extracurricular research I did during my four years at college. Who gave us our decimal system in place of the cumbersome Greek letter-numerals? Who originated the short story, the lyric poem, the beginning of modern medicine, our system of hours and minutes? Plato and

Aristotle had held back science for 2,000 years by their refusal to make experiments.

Bob ignored my attacks on his beloved Greek culture but they may have had something to do with his becoming a lawyer instead of a Greek instructor. Politics compelled me to oppose his election as mayor on the Republican ticket, in 1939. The Record never attacked him personally, even came to his defense when his conduct as sheriff, some years before, was questioned. He was a good mayor. His promising career was cut short by his death in 1941, at the age of fifty-four.

My closest friend on the swimming squad was Dan Renear, fastest swimmer and most powerful man on the polo team. I was the smallest. Whenever I got into a fight because of underwater tactics, which was quite often, Dan came to my rescue. After graduation, we set out together to hobo around the world.

There were many great teachers at the University. But George Kistler, an uneducated coal miner, left the strongest impression on me. His uncanny faculty for knowing what I was thinking made me suspect him of being endowed with second sight. Concentrating on what the other fellow is thinking is the valuable trick George taught me. More important, he developed my physical self-assurance.

Professor Felix Schelling, noted Shakespearean scholar and head of the English Department, did me a great service. For the Senior English Literature Prize, I wrote an essay on Arthur Wilson, one of the lesser Elizabethan dramatists. Schelling used this essay as the theme of a lecture on how English should not be written. He read passages of "the most flowery, flamboyant Oriental prose I have ever encountered," then showed how the same thought could be expressed in clear and simple language. He did not reveal the name of the essayist, but many of my classmates knew I was the author. That lecture was an ordeal, but it cured me of fancy writing.

A course in historical research shaped my political thinking. "Fourierism in America" was the subject assigned to me and to Scott Nearing, later to become a noted sociologist and author of a score of controversial books. A brilliant student, he stayed on at the University to take his Ph.D. and join the faculty as assistant professor. Because of his radical views, he was forced to resign his chair in 1915 and went on to teach at more liberal institutions.

François Marie Charles Fourier (1772-1837), a French philosopher, concocted a fantastic amalgam of socialism and capitalism. Society was to be divided into self-sustaining "phalanxes" of approximately sixteen hundred members, four hundred families. The profits of their industry were to be divided according to Fourier's formula, five parts to labor, four parts to capital (the stockholders who had furnished the original investment), and three parts to talent or managerial ability. Fourier explained that living together in one big house would be much cheaper than maintaining separate households. By growing and manufacturing most of its needs the phalanx would save the enormous cost of middleman and retailer.

The weirdest aspect of this scheme was that so many thoughtful citizens, here and abroad, fell for it. Adults, who knew from experience how difficult it is for two families to live in one house, swallowed this idea that four hundred families could work smoothly and happily together in one huge caravansary or dormitory. The governors, elected by votes of labor, capital, and talent, in proportion to their interests, were to be absolute. Fourier took it for granted that these governors would always be fair and wise. Incidentally he believed that permanent marriages were an improper interference with natural instincts. In many of the phalanxes the governors took it upon themselves to promote eugenics by directing who should sleep with whom.

After long and heated arguments, Scott and I turned in separate reports. Scott held that the forty-six Fourier colonies in the United States had failed because of pressure by their neighbors who resented this new way of life, especially the free love practiced in some of the colonies. I wrote that Fourierism had failed because it was a false and degrading system which reduced all members of the phalanx (Fourier's word for community), except the governors, to the level of ants in an anthill. In the few instances where a phalanx prospered, as in the Oneida Community, the members voted to return to private property and capitalism. This early exposure to Fourierism made me wary of radical social panaceas, the magic formulas for Utopia which hypnotize so many adolescents.

Why is Fourierism the most neglected phase of American history? Why do educators ignore this antidote to radicalism? Why do they hesitate to recall the most famous Fourier colony, Brook Farm in West Roxbury, Massachusetts, where a score of intellectual leaders of the 1840's—Ralph Waldo Emerson, Nathaniel Hawthorne, Charles A. Dana, Horace Greeley, Albert Brisbane (Arthur's father), et al.—fell for this false idealism?

Horace Greeley, most prominent and influential newspaper editor of his time, was so shocked by the suffering of the unemployed in New York, during the depression of 1837, that he turned socialist. At this time Albert Brisbane returned from studies abroad to give Greeley an account of three socialistic systems—of Robert Owen, of Saint-Simon, and of Fourier. Greeley chose Fourierism, the most impractical of the three, as the best way to cure the human misery he had witnessed. He engaged Brisbane to write a weekly column on Fourierism. Through Greeley's and Brisbane's influence forty-six Fourier colonies were established in the United States. Later Brisbane persuaded Greeley to run a weekly column by Karl Marx. This all seems a buried chapter in the annals of our country. Historical prudery, like sex prudery, makes us reticent on some embarrassing subjects.

While I had such occasional flashes of intellectual interest, I was too busy with amateur journalism, athletics, and a growing interest in girls, to study. Father was indirectly to blame for this attitude. I won the entrance prize in mathematics, the only subject for which I showed aptitude. Because Father loved languages he insisted I major in Latin and Greek, for which I had neither liking nor capacity. When I consented to desert mathematics as a major, I told him I wanted to be a reporter.

"Most of the reporters I have met are drunken bums," Father said, and decreed that I become a lawyer. In those days, believe it or not, children obeyed their parents.

Because of this experience I have leaned over backward not to interfere with my children's careers. The one time I tried to I was 100 per cent wrong. Exasperated at the way Tom was loafing through his junior year at Penn, I told him to report for work at the Record.

Langdon Mitchell, the distinguished playwright (*New York Idea; Becky Sharp;* etc.), phoned he wanted to see me. Tom had been taking Mitchell's course in drama.

"Tom shows real promise in writing dialogue," Mitchell told me when we lunched together. "It would be a crime to take him out of college."

I was so impressed by Mitchell's interest that I accepted his offer to assume personal charge of Tom's education. Mitchell transferred him to Harvard, where Tom worked hard at writing a play, but neglected his other courses. The play was a flop and Tom was glad to come to work for me. I told Mitchell he had wasted two years of Tom's life.

I was so wrong. Ten years later, Tom developed a character— Francis, the Talking Mule—whose pungent dialogue was hailed by critics as sparkling satire. After two books, *Francis* and *Francis Goes to Washington,* were published, Hollywood paid Tom a fortune for a series of eight Francis pictures, which grossed more than any other series in motion picture history. My happiness in Tom's success was marred by Mitchell's death before he could have the satisfaction of telling me, "I told you so."

❀　　❀　　❀　　❀　　❀

I was fifteen before I had the courage to call on a girl. The smallest boy of our group, my interest centered on the smallest girl. She had a positive way of stomping into a room on her recently acquired high heels, and an equally positive way of talking.

"I'll tell you what we're doing tomorrow," I overheard her say to the other girls at a Friday night party. "We're going to the matinée and then to Whitman's for ice-cream sodas."

"Isn't she the bossy little thing?" a big girl remarked.

"What's your plan?" the little girl shot back, quick as a wink. She caught her heckler off balance. The big girl hesitated and then said meekly, "I'll go along." My curiosity was aroused by this beautiful and forceful little boss who ordered big girls around. I was too inexperienced to foresee that if she dominated girls she would do the same with boys, and that eventually I would be it. So at fifteen I went to call on Jill Lit; at sixteen I proposed and was accepted. We married when Jill was twenty-one and I was twenty-two.

The years of courtship and engagement were happy ones, laced with storm and strife. I was forever wanting to elope. Jill insisted that we be married in her home as, at long last, we were, on November 22, 1908.

The seven years were divided into periods when we were under the spell of a particular poet or playwright—Browning, Coleridge, Yeats, Swinburne, Barrie. We would read them together, quote them, imitate their style in letters and conversation. The Barrie phase left a lasting mark. Jill called me Sentimental Tommy. My older son's nickname is Tom. His son's name is David Thomas Stern.

Jill's father, Jonker D. Lit, and my father collaborated to keep the youthful romance in check. When I graduated from college in June of 1906, I was sent abroad for a tour of Europe, to be followed by a year at the University of Berlin. My traveling companion was a long-time friend, Las (Elias) Sunstein, of Pittsburgh, who had just graduated from Princeton. We spent much time at the Marble Arch in Hyde Park, London. I cannot recall the subject which interested us but, by a quirk of memory, I recollect the speakers to whom we did not listen because their ideas were too absurd—advocates of prohibition, women's suffrage and freedom for India. How forward-looking I was, half a century ago.

Las, who had graduated with high honors and a Phi Beta Kappa key, worked conscientiously at visiting all the places starred in Baedeker. I preferred to explore night life, and sleep during the day. Great Britain was in the grip of a severe depression which, the following year, engulfed the United States. An army of unemployed, men, women, and children, wandered through the streets of London. From sunrise to sunset they were allowed to rest in the parks, but all night they were forced to walk the streets, not permitted to sit down or even to stop moving. It was a cruel, heartrending spectacle. The government wanted the unemployed to return to where they came from, and to discourage others from coming to London. One night on the Thames Embankment, I saw a bobby drive half a dozen men and women from a bench. In defiance I seated myself on the bench. "Go ahead and arrest me," I told the bobby. When he made no move, I shouted, "I dare you to arrest me. I'm an American citizen and I want to prove my right, anybody's right, to sit on this bench." I had heard so much about the efficiency of the London police, their resourcefulness in any situation, I was putting it to the test. Finally, the bobby spoke: "Sit there as long as you like, my fine young American, and get your bottom full of lice." I jumped from the bench and joined the bobby in laughing at myself. He admitted it was "grim business," but otherwise the streets would be "clogged with vagrants." That night were sown the seeds of my future advocacy of unemployment insurance and social security.

I insisted on visiting Kerrie-Muir, birthplace and home of James Barrie. When Las could not find Kerrie-Muir even mentioned, let alone starred, in his Baedeker, he refused to join me in this sentimental journey. We parted company. Barrie had left for London the day before I arrived, so I never met my hero. The innkeeper drove me around to see the sights. The Cuttle Well, background of *Sentimental Tommy*, was a muddy hole in an unkempt little park. The window in Thrums had nothing to distinguish it from the many other windows in the quaint but drab village. Barrie had made magic with the commonplace.

"What kind of a man is Barrie?" I asked the innkeeper.

"Not much to my mind," was his reply. "When I was collecting for the village band last week not a shilling would he give, and him rolling in royalties." So my sentimental journey came to a dead end.

❖ ❖ ❖ ❖ ❖

When I *immatrikulierte* at the University of Berlin in September, I was informed that a student was not expected to study the first semester, but to *bummel*, have a good time. I was most conscientious in conforming to this custom. At that time Berlin was trying to outdo Paris as a city of gaiety. The leading cafés advertised "music and dancing until 8:30 A.M." In the forty theaters there were at least three Shakespearean performances every night. The Germans were greater Shakespeare enthusiasts than English-speaking peoples. Curtain time at theater and opera was seven-thirty. You met your friends after theater for dinner at ten. If I got to bed by 5 A.M., I was up in time to do some studying before lectures began at three, but this was not often. My "studies" were cut short in January when Agnes cabled me to come home. Father had suffered a severe heart attack.

I found him partially recovered. He begged me to enter law school, which I immediately did. He was in no condition to be subjected to an argument. Father died three months later. Mercifully he was in a coma the last week. His labored breathing could be heard throughout the house. I sat in the coal cellar to get away from the nerve-racking sound. When his tired heart finally stopped, the immediate feeling was relief. Grief came after the funeral. He had been so kind and devoted, so patient and forgiving. I had repaid him with grudging obedience. We had never come to know each other, never had a man-to-man talk on religion, sex, politics or any other subject. My knowledge of my father came from overhearing his conversation with others, or as he revealed himself in casual remarks at the dinner table.

What causes such reticence between two men who love each other? Was it due to the intense prudery which stultified society at the turn of the century, and which is now rapidly, and I think fortunately, disappearing? It is natural for a father to think of his son as a child long after he has ceased to be one. It requires a conscious effort on the part of the parent to break this habit of thought. Father never recovered from Mother's death. The last twenty years of his life were devoted to earning a living so that his children should have every comfort and the best of educations. He had neither heart nor energy to cope with the spiritual problems of adolescence.

After Father's death, I wanted to leave law school, become a reporter and get married. Jill insisted that I complete my law course while she continued at Bryn Mawr. Angered by this postponement of our marriage, I declared, "For the rest of my life I will wander the world as a hobo," and went out West. What a romantic poseur I was at twenty-one.

V

Almost a Hobo

I had to make good my threat to be a hobo.

While Dan Renear and I were talking about working our way around the world, he received a letter offering him a job as cashier of a keno (bingo) game in Goldfield, Nevada. Dan was sure he could get me placed in that boom town, center of a gold rush. I wanted to work my way west via the wheat fields. Dan would go directly to Goldfield and wait for me.

Daniel Bethel Renear, son of a missionary who served in Hawaii and the South Seas, was born at Millville, New Jersey, in 1879. At fifteen he perfected the double overarm with scissors kick, later known as the trudgen stroke. At seventeen he won a world championship by swimming one hundred yards in one minute, seven seconds. At twenty-five, in 1904, he was the first man to swim the hundred in one minute flat. That record stood until the Australian crawl displaced the trudgen, as the trudgen had displaced the English side stroke (one arm over).

Dan's swimming laurels earned him an athletic scholarship at Penn. He was taking the pre-med course with the idea of becoming an athletic director. A powerfully built man with extra-long arms hanging from bulging shoulders, he had hair on his back as well as his chest, so he came naturally by his nickname of Gorilla, "Gore" for short.

Our only preparation for the trip was a visit to Tryon's gun shop to buy shooting irons. Dan insisted that I carry a Smith & Wesson .45 with a gallery sight. I did not wear a holster and toted this heavy revolver in my pants pocket. The gallery sight wore a sore spot on my thigh. I still have the scar to remind me what a rattle-brained kid I was.

With a roll of blankets and my six-shooter, I took the train to

Kansas City. Dan and I had agreed to go without money, and to earn our way. I cheated. I stuck a ten-dollar gold piece in the toe of my shoe. I did not tell Dan, but my conscience was partially cleared when I brought the gold piece back intact.

In Kansas City harvest workers were in demand. Bulletin boards on a street full of employment offices offered jobs at "$3 a day and keep"—high wages in 1907. I was meandering from sign to sign when someone called to me, "Stop gawking at those signs, youngster. I pay three-fifty and all you can eat." This smart farmer was recruiting from his spring wagon to avoid paying the agency commission. I climbed into the seat beside him. After he had filled the back seat with three more recruits, we headed into endless tawny wheat fields.

"Ever harvested?" the farmer asked.

"No."

"Whereyufrom?"

"Philadelphia."

"Ever been to Independence Hall?"

"Many times. It's the most beautiful building in Philadelphia."

"Got a town named Independence nigh here."

"It's an inspiring word."

No response from the boss. I tried to shatter the silence. "I guess 'independence' is the most important word in our language and history."

Another long silence. But my new boss felt he must make some response to such patriotic sentiments, so he finally said, "Harvest time we ain't got time for such."

No more talk the rest of the way. When we arrived at the farm, where enormous barns towered over the farmhouse, we went right to work. My job was to push sheaves into the thresher after the binders had been cut, work which is now done by machine. I was warned to avoid the knife-slash of the worker who cut the binder. The fellow I was replacing had not.

We worked stripped to the waist in the 100° heat. The air was thick with dust from the raucous thresher. I was glad for the lunch break. We were all too tired to try to get acquainted, so we silently wolfed fried pork, bread, jam and coffee. Then back to the thresher until four, and a coffee break. Work again until seven when we were served another big meal. All I could do was eat my fill and climb into the hay loft.

They had me up at five the next morning for another fourteen hours' workout. I stood it for five days, collected my $17.50, and hitchhiked back to Kansas City. I cannot remember overhearing a conversation, let alone taking part in one. "Pass the pork" or "More pie" was about all anybody said—hired hands or family. I should have stayed over to see whether this taciturnity prevailed on Sunday.

From Kansas City I made my way west toward Salt Lake City. I paid brakemen four bits to "ride plush" in an empty boxcar. This was the established rate per division of about a hundred and fifty miles. I never had the nerve to ride the rods. Hobos I met rubbed it in that I was not one of them. "Riding plush" and taking odd jobs put me in a lower social category. I was a floater.

I woke up one Sunday morning on the porch of a saloon at the entrance to the Moffatt Tunnel in the Colorado mountains. I had a hangover and was freezing. To make matters worse, I was broke. I had been cleaned in a crap game. While I was debating whether to break the ten-dollar gold piece, the only other occupant of the porch came to. He was in the same fix. He had lost $120. He offered me breakfast at his cabin five miles away. Ron Johnson, a lanky lumberman, had a contract to pull railroad ties down the steep sides of the mountain into the river. His one object in life was to get enough dough to bring his wife on from Minneapolis. He was earning good money but every Saturday night he had bad luck.

We spent the day sleeping off our hangovers in his snug log cabin high in the mountains. Piles of ties dotted the clearing carved out of the forest. Ron's nearest neighbor was three miles away.

"Ron Johnson, you're a stinking son of a bitch," he blurted out, while we were watching a breathtaking sunset. During my Western wanderings I saw many wonderful sunsets but except for Ron and a Mrs. Stewart, I recall no one else reacting to the grandeur of the scenery.

"I've treated Clara shamefully," he went on. "The best wife a

man ever had. Sensible, loyal, beautiful, and lots of fun in bed."
He had worked hard to build and equip his cabin. Now that he
was making good money he was wasting it on booze and gambling,
"while poor Clara's stuck in Minneapolis."

At supper Ron proposed I work with him to make enough money
to get Clara. "Together we can skid two thousand ties. At eight
cents apiece that's a hundred sixty dollars. Forty dollars for you;
twenty for next week's grub and horse feed; and a hundred for
Clara." The Sentimental Tommy in me had to say, "It's a deal."

At dawn we were on the job. With sledge hammers we drove
dogs, three-cornered spikes, into ties. The dogs were attached to
chains harnessed to a horse. With long reins you stood behind
the ties and started the horse on the steep trail to the river. The
trick was to reach the bank in the same order—horse first, followed by ties and driver. Occasionally I made it but more often
the ties slid down on the horse. The horse bolted to one side,
swinging me around so that we arrived all of a heap, in reverse
order. I was a mass of bruises and cuts. It was a most painful job.
But spurred on by the thought of Clara stranded in Minneapolis,
we kept at it from dawn till dusk for five days. The railroad tug
came up the river Saturday morning. We helped the crew rope and
count the ties. The paymaster handed Ron one hundred sixty-eight
dollars for twenty-one hundred ties, one hundred more than our
goal. Ron gave me my share, forty-two dollars.

We set off for town to send Clara a money order. At the first
saloon we stopped to celebrate our achievement. After a bottle of
eight-year-old bourbon and T-bone steaks, Ron made for the crap
table.

I caught his arm. "Ron, we got to send that money order to
Clara."

"To hell with Clara," was his curt response.

We woke up the next morning on the same porch and in the
same condition as the week before. I was deaf to Ron's pleadings
to make another attempt. I went back to my job on a railroad track
gang at two dollars a day. I never saw Ron again. I wonder
whether Clara ever escaped from Minneapolis.

It took me a couple of weeks to accumulate ten dollars. Then I continued west as far as Salt Lake City. There, an employment office was recruiting laborers for the railroad being built from Salt Lake City to Los Angeles. I signed up for a job in Caliente, Nevada, which was on the way to Dan in Goldfield. Together with a hundred tough bums I was herded into a day coach. It was a wild night. Before the train pulled out the drinking and brawling started. Whenever the pandemonium subsided someone fired his revolver out the window to start it again. I had made the mistake of wearing glasses. Several drunks began to pick on the "four-eyed runt." Fortunately I sat next to a tough veteran of the road who told them, "Let the kid alone." But I never was so glad to arrive at journey's end as when we piled out at Caliente the next morning.

Suddenly I found myself alone on the platform. My traveling companions had evaporated. I was the only one to turn up at the construction camp. The rest had enjoyed a free ride. I was put to work holding a rock drill for a fat Mexican. He kept missing the head of the drill. The heavy sledge was coming too close to my hands. "Too much to drink. When I sober never miss," the Mexican explained. I quit at noon without collecting any pay and caught a freight to Las Vegas where I got a job as hostler's helper. The hostler, foreman of the roundhouse, takes charge of a locomotive at the end of a run to condition it for the next trip. There were four helpers and a dozen Mexicans to do wiping and cleaning. A helper's job was to fill oil and water tanks, sandblast the boiler tubes, see to grease cups and lubrication as well as supervise the cleaning. When I was allowed to guide these mammoth machines, weighing nearly 100 tons, around the yard, from water tower to oil tanks, I enjoyed a big thrill, even though I was limited to a snail's pace.

Las Vegas in 1907 gave no indication of its exciting future. It was little more than a construction camp of the San Pedro–Los Angeles–Salt Lake City Railroad, which was later absorbed by the Union Pacific. A Mormon settlement had been established there in 1855 but the few adobe relics of those days were lost in the growing town. Most of the population lived under canvas. Conspicuous were a dozen rooming tents, old circus big tops, filled with cots which rented at a quarter a night. You supplied your own blankets and you needed them. The temperature would drop from 100 degrees at midday to the forties at night.

There were fewer than fifty buildings, half of them saloons, or rather combinations of drinking, eating, gambling, and dancing establishments. In all of them the layout was much the same. As you entered, the bar was on the right, lunch counter on the left. These were backed by the roulette, crap, blackjack, and poker tables. In the far rear was the dance floor, surrounded on three sides by cribs, usually two stories high, to provide rooms for a score of prostitutes. On Saturday nights, waiting lines clogged the dancing space.

There was no attempt at decoration. Bare rafters and planked walls were unpainted. But with the women in bright kimonos standing on the balcony, the effect had the chrome and tinsel of present-day Las Vegas beat—which would seem to confirm the dogma of some modern architects that beauty is to be found only in the strictly functional. A plant engineer, expert in straight-line production, could not have devised a more efficient floor plan for separating a customer from his money. If, by small chance, you did come out ahead, you were a marked man to help your less fortunate fellow workers with grub money until next payday.

I am sorry to disillusion TV-Western fans, but in my six weeks in the Las Vegas of 1907 I never saw a fight, with fists or guns. The moment a drunk became obstreperous he was hustled out by the bouncers. While they were being separated from their money the patrons of half a century ago were just as sheeplike as they are today.

The only shooting I did myself. Sleeping in a rooming tent, I was awakened by two men trying to make off with my blankets. Thanks to Jack Bones, the blankets were twisted around my head. I grabbed my revolver from under the pillow and fired twice in the air. The thieves ran but the owner of the tent made me pay five dollars to repair the holes in the canvas roof. Later, when I told Dan Renear, he said, "I can't believe you hit the top of a circus tent. Your aim must be improving." After lugging that heavy gun across the continent and back two holes in a tent is my shooting record.

In Goldfield I saw one other shooting. An Irish saloonkeeper, sweeping out before closing, refused to let a drunk come in. When the drunk pulled a gun, the Irishman went after him with his broom. The drunk fired two shots, one of which wounded the saloonkeeper in the arm. But that did not slow up the Irishman. He beat the drunk into submission and turned him over to the police.

While the conduct of men in Las Vegas then was much the same as today, the rules about women were different. Prostitutes never strayed beyond the line which separated dance floor and cribs from the rest of the establishment. The bar, the lunch counter, the gambling section, were forbidden territory. B-girls, women who hang around bars, and streetwalkers were not permitted. In the Las Vegas of 1907, a man could have his fill of food, drink, and gambling without even seeing, let alone being accosted by, a woman. It was up to him whether he crossed the line to the other sex.

Of the many characters I met in Las Vegas only two stick in my memory: one was my boss, Ed Scott, foreman of the roundhouse; the other, Mrs. Helen Stewart, who lived on a ranch a couple of miles from the center of town. An oasis with lush grass and shade from hundreds of large fruit trees, it was located at the low point of a wide shallow valley. Its copious springs were Las Vegas' sole source of water for many years. When I wandered into it one afternoon, the contrast with the surrounding desert sagebrush and Joshua trees was startling.

"Is this a mirage or the real thing?" I asked the elderly woman sitting on the veranda of the ranch house.

"The real thing," she said. "Come and sit down."

"Perhaps it is the sudden change from the desert, but this strikes me as the most beautiful garden I have ever seen."

"That is the way I feel about it," she told me. "But it makes me sad to hear you say it. I've just sold the place to Copper King Clark." She asked me to stay for supper and told me her story. She had been a school teacher in San Francisco. As the bride of the ranch owner, she had come to the oasis in 1870 and had been living there ever since. Her husband had been killed by the Indians thirty years before. With her four children and Indian hired hands, she had run the ranch, sent her two sons to college, and written poetry when she could find the time and the paper.

"Weren't you afraid of the Indians?" I asked.

"Whenever they went on the warpath," she said, "half a dozen miners would come over from Colorado Gulch and stay with us until the redskins quieted down. As the only white woman within fifty miles, I was a public responsibility. And living on the ranch was a pleasant change for the miners."

After supper she showed me poetry she had written, much of it in blank spaces of the ranch account book. "In the early days we were always short of paper. This was the only place I could find to write. Lumber was so scarce when my husband died, we had to cut down doors to make a coffin."

In the poems I noted many references to "voices of the night" and "the voice of God directs me through the night." Mrs. Stewart explained, "I used to believe I had psychic power, that I could hear the voice of God directing me to help travelers in distress. I would sit on this bench at night and hear mysterious voices. I would send a couple of Indian boys out on the trail. Nine times out of ten they brought back victims of desert heat and thirst.

"But the railroad replaced my illusion with a rational explanation. We can hear a train more than twenty miles away. We are at the center of a tremendous natural sounding board. I must have actually heard the poor souls trying to plod through the night instead of making camp and quieting down."

I enjoyed several more meals with Mrs. Stewart. She said I was the only person with any literary interest to whom she had talked in six months. "You ought to be glad to be getting back to San Francisco," I told her. "You'll find a circle of friends who talk your language, go to lectures, concerts, and plays. It will be a whole new life."

"Yes, you're right," she said dispiritedly. "But I cannot bear to leave this oasis." She was an authentic pioneer.

My boss, Ed Scott, a retired railroad engineer, preferred the solitude of the desert to family life in San Francisco with his wife and three grown daughters. "Too many women messing around and taking care of me," was the way he put it.

I thought I had mastered the local lingo by talking as sloppily and with as limited a vocabulary as my fellow workers. But Ed sensed a difference and was curious. He invited me to dinner. His large tent was side-boarded—a cabin with a canvas roof. Shelves were filled with books. One of Ed's hobbies was cooking. After a fine meal he wanted to know all about me and why I was out on the desert.

He could not believe my story. A college graduate as hostler's helper was too absurd. He felt sure I was not telling the whole story and became obsessed with the idea I was running away from some crime or disgrace. He begged me to go back and face the music, offered to lend me money and even go with me if he could help. He was more persistent in trying to save me than my Big Brother Charlie Fox. Then he took to reading the Bible with special emphasis on confess and be saved. These were tedious nights, when I wanted to be out on the town with the boys, but I could not refuse the boss's invitations.

He was such a kind old fellow and was having such a good time, I hated to tell him that, like Huck Finn, he was trying to "free a free nigger." I was in a fix because I was not in a fix. So I threw up my cushy job and hopped a freight for Goldfield.

Goldfield was all that Dan's friend had described, an overexcited boom town: everyone, drunk or sober, talking big and loud; streets crowded with old-timers and newcomers, all lured by gold; towering office buildings next to mud caves, dug out of the sides of hills and closed in with boards and tar paper; a few streets paved; the rest a mixture of garbage and mire. The most hectic spot in town was the curb market for mining claims, where speculators screamed at one another. Claims were endorsed and re-endorsed a dozen times at mounting prices, with less than five per cent down on each transfer. When the boom burst, these houses of cards collapsed and the claims came back to the original owners. While it lasted everybody was having a ball but they were all too excited to enjoy their happiness.

Dan had everything fixed for me, a job as dishwasher at three dollars a day, with meals thrown in. This was a good deal. Meals were two dollars up. A laborer earning eight dollars a day could barely get by. I bunked with Dan in a room above the combination saloon, restaurant and gambling joint where he worked as cashier. I had brought thirty dollars from Las Vegas. It was fun while the thirty dollars lasted, which was a couple of nights. Without money Goldfield was dull. Dan lined up a better job at ten dollars a day, but I figured that, after paying for meals, I would be no better off than as dishwasher.

I wrote Agnes. She had not heard from me for four months. I received wires and letters. She insisted I come home immediately to help settle my father's estate.

Dan sensed what was up and proposed we move on to Los Angeles where we could ship to the South Seas. It sounded glamorous. But by this time, I knew how much hard work and unpleasant living had to be endured between the excitement of new scenes. "I'll be back in three weeks," I promised.

"You're a yellow-bellied quitter," said Dan in disgust. "Once you see that girl you're stuck on, you'll never come back. You weren't a quitter in polo. What's turned you soft?"

"I swear I'll be back in three weeks," I kept repeating while Dan muttered, "Quitter." As I boarded the train I held up my hand, "Dan, you have my solemn oath I'll be back." Dan only shook his head. As the train pulled out, I could still hear him shouting, "Quitter."

❊   ❊   ❊   ❊   ❊

Twenty-five years later my son arrived home from Harvard, for the Christmas vacation, with his roommate, Buck Adams of Reno, Nevada.

"Many years ago I was in Nevada with a college chum, Dan Renear," I told Buck.

"He lives across the street from us," Buck said. "He's Chief Inspector of State Police."

In a few minutes I had Dan on the phone.

"This is Dave Stern, Dan. I don't know whether you remember me."

"Remember you, hell! I've been waiting twenty-five years for you to come back as you promised. I'm looking at your picture on my desk as I'm talking."

That was in 1932. We have been visiting each other at least once a year ever since. While he was waiting for me in Nevada, Dan served as head of State Police for eighteen years under six governors. He achieved a national reputation as a fearless police officer, able to handle mine strikes, prison riots, cattle rustlers and any situation which required steady nerves. He organized the Nevada National Guard, in which he held the rank of colonel. He also found time to be married four times. Now eighty, he has just been married the fifth time. He is still skin-diving, hunting, and fishing. He admits he was glad that I stayed home. As he puts it, "You were play-acting at being a tough guy. With me it came natural."

VI

Marriage

The prodigal brother enjoyed a warm welcome from Agnes and my brother-in-law, Ludwig Loeb. Never before had I appreciated the comforts of sleeping between sheets, bathing in a modern bathroom, wearing clean underwear. Meeting old friends, who had as much to tell me as I had them, was a pleasant relief from my taciturn companions in the West. My drab native city looked good to me; but I kept insisting that I must return to Goldfield in three weeks.

Then I went to see Jill. My promise to Dan and our globe-encircling project were forgotten. The one and only adventure which interested me was marriage. Jill's father told me to "forget that hobo nonsense and complete your law course." On the joint promise by Jill and me to return to Bryn Mawr College and to law school, her parents gave their consent. In those days marriage before graduation was almost unheard of. But on November 22, 1908, Jill and I were married in her home at Glenside, a suburb of Philadelphia.

After a week's honeymoon in New York we went to live in Ardmore, halfway between Bryn Mawr and the University of Pennsylvania Law School. We boarded with a Mrs. Morgan, a widow, with whom we became close friends. Her spacious home was a center for the Saturday Evening Post staff—Frederick S. Bigelow, assistant editor, Isaac F. Marcosson, special writer, and others. Jill and I could not have found a more congenial place in which to begin our married life. But I made both of us miserable fretting over my studies and threatening to leave law school. I cussed professors, authors of textbooks, judges whose opinions I had to read, and the law in general. My griping was so loud and profane,

Jill could not study in the same room. I kept harping on how the Pennsylvania courts had split hairs to favor big business, especially the Pennsylvania Railroad. This did not endear me to the faculty.

The Dean of the Law School, William Draper Lewis, sent for me. "Mr. Stern, your notebook was open on my desk. I could not help noticing, 'Thus decided the Supreme Court of the Pennsylvania Railroad.' Was that an inadvertent error, or does it reflect your state of mind?"

I explained I was completing the course to fulfill the wish of my dead father. I admitted mine was not the proper attitude for a member of the bar, but I assured the Dean, "You need have no misgivings in permitting the devil's advocate to graduate. I promise never to practice law."

That promise did not include never criticising the courts. In 1940 I wrote an editorial for the Philadelphia Record, accusing the Pennsylvania Supreme Court of playing politics by interfering with the organization of the State legislature. Chief Justice John W. Kephart was so infuriated that, without consulting his colleagues, he declared me in contempt of court and ordered the District Attorney of Philadelphia to arrest me. The District Attorney delayed carrying out the Chief Justice's order. After several months, the other members of the court calmed Kephart down and persuaded him to vacate the contempt citation. But when the story first broke, Dr. Lewis and several other nationally recognized leaders of the bar—among them Arthur T. Vanderbilt and Frank Hogan—phoned, offering their services to defend me from what they considered interference with freedom of the press. To thank Dr. Lewis for his friendly gesture, I invited him to lunch. We recalled our conversation about "the Supreme Court of the Pennsylvania Railroad" thirty years before. Lewis confessed that he was as critical of the court as I was, but as Dean he had to uphold the traditional respect.

❖　　❖　　❖　　❖　　❖

In June of 1909 I graduated, passed my bar examination, and was admitted to practice before the Supreme Court of Pennsylvania. The ordeal was over. After a week at the shore, I planned to go back to my job as reporter on the North American, while Jill completed her senior year at Bryn Mawr. Everything seemed hunky-dory. My salary of forty dollars plus the sixty from my inheritance would give us a hundred a week—more than sufficient fifty years ago. We would continue to live in our comfortable suite at Mrs. Morgan's.

Then Jill told me she was pregnant. Instead of rejoicing at the good news, I was scared and worried. A hundred a week was plenty for two, but not for three. I must earn more money. I went to my friend van Valkenburg. He congratulated me on becoming a member of the bar, adding, "Your old job is waiting for you."

"I want a new job," I told him. "I want to sell advertising."

"Why this sudden change?"

"Advertising men earn more than reporters. I want more money. We're expecting a baby."

"You've had no experience in advertising." Van was both annoyed and amused. "It takes years to learn. How do you know you'll make good?"

"I'll make good. If I can talk people into giving me news, I can talk them into advertising."

"We have no opening in advertising." Van started to swing his chair around, a sign that the interview was finished.

"George McDevitt is hiring men every day," I said to the back of his neck.

"Yes, at ten dollars a week."

"I'll start at ten," I persisted. "I just want a chance to show you."

Van swung back to face me. "Throw up a good forty-dollar job for which you are trained, to take a poor one at ten? Go to it, Simple Simon." I went to work soliciting room-for-rent ads in a slum section of the city.

George A. McDevitt, classified-advertising manager, was tall, good-looking. A meticulous dresser, he wore old-fashioned wing collars not only then, but until the day he died. He looked and acted like a formal mid-Victorian gentleman. But for all his stilted manner, he was an able sales executive. In later years George became national representative of all my newspapers. I paid him more a day than he had paid me a year.

Van had given George the difficult task of developing classified advertising against the competition of the Inquirer, which virtually monopolized the field. George handled his twenty-five solicitors with skill. Every week it was a game to "beat the figures," or quota he set. We were supposed to work from eight to six, six days a week. Often it was nine P.M. before we completed our orders.

Determined to make good, I worked harder than ever before. I did not walk between calls. I ran. I was advanced to real estate advertising. In six weeks I was drawing twenty dollars with a promise from George of more.

Never one to let well enough alone, I pestered George to recommend me to the display advertising department. George insisted I stay with him for a year. I refused to accept his sensible advice. Finally, George lost patience. He decided to teach me a lesson.

"Report tomorrow to Mr. McGuckin in Display," he told me. I thanked him profusely. I was not aware that George had told his friend, Gene (Eugene) McGuckin, assistant advertising manager, to give Smart-Aleck Stern the works.

Gene was the antithesis of George. Volatile, nervous, his long, thin arms and hands seemed to be in perpetual motion. His torrent of words could not keep pace with his quick mind. Every few minutes he would reach his own supersonic barrier. His arms would go on flailing while no words came forth. He was a high-pressure supersalesman who never took no for an answer.

My first briefing by Gene was startling. "One call is all you need to make a sale and that is all you get. After one call the prospect will be taken away and failure will be marked against you. Make up your mind when you walk into a man's office you are going to stay there until you get his signature, or are thrown out, and I mean literally thrown out. Stick until you wear him down. It's your will power against his."

I was too inexperienced to realize how absurd these instructions were. I did make some sales but they were more than offset by the businessmen I offended when I insisted they sign immediately or never again would they be asked to advertise in the North American. The harder I fought for business, the more critical and sarcastic Gene became. It was a nightmare. After three months I couldn't take any more and quit. That was the first in a string of false starts. At the time, I could not know it was another instance when what appeared to be the worst turned out for the best.

If it had not been for my panic when I learned I was to be a father, I would never have crossed the Rubicon from reporting to advertising. In those days there was intense caste cleavage between editorial and advertising men, who looked upon one another as untouchables. For a college professor to become janitor, for an architect to turn bricklayer would have been no more unusual than for a reporter to turn ad-solicitor. Not one metropolitan newspaperman in a thousand serves apprenticeships in both departments. That training under two master salesmen of opposite types was to pay off in later years.

Meanwhile the baby had arrived, a wonderful boy who was to work with me on my newspapers—as publisher of the Philadelphia Record and the Courier-Post; and after I retired, as publisher of the New Orleans Item and the Philadelphia News. My failure as an advertising salesman clouded this happiness. I was a family man out of work. I could not swallow my pride and ask Van for my old job as reporter. I was afraid to apply at other offices. I imagined all Philadelphia newspaperdom was talking about how Stern had flopped.

Jill urged me to make a fresh start in another city, "A young growing city of the Far West." We both shared an aversion to the "bricks and marble of Philadelphia," the endless rows of houses as alike as peas in a pod, red brick with white marble steps, repeated over and over again until it got on one's nerves like a stuck phonograph. Mass production of cheap dwellings did not explain this architectural regimentation. In better sections of the city, homes for the wealthy had also been built in blocks all alike. A spirit of conformity gripped the town. To be different from one's neighbor was taboo.

This ultraconservatism cost the city plenty. When the Federal Government offered interest-free loans for slum clearance, Philadelphia's allotment was two hundred million dollars. Nathan Straus, Housing Authority Administrator, declared that Philadelphia was afflicted with the worst slums in America. But Joe

(Joseph N., Jr.) Pew, Republican boss, advised the City Council not to besmirch the City of Brotherly Love with New Deal money. So Philadelphia was the only large city in the nation to refuse its allotment. When John Gunther was writing *Inside U.S.A.* he asked me to describe Philadelphia in a phrase. "The greatest Chinese city in America," was my answer. I am glad that, at long last, my native city has broken the grip of stodginess. In the past decade, under a Democratic city government, Philadelphia has improved more than in the century before.

"Let's get away from this stuffy atmosphere," Jill kept urging. "You go ahead. As soon as you find a job I'll follow with the baby." The spirit of adventure which had lured me west once before again gripped me. In January, 1910, against the advice of friends and family, I went to Seattle.

Enjoying a boom, Seattle was hungry for skilled workers. I was offered jobs on all of the three newspapers—the Post-Intelligencer, the only morning paper; the Times and the Star, evening papers. I chose the one with the best pay, forty dollars a week as advertising solicitor on the Star. Smallest of the three, the Star was a member of the Scripps-Lee chain. Like all Scripps papers in those days, the Star was run on a pinchpenny basis. If an employee stepped into the pressroom for a paper, he dropped a penny into a box which hung beside the delivery table. The staff was so small, I wondered how it managed to get out the sheet. Everyone worked hard doing three men's jobs, in a catch-as-catch-can way. I found I was the entire local staff. The advertising director handled department stores. Two men covered amusement, shipping, railroad, and other special advertising. The rest of the town was up to me. Thanks to the boom, I did well. With low advertising rates, the Star was a natural for smaller stores which were springing up like mushrooms. Within two weeks I had a couple of copy boys helping me gather and mark up copy.

I was given the title of local advertising manager. As a department head, I made out the weekly payroll for myself and my two assistants. When I asked for a raise, I was told that it was up to me to make out my payroll for whatever I thought fair. I handed myself a five-dollar raise each week. When I was drawing sixty dollars

I boasted to the business manager that I had signed up practically every specialty store on a stated-space contract—to use a certain minimum space each week for a year.

The next week the pink slip was in my envelope. I had done such a good job they did not need my services. My boys could handle the copy. Later I learned I had raised myself to the advertising director's salary. If I had passed him, his job would have been in jeopardy.

Now it all has a comic-opera quality. But at the time it was tragic. My wife and baby were arriving the next day. I had written glowing accounts of how well I was doing in this wonder town. It was bad enough to be fired when I was making good. To have my family on my hands was piling Pelion on Ossa.

My joy at being united with my wife and baby son drove away the gloom. I was glad to accept a job as reporter on the Post-Intelligencer at thirty dollars a week. Between jobs I had a week to show Jill the wonders of Seattle. She had never seen snow-capped mountains before. We enjoyed steamboat trips on Puget Sound, with the lofty white-topped Olympics as a backdrop, and explored the harbor with its clutter of strange craft from the Orient. We were happy to be adventuring together in this vibrant new land.

On the Post-Intelligencer, I was assigned to the waterfront. I admitted to no experience in ship-news reporting but was told the work was routine, picking up reports of incoming and outgoing vessels, interviewing prominent citizens who arrived. The Post-Intelligencer maintained a motorboat to meet ships at Quarantine.

On one trip to board a trans-Pacific liner I had, as fellow passenger, a dignified individual, who looked like a college professor and carried a brief case. He introduced himself as "Rufus Rohrbacher, official biographer for the Post-Intelligencer." When I admitted that I had never heard of such an "animal," he turned silent. It was not until later, when we became friends, that he satisfied my curiosity. Rufus wrote flattering biographies of men who had recently become successful and wealthy. He would call on them to verify his facts and for permission to publish. After he had read the eulogy, his victim was in such a state of euphoria that Rufus put in the touch for a "contribution" to cover expenses. He seldom failed to bring back a fat check, between a hundred and a thousand dollars, which he split with the paper. He was netting $10,000 a year, double what he had earned as a city editor.

Off the job Rufus discarded his professorial dignity and became the jolliest, fun-loving, story-telling companion. He had a beautiful wife, Annabelle, and a daughter of three. We became such good friends we rented a bungalow on Lake Washington. The two families spent six weeks together.

"I sell inspiration and incentive," Rufus would tell me in justifying his means of livelihood. "Perhaps a man has not quite attained the high perch on which I place him, but I stimulate him to reach for it." Then he would discount this big talk by telling funny stories about the "fat cats" as he called his customers.

Interviewing passengers was seldom productive of good copy. Trying to develop news which was different, I took to gossiping with the captains of tramp steamers. I found they would let me use their names for tall yarns I made up. They welcomed press notices they could mail to their folks back home.

I bought an old canoe. Instead of using the motor boat, Jill and I would paddle out to a tramp, lying at anchor. The skipper would shout, "What kind of a fool are you to risk a girl's life in that cockleshell? I ought to send for the shore authorities." But out of curiosity he would invite us aboard and help to concoct a humdinger of a story. It was the most fun of any job I have ever had.

It was not so much fun for Jill. I had to work nights and seldom finished before ten o'clock. She used to wait for me in the hall outside the newsroom. Nell Siddons, the woman's page editor, invited Jill to sit in her office. Jill offered to help Nell and before we returned to the East, had learned the technique of editing a woman's page.

At first the copy desk fell for my tall tales. But when it became obvious I was faking, instead of being reprimanded, my salty yarns were handled as humorous features to lighten up the front page. Toward the end of my stay on the Post-Intelligencer, I was turning out three a week.

Only one of these stories caused trouble. It started with a classified ad for partners to join in equipping the good ship *Vera* for a cruise to Peru in search of gold. The advertiser was a barber, on the waterfront, who had been mate on tramp steamers until he married and promised to give up the sea. He hated shore life but did not want to desert the missus and his two kids. Here was a way to have his penny and his cake, his family and the sea.

He had just bought the hull of an old contraband sealer and named it *Vera,* after his wife. For $20,000 he could fit it for a trip to Peru to search for gold. As a young man he had prospected there. He wanted twenty fellow-adventurers to put up a thousand dollars each.

My story was given a play with art in the Sunday Post-Intelligencer. At the first meeting of the adventurers, Vera, the lady, not the ship, was present. The old sailor had picked himself a comely wife, a Norwegian girl, blond and buxom enough to model for a beer calendar. After lengthy discussion of reconditioning, I ventured the suggestion that Peru offered inducements to agricultural colonists. It would be safer to enter as agriculturists and do prospecting on the side. They did not cotton to this idea. Vera served a few rounds of beer. I mentioned that the Peruvian government allowed agricultural colonists to establish their own local government, with mayor, justice of the peace, and all the rest. This interested the adventurers.

"I could be mayor," exclaimed the barber. The titles were divided among those present. By the fifth round of beer, the village government had expanded to a republic. The barber had advanced from mayor to president. I accepted his appointment as secretary of state. The new nation was christened Republic of Kashkopitonka—"hard cash" in Indian talk.

My stories about Kashkopitonka brought more screwballs into the great adventure. Finally, the *Vera* was shipshape. All that was lacking was enough money to pay for equipment and provisions. A ship chandler libeled the *Vera*—obtained a court order forbidding the ship to sail until he was paid. A deputy marshal was put on board. One summer evening the marshal was invited ashore for a drink. Meanwhile a painter changed the name *Vera* to *Vida.* When the marshal returned to the pier, his bird had flown.

A revenue cutter soon overtook the *Vera-Vida* and brought her back to Seattle. The ship's company was jailed. Off duty that day, I read about it the next morning and hurried to the jail to find my president and fellow cabinet members very low.

To cheer them I put up a bluff. "They cannot do this to our Republic. Mr. President, as Kashkopitonka's Secretary of State, I shall protest to Secretary of State Knox and demand your immediate release as well as warships to convoy you to neutral waters." I sent a wire to Philander Knox threatening to break off diplomatic relations. I told the story in the Post-Intelligencer.

When I reported the next day, the city editor told me to see the publisher, William C. Chapin. With him I found the U.S. Attorney, who had received a request from the State Department to investigate my wire. I had left out of my calculations the State Department's lack of humor. Instead of dismissing my message as a prank, the protocol specialists had been up all hours trying to find the whereabouts of Kashkopitonka.

I had carried the joke too far. My only excuse was that I figured the hoax was so obvious no sane person would be taken in by it. I said all the fault was mine for suggesting this *opéra bouffe* to a group of grown-up children.

"If anyone should go to jail, it's you," said the U.S. Attorney. "Sorry there's no statute to cover playing practical jokes on the State Department."

Fortunately, Chapin had the sense of humor which the State Department lacked. I was let off with a letter of apology to Secretary Knox. I did persuade the U.S. Attorney that the barber and his pals were harmless. They were released on suspended sentences. The *Vera* was sold at auction for enough to satisfy creditors and return to the adventurers a third of their original investment. Thus died aborning the great Republic of Kashkopitonka.

This fiasco made me realize I was playing the newspaper clown and, in four months, had not handled an important story. I asked to be transferred to general assignments. Instead I was given a raise and told to go on writing tall tales of the waterfront.

Meanwhile I was in financial difficulties. My Uncle Edward Stern, my guardian until I reached thirty, refused to help me. He had disapproved of my going west. He wanted me to practice law. Again I was in the doldrums. Jill had shipped our furniture to Seattle and it was still in the warehouse. I hocked it for enough to pay my debts and railroad fare to Philadelphia. So ended my second futile foray to the Far West.

VII

Tryouts in the Styx

Returning from Seattle with my wife and son, I was embarrassed by the cordial welcome of Jill's parents to their home in Glenside. I knew they were worrying about their feckless son-in-law, and so was I. After making the rounds of the Philadelphia papers, I was glad to accept a job on the Bulletin as rewrite man. (The rewrite man's original job was rewriting unsatisfactory copy. Nowadays his main work is taking news on the phone from legmen, reporters who stay out on their beats.)

This inside position on an evening paper was very different from my previous experience. Most of the Bulletin staff worked from eight to five and then went home. There was little afterhours camaraderie. Relations with the city desk were stiff and formal. It was a smoothly efficient machine geared to gather neighborhood items and news. Every fire, accident, and street fight, however trivial, was covered by an army of legmen who kept in constant touch with the office. The saying was that Bulletin reporters arrived at a fire before the firemen and in greater numbers. Little effort was made to inject human interest or dramatize the news. The more names the better was the formula devised by our publisher, William L. McLean, who had started his newspaper career in the circulation department. His formula worked. The Bulletin was dull but most profitable, with the largest circulation in Philadelphia.

One of my duties was to serve as "nut editor." When an unknown asked to see the editor, the receptionist phoned for me. Most of the callers were cranks who were tactfully turned away with the suggestion they write the editor.

Only once, as nut editor, did I discover a story. An attractive girl wanted to see "the boss." She was a model at the Academy of

Fine Arts, Philadelphia's oldest and leading art school. The models had received notice the Academy would continue to pay seventy-five cents an hour for posing in the nude, but only fifty cents if they wore clothes. The young lady complained, "We got to eat, clothes or no clothes. Besides, it's more relaxing in the nude." The models were ready to fight this injustice. Would the Bulletin help?

After an O.K. from the desk, I assured her the Bulletin would come to the rescue. With a photographer I met a half dozen of the models that afternoon. At my suggestion they applied to the A.F. of L. for an artist's models' union charter. On this news lead I wrote a series of stories which made a hit with the desk because it gave the prim Bulletin an excuse to run pictures and stories of pretty girls.

This incident earned me similar assignments. Trouser skirts, creating a furor in Paris, were imported by a department store. When I hired a model to wear culottes on the street so that we could score a beat, police had to rescue the girl from the mob. It did not take the kidding of friends to disgust me with my work. Here I was again playing the clown, as I had in Seattle. "You started as nut editor," Ben Raleigh told me. "Now you're artist's-model editor. If you keep at it, they'll promote you to out-house editor." I resigned from the Bulletin to take an advertising job with the Record, of which I was to become publisher eighteen years later.

When I left the Bulletin I was even more discouraged than on my return to Philadelphia from Seattle. I did not appreciate the training I had received in one of the best organized news departments in the country, exactly the experience I needed for my future work. What was to prove even more valuable, my interest in Camden, New Jersey, was aroused. I took news on the phone from the editor of the Post-Telegram, one of the two Camden dailies, neighborhood sheets which made no attempt to cover national or world news. One evening I stationed myself at the Delaware River ferry newsstand. Nearly everyone bought both a Philadelphia and a Camden paper. If a Camden paper gave complete news coverage, I was convinced it would take South Jersey circu-

lation from the Philadelphia papers. Eight years later I proved my
hunch was right.

On the Record I solicited automobile advertising as assistant to
Charlie Gilchrist, a veteran in this special field. M. F. Hanson, the
publisher, told me I would inherit Gilchrist's job on his retirement.
This prospect depressed me. "When I'm twenty-eight I may be
making seventy-five dollars a week as an auto ad-man," I told Jill.
"I should have kept on hoboing with Dan Renear."

My discontent drove me to newspaper brokers. I wanted a job
on a small daily with option to buy in five years when I would
come into control of my inheritance. A New York publication
broker had on his list the Providence (R.I.) News, a dog so run-
down he had no hope of selling it. D. Russell Brown, head of a mill
supply company, and formerly Governor of Rhode Island, had
bought the paper when he was active in politics. Now, out of
politics, he had lost interest and had allowed the News to deteriorate. The broker figured he had nothing to lose by getting me into
the picture. If, by a miracle, I made good and exercised my option,
he would earn a commission. So he introduced me to the Governor.

"It is an honor to shake the hand of such a distinguished citizen
of New England," was my greeting to Governor Brown, when I
met him in the broker's office. Having done a thorough research
job, I was able to feed his vanity. The Governor was a dead ringer
for Tenniel's White Knight in *Alice Through the Looking Glass*,
long—six foot four—thin, stooped with seventy years. His white
hair and long mustache were usually unkempt. His pale blue eyes
were as vague and his speech as rambling as Lewis Carroll's character. I was hired as general manager at seventy-five a week, with
an option to buy a half interest for fifty thousand dollars within
five years.

A week later I took over. At the start of that day's run, I went
to the pressroom to enjoy the thrill of seeing my name as "General
Manager" on the masthead. The towering press stretched the
length of the room. The foreman handed me the first copy off the
folder. To show my authority I hollered above the roar of the
press, "Give her more ink."

The press stopped.

"What's the matter?" I asked.

"Nothing," answered the foreman. "We're through. We can't regulate the ink. The run's too short."

"What's your press run?"

"Fifteen hundred."

The News claimed 15,000 circulation; The Providence Journal 75,000; the Tribune 25,000. This was before A.B.C., the Audit Bureau of Circulations, which audits and certifies newspaper and magazine net paid circulation. The News was just a ghost of a newspaper, and it was costing five thousand a month to keep this ghost going. The old-fashioned, conservative make-up of the front page accentuated its dullness. I wondered why anyone chose the News. To find out I stood near the busiest newsstand.

"Give me all three, and the Boston American," was repeated time and again. Often the multiple-newspaper buyer would toss down a nickel and not wait for his penny change. So that was it. What little circulation the News had was largely duplicate. The out-of-town choice was Hearst's American, with a sale, in Providence, of 30,000. Its front page, screaming of crime and scandal, was in striking contrast to the conservative make-up of the local papers.

If lurid headlines was what Providence wanted, lurid headlines it would get. But I found my managing editor was no more capable of such type juggling than I was. It takes experience in the technique of blowing little up into much, to produce sensational front pages. I remembered that Walter Clarke, whom I had come to know as night editor of the Philadelphia Public Ledger, was now assistant managing editor of the Boston American. I took the next train to Boston and found Walter putting the last edition to press with Cuts Sweetheart into Pieces as the top head. He was the son of a minister, looked and talked like a minister, and ended his days as editor of a church magazine—but he was as expert in yellow journalism as in theology. Walter laughed at my suggestion that he become editor of the News. The News was a joke. I did not have a chance to put it over. I offered him a hundred a week, although

I knew I would have to pay twenty-five of this out of my own pocket. I gave him my personal guarantee that if the project blew up within a year, I would pay him three months' salary. He agreed to join me.

Clarke was to give us a sensational front page à la Hearst. But we had no big type, a detail I had overlooked. The fonts Clarke specified would cost two thousand dollars. I had no chance of getting it from the Governor who disapproved of any change in the dignified style of the News.

Elmer C. Pratt, foreman of the composing room, came to the rescue. A friend of his, at the Boston American, pulled mats (papier-mâché matrices or molds) of the type faces we required. Then Elmer had the type cast in the stereotype room.

Elmer was the only live wire I found on the News. He remained with me as mechanical superintendent of my newspapers for thirty-five years until he retired on pension. A wisp of a down-East Yankee, always tense, he had remarkable ingenuity and drive. Considerate of subordinates, he commanded their loyalty and devotion. But he had a chip on his shoulder for his superiors. Editor or business manager entered the composing room at his peril. In later years, when Elmer was especially nasty to a new editor, Neal Dyer, Elmer's assistant, would take the newcomer aside to explain, "Yankees are like that—dyspepsia from eating pie for breakfast." Nor was I immune from Elmer's terrible temper, but over the years our squabbles became routine. Passing Elmer in the hall one day, I asked, "Are you feeling O.K.?" Puzzled, Elmer replied, "Yes, why do you ask?" "You haven't raised hell with me in a week." I hurried down the hall to avoid his tirade.

With our homemade type, Clarke out-headlined the American and gave us the hottest front page in New England. Sales began to mount. By the second month, circulation had reached 10,000. Then the awakening: Joe Silverman, Providence agent for the Hearst newspapers, came to see me. If we did not stop making the News look like the American, he was going to order his newsboys not to handle our newspaper. Our front page was so much like the American's it was hard, at first glance, to tell one from the other. The newsboys were pushing the News, which they bought for forty cents a hundred as against sixty cents for the American. That explained our sudden growth.

I told Silverman I would give him my answer the next day. Our circulation manager confirmed my fears. If Silverman forced the boys to make a choice between selling one paper or the other, they would stay with the American. Its Providence circulation was still double ours, and the Sunday American brought them more money than weekday sales. If we changed our front page so that it did not look like the Hearst paper, our circulation would take a dive. When Silverman returned, I asked his peace terms. He was not prepared for such a ready surrender.

"Just make your front page different," he said.

"That's indefinite," I replied. "First thing you know, we'll be wrangling as to whether it's different enough. Write us a letter telling just what you want."

"I don't know how to say it. I don't know the names of the big types on the front page."

I offered to dictate a letter. It specified the sizes of type we were to use and the penalty for noncompliance. Silverman signed it as "Agent for Hearst American."

This letter was reproduced on our front page under screaming headlines, HEARST ORDERS NEWS OFF STREETS OF PROVIDENCE. An editorial defied Hearst to dictate to the free press of Providence and threatened legal action. It was a cheap trick. I had pretended friendship and co-operation to entrap Silverman.

The Hearst management was too smart to be drawn into battle. They told Silverman not to cut us off from the newsboys. Instead, he gave them bonuses which offset the difference in the wholesale rate.

But our circulation held. The public loves a fight and usually sides with the smaller guy. The News had been livened with comic strips and syndicated features. We scored editorially on several local issues and I managed to get some department store advertising at a low rate. But we could not hope to show a profit until we reached 25,000 circulation.

Meanwhile I was having trouble with the Governor. My pressure tactics, which had increased circulation, had also increased the monthly deficit. I had not had time to develop compensating advertising. I tried to convince the old gentleman that we would have the paper on a paying basis within a year.

"I've heard that before," was his reply. "I'm tired of throwing good money after bad. If you're so sure you'll make good, buy me out."

I explained again, as I had before, that I would not receive my inheritance until I was thirty. In spite of Brown's continuous harassment, I did stick it out until the fourth month, with circulation mounting to 15,000. The finale was as trivial as it was ludicrous. Elmer sent a printer's devil to the Governor's supply house for a dozen belt lacings which cost ten cents each. The boy came back with six. The Governor wanted to know what we were doing with belt lacings. He had sent us a dozen the month before!

Elmer burst into my office livid with rage, waving the six leather thongs like a battle flag. "Quit now while you still have your self-respect. This fellow will drive you nuts. I'm a Yankee, and I know that when a Yankee sets out to be mean, he can outdo a skunk."

I knew Elmer was right. I sent in my resignation. A controversy over six strips of leather was the humiliating end of my first experience as publisher. But my efforts were not entirely futile. The Tribune was so impressed by our sudden spurt that it paid Brown fifty thousand dollars to merge the News with the Tribune, which was in turn eventually absorbed by the Journal, now the monopoly newspaper in Providence.

When I went home that evening I was dejected. We were sharing a small cottage on Narragansett Bay with Elva and Mick (Milton R.) Katzenberg, our closest friends. The two families had had a lot of fun together that summer. When Mick heard the bad news he insisted on taking us to a fancy dinner with champagne at which he announced, "I'm ready to invest ten thousand dollars in your next newspaper." An unusually able businessman, he was already making good in his father's hide company.

How much I owe my loyal wife and friends. They kept me from deserting journalism for law. At the time I saw only the negative side, four months of intense effort wasted, a great opportunity muffed—not the positive side that I had had experience in running a newspaper at Governor Brown's expense.

After the Providence debacle, I was ashamed to go back to Philadelphia and admit another failure. I took an advertising job on the New York Globe. We moved to a small apartment overhanging the Columbus Avenue elevated where eventually we became accustomed to the roar of the trains.

Clarke had resigned with me. I owed him thirteen hundred dollars, the three months' salary I had promised in case I quit within the first year. Persuading Uncle Ed to advance thirteen hundred dollars was tougher than trying to get belt lacings from the Governor. After a long lecture, Uncle Ed had me almost ready to surrender and join a law office. But I was determined not to throw away three years' experience without one more try.

My chance came sooner than expected and in a peculiar way. One of my regular calls for the Globe was on the James O'Flaherty Advertising Agency. A big handsome buckaroo was Jim O'Flaherty. His hair was red. So was his handle-bar mustache. He was a professional Irishman. While he normally talked without accent, when he put on his Irish act you could cut his brogue with a knife.

One morning, as I walked into his office, I found him ranting. "The miserable blankety-blank of an A.P.A.—that blankety-blank Hugh Boyd. I'll be damned if I ever give that no-good double-crossing Protestant another line out of this agency." O'Flaherty was addressing his secretary at a pitch which would have filled Madison Square Garden. When he noticed me standing in the doorway he stopped his tirade. A bright idea seemed to strike him.

"I'll tell you what to do, my boy." It was a command, not a request. "Go down to New Brunswick. Buy that miserable good-for-nothing Times. I'll give you every line of advertising. Not an ink blot to that goddamned A.P.A. That'll make Boyd twice as mad as if I just cut the town off." Jim's well-rounded face relaxed into a gleeful grin.

"Do you mean that, Mr. O'Flaherty?" His manner was so theatrical I seemed to be playing straight man in a farce.

"Sure, I mean it, and Jim O'Flaherty's word is as good as his bond." Then he cut off the brogue. "You can buy the New Brunswick Times for a song. I promise you all the advertising out of this office. With your experience you're just the lad to make good."

He looked at a memorandum on his desk.

"Now here's what you do," he continued. "See a Mr. George Viehman, head of an insurance agency. Tell him I sent you. He asked me to find him a buyer. Let me know what kind of deal you can make."

Here was a real opportunity. James O'Flaherty had developed a unique business. He held a monopoly of out-of-town advertising by New York and Newark department stores. Suburban newspapers were not equipped to handle the difficult typography of metropolitan retail advertising. O'Flaherty supplied these suburban dailies with mats of New York ads, from which they cast stereotype plates. He owned the Bronx Home News, a successful neighborhood daily, which set the ads, made and distributed the mats. Because he performed this mechanical service, O'Flaherty was not limited to the usual 15 per cent agency commission. He bought space in bulk from suburban papers and sold it to New York stores in the same way. The spread between the two figures was a trade secret. To preserve it he had a strict rule that his suburban newspaper clients were not to solicit advertising from New York stores. It was part of his stock-in-trade that he protected the department store advertising managers from solicitation by forty small-town advertising men. The New Brunswick Home News had broken this rule. Gimbel's advertising manager mentioned to O'Flaherty he had met Arthur Boyd, a son of Hugh Boyd, publisher of the New Brunswick Home News, at a cocktail party and they had discussed advertising. Hugh Boyd happened to be a Protestant Irishman, which seemed to add fuel to the flame.

I took the next train to New Brunswick, a delightful, old-fashioned New Jersey town of 25,000, forty miles from New York. Viehman talked astronomical figures. After three days he agreed to let me have his 80 per cent interest "practically as a gift" for $2,500 cash and a $10,000 mortgage. The other 20 per cent was owned by the editor, Sam Christy. The Times plant was in good condition, flatbed Duplex and five linotypes, housed in a sound and centrally located building. But it had only 1,500 circulation against 8,000 guaranteed by the Home News. The New York and Newark advertising, promised by O'Flaherty, would increase circulation and decrease the annual deficit of $10,000. I was confident I could put the Times on a paying basis.

Where to get the $2,500? Uncle Ed was impossible. I went to Agnes and Dr. Ludwig Loeb, my sister and brother-in-law. I should not have asked them to risk money on this gamble. Ludwig had a good practice but he had a growing family to support. Against the advice of uncles and aunts, Agnes and Ludwig lent it to me. They alone had confidence in me and let their initial investment ride in my subsequent ventures. Fortunately, it turned out all right. When I retired, thirty-five years later, they received $400,000 for their stock.

* * * * *

That first morning as publisher-owner of the Times, while I appeared to be sitting in my office, I was really floating on a cloud. At last I had reached the summit. My first caller, a syndicate salesman, pulled me down to earth.

"I want to see your father" was his greeting.

"My father died five years ago," I said. He was as embarrassed as I was annoyed. At twenty-six I looked eighteen. To camouflage my youthful appearance and prevent a recurrence of such incidents I kept a big cigar in my mouth almost continuously. What started as "protective coloring" developed into a fixed habit. I became a chain smoker, consuming a dozen or more big ones a day. I kept this up until I developed cancer of the throat in 1956. Fortunately, Dr. Eugene P. Pendergrass, the radiologist, was able to catch it in time so I am still in circulation—but not smoking. That morning on Olympus in a state of euphoria, a trivial misunderstanding started a bad habit which nearly cost me my life. Through what a chancy channel we navigate.

Sam Christie proved an able editor whose liberalism had been nullified by Viehman's conservatism. A wiry, high-strung Scotchman, he had a dogmatic way of writing and talking. His favorite expression, "Never was wrong in my life," irritated me at first but his quick decisions were usually correct and I came to accept his cocksureness with his other idiosyncrasies—one of them to compose his editorials on a linotype machine, without writing them out first. He had been a "swift" (fast linotype operator) in his younger days. His slash-bang liberal editorials in support of Governor Woodrow Wilson for President made a hit with the industrial workers who were 40 per cent of New Brunswick's population.

Thanks to her experience with Nell Siddons, Jill gave us an excellent woman's page, as well as a daily book review and a weekly church page. In her usual thorough way she compiled a complete roster of women's social clubs and church societies. We published such a complete, accurate calendar of meetings that clubwomen just had to buy the Times. It was the kind of job Jill disliked, but she worked so hard and conscientiously she brought us important circulation among the "upper crust" who had never before read the Democratic paper.

We all worked hard. It was a small force, as small as could get out a daily—twenty-five on a payroll of five hundred dollars a week. As they say in the circus, we doubled in brass. When they were not printing the paper, the two pressmen did stereotyping and job work. The five linotype operators helped on make-up and handsetting. Everyone was intent on making each minute count. They complained when they were not kept busy. Standing time was taboo.

In addition to my other duties I set myself the task of building suburban circulation. I visited the twenty small towns and villages within a twelve-mile radius of New Brunswick to hire correspondents. To handle this suburban news I would call at the post office by 6 A.M., and have copy on the hook when the linotype operators came to work at 7:30. By 9:00 I was on the street soliciting advertising and job work. At night I kept the books and wrote ads. I saw my wife and son only at meal times, or when I took them in my Model T to make the rounds of the country correspondents.

I was enjoying myself so much that hard work and long hours did not tire me. We were making good. The Times was better than breaking even. Circulation had doubled within the first six months. O'Flaherty proved a man of his word. The Times carried all the big-city advertising; the Home News, not a line. O'Flaherty's check for six hundred dollars a month was a great help.

Then there was Barney Gannon, Democratic boss of Middlesex County. Many political leaders have promised me support. Barney not only promised, but delivered. A small stout man, built like a kewpie, Barney had only one eye. The saying was that Barney saw more out of one eye than anyone else out of two. His political strength was in the factory and oil-refinery districts of Perth Amboy, South Amboy and South River. The silk-stocking, commuting population was the obstacle to his control of New Brunswick. He did have a toe hold in the city government. Of the twelve councilmen, five, elected by industrial wards, were Democrats.

To get rid of Barney's obstreperous councilmen, the Republicans initiated a referendum to change the city government from councilmanic to commission, an innovation which had just been introduced by Governor Wilson. Commissioners are elected at large, not by wards. With a 60-40 majority in the city as a whole, the Republicans could elect all five commissioners. I was so busy pulling the Times out of the red I left politics to Sam. But both Sam and Barney enlisted my help in the referendum contest. I wrote front-page editorials to warn that commission government was a new-fangled scheme which breached the fundamentals of democracy by depriving the wards of representation. I gave big play to stories of municipal house cleanings which inevitably followed the shift to commission rule. No city employee's job would be safe if the municipal system were altered. This worried Republican officeholders, the backbone of the opposition.

The dignified Republican Home News did not deign to answer my editorial blasts, but I had evidence I was making a dent. New Brunswick's leading department store, our largest customer, stopped advertising because "The Times is too full of politics." I phoned Barney. "Leave it to me," was his curt and characteristic reply. Late that afternoon the head of the store came to my office with copy for the next day. He explained there had been a misunderstanding. Barney had recruited fifty women to phone the store they were closing their accounts!

The referendum was defeated by 143 votes. Sam and I joined Barney and his lieutenants at a celebration which lasted until dawn. Barney gave all credit to my editorials. He kept repeating a toast to "My frien' Dave, greatush editor in th' worl'." All very silly—but I ate it up.

The next morning brought more tangible proof of victory. Into my office came Charles McCormick, treasurer of Johnson & Johnson, the city's leading industry. He looked and acted the crisp, tense, come-to-the-point executive talking to the hick publisher.

"Congratulations, Stern. You certainly put it over. Great work. Barney never could have done it without your editorials. Stern, how much do you want for your stock in this paper?"

This abrupt approach struck me dumb. To gain time and gather my wits I said, "Won't you sit down?"

"Yes, I'll sit down, but how much do you want for your stock?"

"I owe it to Sam Christy to ask him how he feels about it."

"Sam's for it. We'll retain him at an increased salary. Ask him." McCormick did not waste words. So Sam had been consulted and not told me. I called Sam into my office.

"It's all right with me," he said. "Dave, I advise you to sell. We're doing fine, but it will take years to overtake the Home News. Until then, you'll never make real money. Your energy and ability can earn ten times as much in a larger city."

I named what appeared to me a high figure, twenty-five thousand dollars. Later I learned McCormick had been authorized to pay up to fifty thousand—my nuisance value to the big business interests of the town.

McCormick wrote a check. We walked to the bank where I had the stock certificates, which I endorsed and handed to him.

When I returned to the office, Jill was hard at work.

"Let's go home to lunch."

"Why so early? I want to finish this piece."

"I'll tell you on the way home. It's important."

"You have no plan for the future," was Jill's first reaction. "Why get out of one enterprise before you know what you're going to do next?"

"I have it all planned," was my reply. "You and I have worked awfully hard. We haven't had any real fun, and only a week's honeymoon. We've knocked around from one job to another. We're going to Europe. Your mother and father will be glad to take care of Tommy for a couple of months. Now we'll have a real honeymoon. When we come back, I'll get a bigger paper in a bigger town. Now I know I can do it."

Under Johnson & Johnson ownership the Times lost so much money, after six months they sold it to the Home News, which has maintained its monopoly ever since.

❖   ❖   ❖   ❖   ❖

It was thirty years before I returned to New Brunswick. I had an hour to spare after a business appointment. I looked up some of my old friends.

"Dave Stern, I remember you. You got out your newspaper with a Ford," was the usual greeting. During a sleet storm which shut off power throughout the town, I had managed to get my Model T into the plant, jacked up the back wheels, clamped a belt on them to run the linotypes in the morning, the press in the afternoon. Boyd's big Packard stuck in the door, so the Home News did not publish. The spectacle of the little newspaper beating its big competitor struck the town as a great joke, and was fixed in its memory. Forgotten were my editorials, my championship of factory workers versus commuters, my victory in the commission government referendum.

Max Strassburger, the friend I had most hoped to see, had died. Max had been foreman of that hard-working composing room and job shop. Ten years after I left New Brunswick, when he was foreman of the Home News, he had taken the trouble to phone me in Camden, "Two young fellows from the Camden Post-Telegram are in the morgue copying your editorials against commission government. I thought you might want to know."

It was a most important message. The Camden Courier was supporting a referendum for commission government. I lost no time in writing an editorial explaining that I had opposed commission government ten years before when it was an experiment, but now that I had seen how well it worked in other cities, I was for it. It took the wind out of the opposition's blast at my change of front.

What a loyal crew helped me put over the Times.

VIII

A Third Tryout

My experience in Providence and New Brunswick developed self-confidence out of all proportion to actual accomplishment. I thought I knew the newspaper business from A to Z. Fortunately, the "veteran publisher" was to have another most valuable five-year tryout in the Middle West.

The outbreak of World War I made a European trip impossible. Instead Jill and I set out, in our Model T, to see the United States. Before we started I had made an analysis of the newspapers in all cities between fifty and one hundred thousand population. Evening dailies were away ahead of their morning competitors in every city except one—Springfield, Illinois, where the two morning papers had double the circulation of the two evenings and carried most of the advertising. Henry F. Henrichs, a newspaper broker then, now head of Henrichs Publications in Litchfield, Illinois, told me both evening papers, the News and the Record, were for sale. When I asked him why the morning-evening ratio was the reverse of that in other cities, his explanation was, "Springfield is the trading center of a vast corn-farming area. Its morning newspapers reach the farmers on the day of publication by rural route mail. The evening papers are delivered a day late."

"But in other agricultural centers the evenings are on top," I said. That stumped Henry. "Why don't you go out and see for yourself?" was his suggestion.

As this was a strictly sight-seeing and pleasure trip I sold Jill on visiting Lincoln's tomb and home town. It was 100 degrees in the shade as we bumped along a dirt road toward Springfield. For hours we seemed to be traveling through one everlasting flat corn-field. Drab farm towns, at ten-mile intervals, did not relieve the monotony. First impressions are lasting. For the five years we lived in Springfield that heat-seared picture of ever repeating rows of corn was fixed in our minds.

Springfield would have been just another Midwestern state capital were it not for the aura of Lincoln—his home, tomb, Mary Todd's home and other historic sites. In the center of a large square stood the usual county courthouse and bandstand, dwarfed by the towering Capitol building a few blocks away. The city was clean and prosperous but not exciting. After a morning of sight-seeing Jill wanted to rest. This gave me an opportunity to call on Victor Bender, publisher of the Springfield News, the larger of the two evening newspapers.

At our first meeting Bender and I hit it off. He was, or rather had been, a handsome man. Now he was fifty-five. Hollow cheeks and dark rings under tired eyes indicated weariness and ill-health. He told me he was anxious to get out. "I have no mind for business details. I hate financial statements, especially when they end in red ink." During the ten years of his ownership, the yearly deficit had gradually grown to $25,000. When he had sunk all his own money, his friend Frank O. Lowden had come to the rescue and lent the Springfield News Company $140,000 on demand notes endorsed by Bender. His personal liability on those notes explained the circles under his eyes.

Frank O. Lowden was a successful Chicago lawyer, general counsel of the Pullman Company. He had married Florence Pullman, heiress to the $50,000,000 Pullman fortune. It was generally rumored Lowden would be the Republican candidate for Governor in 1916.

"You pay Lowden's notes and I'll give you my stock," Bender said.

"Where would that leave you?" I asked.

"Sleeping nights. Perhaps you'd give me a job. I don't need much. My wife is dead. My son, just graduated from college, can fend for himself."

"You're more concerned about Lowden than about yourself," I said. "He's the least of your worries. All his notes are worth is what the machinery would bring in liquidation. Give him preferred stock for his notes. I'll put twenty thousand dollars in the till to keep us going until we turn the corner. You keep forty per cent of the stock and stay on as editor. Give me sixty per cent and control as publisher."

I had a hard time persuading Bender to let me present the plan to Lowden. It went against the grain to ask his friend to compromise a personal obligation. After lengthy arguing, he called Lowden in Chicago and made an appointment, but refused to go with me.

Lowden's face was grim when he greeted me in the outer office. "Mr. Stern, you have a hell of a nerve asking me to swap demand notes for worthless preferred stock."

"I consider it a fair proposition, Mr. Lowden, or I would not have made it. If you think the preferred stock worthless, then I'm a sucker to invest twenty thousand cash, junior to your security."

"As long as you're here," Lowden said, "we might as well talk it over." He led me into his private office.

"So you want to protect old Bender instead of rich Mr. Lowden who can afford to kiss his money goodbye. I know all about your fine plan. Victor came clean with the whole plot."

Before I could interrupt, he went on, "What's more, young man, I like your line of reasoning." A smile replaced the scowl. When Lowden smiled, he was in a class with Franklin Roosevelt and Anthony Eden. They were the three handsomest statesmen of my time, and how they could disarm with their charm! "I like your idea of cutting Victor in. I apologize for calling the preferred stock worthless. What little I have found out about you inclines me to share your confidence that you will pull the News out of the red. But I don't want the preferred. I'll wipe the slate clean. I'll hand the notes to you, marked paid." Then, after a pause:

"No, I won't. I don't want anyone to hold evidence of what a sucker I've been. I'll destroy the notes in your presence and give Victor a quitclaim to restore his peace of mind. You two can make a fresh start out of debt, and, I hope, stay that way."

Unprepared for so generous an arrangement, I was speechless. Lowden leaned back in his chair and laughed. "Young man, has the cat run off with your tongue?" he bantered. "Has Old Scrooge taken you by surprise? I appreciate how disappointed you are. You came to Chicago to drive a bargain. Now you find nothing to bargain about."

This was the beginning of a warm friendship which lasted until Lowden's death in 1943. That I wanted Bender to retain an interest and continue as editor made a hit with Lowden. For years he had realized that the situation was hopeless, but kept on helping his boyhood pal on the chance that some solution would develop. My offer gave him a way out.

After I had phoned Jill and Bender the good news, I took the next train back to Springfield. Jill stayed with me for a few days to find an apartment and then went back to her parents' home to fetch Tom.

Vic Bender was so relieved by his release from the Lowden notes, his lawyer and I had a hard time holding his attention to the agreements and documents we had to sign. While the paper work was being completed, he introduced me to the staff. I cut the flowery language usual on such occasions. I told them I had come to Springfield to find out why it was the only city in the Middle West where morning newspapers had more circulation than evening. Could anyone give me a clue? When there were no answers, I closed the two-minute meeting with, "Let's find out."

During the afternoon I received a courtesy call from Thomas Ries, publisher of the Register, oldest and largest of Springfield's newspapers. After conventional conversation, Ries, a portly, pompous old gentleman, rose to take his leave. He had a final message for me. "Stern, you should know we Springfield publishers never hit below the belt, but we wear our belts around our ankles." It was not long before I found how true this was.

Bender and four executives dined with me that night. I was impressed by the managing editor, Bill Cheedle, and the city editor, Hal Crews. The advertising and circulation managers were obviously punch-drunk from waging a losing battle. Before we broke up, we prepared a front-page statement by Bender, that I had purchased a controlling interest in the News and was now its publisher, while he continued as editor.

I spent the rest of the night studying recent issues of the News.

It was well edited, but pitifully thin—eight to twelve pages against its morning competitors' sixteen to twenty-four. I would have to increase its bulk to gain circulation. I had just learned the real honest-to-God net paid was 9,000, instead of the 12,000 claimed.

At dawn I fell asleep wondering how I could solve the puzzle— sell advertising without circulation, while I increased circulation to get advertising. When I woke a few hours later, I had the solution. I set out on the strangest business adventure of my career. To this day I have not made up my mind whether it was the stupidest or smartest move I ever made.

Without introduction, I called on the six department stores. I was breaking a precedent. In Springfield, newspaper publishers never descended from their ivory towers to call on advertisers. I broke another precedent by telling the truth about circulation. It was 9,000, not 12,000. Before A.B.C., a publisher was expected to exaggerate. I offered these stores advertising at an absurdly low rate, in return for their commitments to run not less than half a page six days a week for a year. "But we have to think this over," was repeated each time I filled out the contract form. "We'll let you know next week."

"I won't be offering space at half cost next week. I'll have come to my senses. The only benefit I can get from selling you advertising below cost is the impact on the smaller stores when you, Springfield's leading merchant, show you want the News to succeed. It's now, or not at all," I would say aloud, while repeating under my breath, "You will sign now." Thanks to Gene McGuckin's training, I returned to my office that evening with the six contracts. The problem of bulk was solved.

Overnight the News doubled in size and boasted the largest volume of advertising in Springfield. This infuriated my competitors, who predicted I would go broke within three months. I was a fake and fly-by-night who sold advertising for anything I could get. My rate card was a joke. Furthermore, I was a crook and drank too much, borrowed from my employees and had affairs with women in my office. They literally knocked me into success.

"The Harder They Knock the Higher We Go," was the caption

of a cartoon I ran in the News depicting a ring-the-bell game at a county fair. The Register and the Journal were swinging mallets which drove the News up the column to ring the bell at the top. Under this picture were figures to show that the News carried more advertising than "both morning newspapers combined." Once a month this page ad appeared and never failed to goad the morning newspapers into fresh attacks.

The battle of the News with its prosperous competitors intrigued the business community. Over the years the Register and the Journal had become a bit stiff and overbearing. Besides, Americans resent knocking. Call a candidate son-of-a-bitch often enough, and you elect him. A new Ford agent, who had just arrived in town, phoned me before our representative had called on him. "I'm ordering all my advertising into the News, and only the News," he said. "I don't like the way the other newspapers in this town solicit business. From what they tell me you must be meaner and tougher than anyone I've ever met." He became a friend and booster, gave us letters stating how many cars he had sold while advertising exclusively in the News. This helped us take the lead in automobile advertising. The other papers retaliated by running pictures of accidents in which Fords were wrecked, even if they had to go fifty miles to find one. Jennings, the Ford agent, was a stubborn cuss. He stood pat for two years.

But there was another side to the picture. I had sold advertising below cost, at ten cents a column inch, $16.80 a page. The News had been averaging forty dollars per advertising page and losing money. By the laws of arithmetic I was bound to go broke as my competitors predicted. I should have foreseen that the composing room would bog down under the sudden increase in business. I phoned Elmer Pratt, who was working in Boston. He caught the next train and pulled us out of our difficulty. But, with all his skill and drive, he had to hire more compositors and we were consuming more newsprint. The twenty thousand dollars I had put in the till was evaporating. I felt the hot breath of the sheriff on the back of my neck.

I phoned Rufus Rohrbacher, the biographer in Seattle. Exploiting people's vanity is a disreputable way to raise money but I was running scared. Rufus worked round the clock preparing his "biographical" material. His first call was on Lowden, who everyone predicted would be the next Governor. "The rest is easy," Rufus said when he brought back Lowden's check for $1,000. Within two weeks he had collected $12,000, of which the News' share was a desperately needed $6,000.

The Gilman Paper Company gave us long credit on newsprint. Mick Katzenberg bought stock. When we could not meet the payroll in any other way there were a few advertisers who would pay in advance. One of these was a Scotchman who always carried a big roll, and enjoyed any "given" number of drinks. On a Friday afternoon, when Alfred Neef, our bookkeeper, told me we were in trouble, I would phone my friend to meet me in our favorite saloon. After I had paid for the fifth round I would help him into my car, parked at the back entrance, and drive him home—but not before he had peeled off the three or four hundred dollars we needed to make the ghost walk on Saturday.

Somehow we always managed to meet the payroll and keep our heads above water, but it was a nerve-racking struggle until we bought the Springfield Record, the other evening newspaper, in 1917.

The Record had been started in 1910 by liquor and brewing interests to stem the growing blight of local option. It had not proven an effective antidote. Most of the central Illinois counties had gone dry and Sangamon County (Springfield) itself was in jeopardy. Backed by big business, prohibitionists were demanding the Eighteenth Amendment. One of their arguments was that, without intoxicants, labor would be more reliable, the nation more efficient. In this way prohibition became linked with the war effort. When war was declared April 6, 1917, it looked as though prohibition was inevitable. The owners of the Record gave up hope and decided there was no reason to keep on meeting the annual deficit of $30,000. They sold its name and goodwill to the Springfield News Company for $50,000 of preferred stock. With great fanfare we changed our name to Springfield News-Record. The merger brought little increase in circulation but it did give us an excuse to raise our ruinously low advertising rates. From then on we maintained a respectable bank balance and the pressure was off.

❊   ❊   ❊   ❊   ❊

Jill had given me the happy news she was expecting our second child. It is her story, but I deny it, that my first reaction was, "You'll have to quit work." Jill had become a most essential member of the staff, editing a weekly book page as well as the daily woman's page, in which she had increased interest by urging the women's clubs to undertake successful campaigns for civic improvements—free garbage collection, watering dusty streets before sweeping, improved health service, and others. In addition to her heavy schedule she was teaching Tom and his playmate, Bobby (Robert) Fitzgerald, aged five, to read. I think it is more than a coincidence that both of her pupils became successful writers. Fitzgerald recently received an award for his poetical translation of the Odyssey.

How she managed to run the house, care for the children, do a day's work at the office and always look well-groomed is beyond me. I was just the opposite, too busy to shave, have my clothes pressed, or my shoes shined. Albert Myers, head of Springfield's leading clothing store, took me to task. As I was passing his door one day he stopped me.

"Dave, I'll give you any suit in this store as a present," he said, "if you promise me to clean up. The way you go around, you're a disgrace to the Jews of this town."

It was absurd the way I drove myself. As in New Brunswick I came to the office at 6 A.M. to handle country correspondence. But my long hours had an important side effect. My staff fell into the same pace. Advertising solicitors reported at 7:30 A.M., were on the street by eight to hit the stores before customers arrived. We paid no overtime but they worked nights, as I did, writing ads. The news and circulation departments followed suit.

Jill was at the office until the day before our baby was born, and back on the job within a month. Our daughter, named Jill, and called Little Jill, a beautiful and delightful child, was a great joy. I took to stealing home for lunch to play with her. Little Jill's one complaint was that she could not go to school with her brother.

So I had to stay on after lunch to conduct a pretend school at which she did so well I told her she would be a novelist and an actress when she grew up. Both predictions came true.

From 1917 on I had another run of luck like my first week as a cub reporter. The six hours' difference between European and Central Time was a most fortunate break for the News-Record. Our 6 P.M. War Extra cleaned up cable news from France and Germany up to midnight European time. In those days, there was no competition from radio.

With this late edition, we were able to break the morning newspapers' hold on rural route mail circulation. Rural carriers left the post office early in the morning. Farmers refused to take a newspaper delivered a day late. So, after the press run for the day was completed, we changed "War Extra" to "Farm Edition," the date on the front page to the next day, and chiseled the date lines off the other plates on the press. As we had to alter our Saturday War Extra to the following Monday's Farm Edition, no one was fooled by our device. But this inexpensive method allowed us to cut in half the then prevailing yearly subscription price of four dollars. A two-dollar saving is a potent argument on an Illinois farm. We signed up 3,000 rural route subscriptions and passed the morning newspapers in circulation as we already had in advertising.

Not the least of these lucky breaks was my chance choice of Pop (Isaac) Gilman as supplier of newsprint. I had ordered my first carload of paper from Pop's son, Fred Gilman, a college friend. That was for the New Brunswick Times, which used five carloads a year. Over thirty-five years my account grew to ten carloads a day. Through all my ups and downs, Pop Gilman backed me, bought stock in my newspapers, extended credit to which I was not entitled, gave wise advice and encouragement.

Pop could scarcely read or write. He spoke broken English, had never read a book. But I enjoyed being with him. Nor was I the only one who found him stimulating. Men like General James G. Harbord and former Attorney General George W. Wickersham sought the company of this unlettered Russian-Jewish peasant who radiated wit, wisdom and charm.

As a child, he had been indentured to a farmer, which was virtual slavery. The brightest boy on the farm, it was his job to go to town to buy supplies. By the time he was eighteen he had saved enough to make his way to New York, where he became a cigar maker. Standing outside the factory one sunny spring noon, he noticed a man, with a horse and wagon, selling paper bags to peddlers. What a wonderful life, out in the sunshine all day, riding about in a fine rig! Gilman bought horse, wagon and stock of paper bags, for the eighty dollars he had saved during his two years in New York.

When I first met Pop, which was twenty-five years after he bought the horse and wagon, he had just purchased a paper mill at Fitzdale, Vermont. The townspeople changed its name to Gilman, not because he had built both a Protestant and a Catholic church, as well as a hospital, but because this remarkable little man had endeared himself to all of them.

One Sunday morning in 1937 Pop and I were taking a ride in the hills overlooking Gilman. Our car became mired a mile from town. A passing farmer went to fetch his team to pull us out. Before he returned he had phoned his neighbors, who strolled up to shake hands. They stood in a circle around Pop, these Vermont farmers, the shortest of them a lanky six feet in contrast to Pop's dumpy five-feet-five. They had not come just to greet the mill owner. They wanted Pop's opinion on world affairs and domestic economy. In 1936, Vermont and Maine were the only two states against Roosevelt. These farmers were worried that the terrible man in the White House would destroy the country "by letting those radical labor unions run wild." When Pop said, "Higher wages means higher prices for the farmer," they cheered up. Before the impromptu confab was over, we were cracking jokes. No other "New York foreigner" could have duplicated this scene. Pop possessed that mysterious magnetism which puts over great actors and orators.

One of Pop's slogans was, "Treat the man you buy from better than the man you sell to." I did not appreciate this reversal of the usual code of business conduct until the depression in 1933. New York banks suddenly called Gilman Company loans. Pop would have lost control of his business if the firms from which he bought pulp, coal, etc., had not come to the rescue and extended long-term credit to their fairest and friendliest customer.

On Pop's death, August 1944, Time Magazine headed his obituary, "A Good Man." "His life stands as proof that in America a poor boy can achieve great material success with grace and kindliness," was part of the Philadelphia Record's tribute.

❊   ❊   ❊   ❊   ❊

There was a fly in the ointment of the News-Record's success. Springfield was two hundred miles away from any vacation spot—trivial today, with modern highways and airplanes. But forty years ago, it required an overnight train trip to reach summer recreation. Jill and I, tied to the daily grind, could not spare time for vacations. Then, Springfield had few parks and no public swimming pools as it has today. So our children had to spend the hot summers —and they were hot as hell—playing in the yard. They were well and contented, but we felt guilty.

I liked the people of Springfield. They were forthright and free of pretense. Comparing them with other sections of the United States, in which I worked, they impressed me as the most commonsensical of Americans. But it was a very literal and matter-of-fact community in which sarcasm and persiflage did not register. At a social gathering, during my first month in Springfield, the conversation turned to higher education. I was critical of American colleges and ended my fault-finding with the quip: "I'd rather have my son go to jail than to college." A year later, Art (Arthur) Fitzgerald, my friend and lawyer, asked me whether I had made such a ridiculous remark. I admitted I had, and added, "I thought it would be understood as an obvious wisecrack."

"They put you down as a complete screwball," Art said. Shades of Mark Twain's autobiographical *Pudd'nhead Wilson*. Twain's humorous sallies must have come bouncing back at him from a stolid wall of literalness. The circle of friends who talked our language was limited—Vachel Lindsay, his friend Edgar Lee Masters, the Fitzgeralds, and the delightfully stimulating Haglers afforded our only social relaxation.

Dr. Elmer Hagler was the leading eye surgeon of central Illinois. His wife, Kent Hagler, a graduate of Wellesley in the days when higher education for women was an innovation, kept her family on their intellectual toes. A small, unassuming woman, quiet of voice and manner, she ruled the roost. She insisted that her two sons attend Harvard, and they both showed brilliance before their untimely deaths. On graduation, the older boy, Elmer Jr., became a reporter on the News-Record. A slight and delicately-built youth, his chief interests were poetry and painting. When I overheard the city editor complain that Hagler was late with news from police headquarters, I made the ill-tempered comment, "Serves you right for assigning that Harvard la-di-da to cover police."

Just then Hagler showed up sporting a black eye and torn collar. He had beaten up a police sergeant and two patrolmen in a battle royal. The News-Record had been highly critical of the Police Department. Hagler's routine request to look at the police blotter had been met with a string of insults for himself and his newspaper. The fat sergeant had been lolling back in his chair when he delivered his billingsgate. Hagler tilted him past the center of gravity and proceeded to read the blotter. The sergeant, reinforced by two patrolmen, charged the enemy. Hagler tipped the desk over on them and took it on the lam.

When the United States declared war, Elmer received a commission in the regular Army. His regiment was one of the earliest to go overseas and into action. He was the first Springfield man reported killed. The city went into mourning. Memorial services were held in many of the churches. The Episcopal bishop referred to him as St. Elmer. Later Elmer claimed this gave him an irrevocable pass to Heaven.

Several weeks after his reported death, his parents received word he was alive. He had been gassed and ordered to the rear. But when action started, the other officers in his company had been killed or wounded, so he led his men over the top. His hip shattered by a bullet, he lay in a shell hole until night, when one of his men, who received the Congressional Medal for his bravery, carried him back to our trenches. Elmer, promoted on the field, was the youngest captain in the regular Army.

When he came home the town turned out to welcome the returning hero. Trust Elmer to make a dramatic entrance. He stepped off the train wearing a bandage around his forehead. His shabby, disheveled uniform, his cane and limp, completed his get-up. The crowd went wild. Since there had been no mention of a head wound, I was puzzled. Elmer explained, in strict confidence, that after a wild party in New York he had made the mistake of diving into the shallow end of the pool at a Turkish bath.

Elmer was the most brilliant boy who ever worked for me. He was a painter of exquisite miniatures, a poet, and a mathematical genius. He could have achieved distinction in any field. Against my advice he remained in the Army after the war. His health and nerves had been shattered by that day in no man's land. Because the Army doctors were not wise enough to insist on a year of complete rest, he died young. Kent Hagler, Elmer's younger brother, rejected by the Army because of a back injury he had received playing football, enlisted in the Ambulance Corps, and died in France. The third child, Clarissa (Mrs. Jorganssen), and her children are the only survivors of the colorful Hagler family.

❀   ❀   ❀   ❀   ❀

By the spring of 1919, the News-Record had made such progress Jill and I planned to take our children to a Michigan lake resort for a month's vacation. Then the Associated Press notified me that Thomas Reis had applied for an evening membership. In 1917 I had signed what I was told was an exclusive Associated Press evening membership, which would protect me in that field. This "exclusiveness" was about to be challenged.

Through Art Fitzgerald, Reis had made several offers to buy me out. These proposals were accompanied by the threat that if I did not sell, one of the two morning papers would move over to the evening field. I had paid no attention to offers or threats. Now it looked as though my competitors meant business.

In protest to granting a second evening membership in Springfield, I appeared before the Associated Press Board of Directors at their annual meeting in New York, April, 1919, to state my case: I had been induced to take A.P. service on assurance that my exclusive membership would protect me from competition in the evening field. The town could not support two evening newspapers. My morning competitors had offered to buy me out, now threatened to drive me out. If the A.P. granted this second evening membership, it would become a party to this attack. From the questions asked and the directors' side remarks, I was sure I had won.

As I left the board room, Tom Reis was ushered in. Then for two hours we sat in the outer office, ignoring each other. Finally, Frank B. Noyes, president of the A.P., came to explain that Reis' forty-year-old founding membership was so worded as to include evening as well as morning and Sunday services. He admitted the A.P. had misrepresented the status of my membership. Later I learned that Reis had won a bare majority of the board by the old-school-tie argument. A member of the A.P. for forty years, he said he was too old to move while I was young enough to establish myself in another city.

My answer to this adverse decision was to tell Noyes, in Reis' presence, "I'm applying for A.P. Sunday service. If they move into the evening field, I'll start a third Sunday newspaper. Both sides can play the game of ruining each other."

Starting a Sunday edition would require additional capital, but the town was with me. Leading citizens offered financial backing. One of them was Logan Hay, senior member of the law firm with which Lincoln had been associated, and president of the Lincoln Association. He was a nephew of John Hay, Lincoln's secretary and biographer, who later served as Secretary of State. A most kindly and devoted friend, an idealistic, pipe-smoking intellectual without a sense of humor, he had the obsession that I was working myself to death. He would come to my office at night to make me quit. Then, while I tried to keep awake, he would sit up still later in prolonged debate on the meaning of life. Hay offered to raise $250,000 to finance my battle with the Register. Another supporter was Dr. Hagler, who handed me his check for $50,000.

"On what terms do you propose to invest this?" I asked.

"On any terms you name," was his answer. "We need you in Springfield."

It was heartening to receive such tangible proof of community acceptance. Meanwhile, Reis was raising his ante. He had started with $100,000 net for "Stern to get out of town." Now Art came to my home one night to report that the latest offer was $250,000.

Jill and Art urged me to accept it. The decision was up to me. Because of ill health, Victor Bender had retired the year before, and I had bought his stock. Agnes and Mick Katzenberg, the only other stockholders, would accept my judgment.

"Dave, I'm sure you'll win out," Art said. "But it will probably take another five years—and I don't know how much longer to accumulate two hundred and fifty thousand dollars. It's up to you whether you want to keep battling or accept this small fortune." In 1919 a quarter of a million was equal to a million dollars today.

Jill said she was tired of living in Springfield. "And I'm tired of having you work five nights out of seven. If you start a Sunday newspaper, it will be six nights."

"It won't take five years," I assured them. "Of course, at the start, we'll lose money on the Sunday, but the Register will be losing more on their evening edition. Within a year Reis will be glad to stop his evening if we stop our Sunday. Then the Register and Journal will consolidate, which is the sensible solution."

"Now we'll have to give up our vacation." Jill kept harping on the personal equation. "The children will spend another hot summer here. They are missing all the summer fun your father gave you when you were a child."

I refused to pay attention to Jill while Art and I discussed issuing more stock to finance the Sunday edition.

"If you accepted, we could rent a cottage in Atlantic City," Jill interrupted. "Little Jill has never seen the ocean."

That got me. I could not dismiss from my mind the contrast of Little Jill and Tom playing on the beach and playing in our back yard.

"You win," I said to Jill. "Art, draw up the agreement with Reis."

As events turned out, I am glad I decided as I did. At the time, I was far from happy about leaving a city which had treated a stranger so kindly, and about saying farewell to my loyal staff. I could not anticipate that most of them were soon to rejoin me in my

next venture. Nor could I foresee the aftermath of my friendship
and admiration for Governor Lowden. I had expected the Springfield News to support President Wilson in 1916, as the New Brunswick Times had in 1912. But Lowden was running for Governor on
the Republican ticket and his campaign managers declared this
would nullify our support of Lowden. I argued that we could win
Democrats to vote for the Republican gubernatorial candidate.
But the records showed that less than five per cent of Illinois voters
split their ballots at Presidential elections. Both Bender and I felt
under heavy obligation to Lowden, so we came out for the straight
Republican ticket, Charles Evans Hughes for President, Lowden
for Governor. Election night Vic and I celebrated our double victory. The next morning we found that Hughes' failure to shake
hands with Hiram Johnson had lost him California and the election. But Lowden had won by a large majority.

Lowden's brilliant record as Governor made him one of the leading candidates for the Republican nomination for President in
1920. He had reorganized the antediluvian State government, in-
augurated a budget system, consolidated fifty graft-ridden State
agencies into twelve departments, began construction of the Great
Lakes-Gulf Waterways. By that time I had bought the Camden
(N.J.) Courier, a Republican newspaper, which supported Lowden for the nomination. I went to the Republican National Convention in Chicago with Senator David Baird, New Jersey's Old
Guard leader. When Harding was nominated I was so disgusted I
said I would not support him.

"You sat in on the game. You can't welch," was Baird's laconic
reply. The Courier supported Harding. Within two years the
Courier broke with Baird, elected a Democratic mayor of Camden, and later, a nonpartisan commission city government. While
Democratic in local politics the Courier continued Republican in
national elections.

When I bought the Democratic Philadelphia Record in 1928 I
went all out for Al Smith. This was duck soup for my critics, who
called me "the two-faced publisher, Democratic on one side of
the Delaware and Republican on the other." Judge John Kates,
one of Camden's elder statesmen, never missed a chance, at public

occasions, to ask me, "At the exact center of the Delaware River bridge, which is your party?"

Looking back it was a careless mistake. The Courier had absorbed its opposition, the Post-Telegram, and could have changed its national politics in 1928. Truth of the matter, I was too occupied with the Record, my first metropolitan newspaper, to give proper thought to the situation—an example of the effect of chain ownership.

In 1932 the Philadelphia Record, the Camden Courier and the Camden Post supported Roosevelt and the Democratic ticket, as did all my newspapers until I retired in 1947.

IX

Camden Dream Comes True

Springfield marked the end of my eleven years of wandering apprenticeship as reporter, advertising solicitor, editor and publisher, in the East, Far West and Middle West. My next newspaper, the Camden Courier, I was to publish for twenty-eight years, until my retirement.

Jill lost no time leaving Springfield with the children to rent a cottage in Atlantic City. I had to stay on to settle my affairs and to see that my loyal staff found positions. Page ads in *Editor and Publisher* brought prompt response. The News-Record had a good reputation. Before I left all my men were placed. Within a year many of them were again working with me in Camden.

My regret in leaving a city which had been so friendly was drowned in a round of parties, or rather one continuous ball. My suite at the Leland Hotel was well stocked with liquor. Friends who dropped in for lunch often stayed until the next morning. I was glad for an excuse to interrupt this carousal. William D. Boyce, publisher of the Chicago Ledger and the Saturday Blade, invited me to visit him. Just before the war he had bought the Indianapolis Star for his son. "I moved it into the finest plant money could buy," he told me. His son was gassed and came back from the war an invalid. "He's in Arizona now, and God knows when, if ever, he'll be able to live East. That's why I never want to see the Star again. That's why I asked you to come and visit me."

I spent three days in Boyce's palatial home getting acquainted. When I said I had to return to Springfield, he made me an unusual proposition: "Dave, go to Indianapolis. If you want the property, write your own ticket. I leave it to you to name a fair price. If you need your money for working capital, pay me off over ten years."

On my way to Atlantic City, I stopped to see the Star. Boyce had not exaggerated. The front of the building and the public office were done in marble. The machinery was as modern and efficient as the decorations were beautiful. The Star's competition, the News, was extremely conservative. It was just the set-up I wanted. I wired Boyce I was interested and would write him from Atlantic City.

"We're going to Indianapolis," were my first words, after greeting Jill and the children.

"Maybe you are, but I'm not!" was Jill's ultimatum. She was tired of the Midwest. There were just as good, if not better, opportunities in the East. I kept stalling Boyce while I tried to persuade Jill that Indianapolis was the chance of a lifetime. I offered summers in Atlantic City, frequent trips East. It got me nowhere.

In spite of this controversy, we had a marvelous summer, our first real vacation since our marriage. My ten-year-old son shared my love of the ocean. Little Jill was at the delightful age of four. The idea of separating myself from my family became less and less to my liking. Finally, I capitulated and told Boyce I had decided to retire.

I did not take Jill's stubbornness in good grace. I told her I was through with newspaper publishing and that I would devote myself to study and writing. Jill's father had died and she wanted to be near her mother, so, in the fall, we moved to Philadelphia.

Atop a high building, our apartment overlooked Camden and its great factories across the Delaware. This reawakened my idea of a Camden newspaper, hatched while I wrote South Jersey news for the Bulletin. I explored Camden and its suburbs. Its industries were expanding, especially the huge plants of the Victor Talking Machine Company and Campbell Soup Company, at that time the two largest advertisers in the world.

My Philadelphia banker suggested I see F. Morse Archer, president of Camden's largest bank, the First National. To Archer I described the kind of newspaper I would like to publish for all South Jersey. He told me there was small chance of buying either of the two newspapers, owned by henchmen of U.S. Senator David Baird, political boss of South Jersey for twenty-five years.

"Control of the press is important to Senator Baird," Archer said. "He would not want an outsider in the picture. I wish Camden could get a live wire like you." I dismissed this last as polite talk, but a week later Archer phoned to make an appointment for the business manager of the Camden Courier, Walter L. Tushingham.

Tushingham was in a fix, as he frankly admitted. His straightforward approach won my interest and liking. His rugged, homely face, as well as his manner, spelled candor and honesty. I was also impressed by the kindliness and consideration with which he talked of his aging publisher, George A. Frey, who was the cause of his present trouble and his visit to me. It was the beginning of a business association which lasted twenty-eight years.

Tush (the nickname with which Camden affectionately dubbed its most popular character) was the son of an itinerant preacher. Because of the family wanderings, he had grown up with little or no education. He had saved enough to attend night classes in a Philadelphia business school. On graduation, in 1894, he became bookkeeper of the Courier at five dollars a week. Frey, a prosperous wholesale grocer, had bought the Camden Daily Courier in 1888. It had been started as a weekly in 1878. As Frey became occupied with banking and other interests, he left the management of the Courier largely to Tush. But while quick to add to Tush's responsibilities, Frey was slow to increase his salary. It was not until 1900, when Tush had attained the title of business manager and the princely salary of fourteen dollars a week, that he had felt able to marry. Then Frey, who was goodhearted although penurious, had presented Tush with a 20 per cent interest in the Courier.

Tush had persuaded Frey, now in his late seventies, to build an addition to the plant and install a new press. This $75,000 investment had preyed on the old man's mind. In a fit of melancholy, owing to his age and not to his financial condition, he had suddenly stopped work on the unfinished building. Meanwhile the new press was rusting in freight cars on a siding. It would require less than $15,000 to complete the new plant, but Tush had given up hope of installing the press while Frey was in control. Would I buy Frey out?

"We have all the advertising we can carry on our old press," Tush explained. "The last years, little effort has been made to sell more. We haven't grown with the town. When the new press is in operation, we'll make a drive for business and increase our earnings. The population of South Jersey will double when a bridge is built across the Delaware, which is bound to happen within the next ten years."

The Courier was making a net profit of $20,000 on an annual volume of $100,000—20 per cent against the usual 10 per cent. When Tush described Frey's stringent economies, I wasn't surprised at the high rate of profit. One of Frey's rules was that no toll call could be made on the Courier's single phone line. Instead, the reporter or editor had to walk two blocks to Frey's office. As city treasurer, Frey received free telephone service. This rule applied to suburban calls costing ten cents. The five members of the editorial staff had side jobs with the city and county government, as secretary to the mayor, clerk of the City Council, etc., so Frey paid them little or no money.

I asked Tush what it would cost to buy Frey out. He replied, "Two hundred thousand dollars."

"Half that figure would be too much," I said.

"The price is high," Tush admitted. "If it were less, someone in Senator Baird's organization would take it over. Frey is sure to consult the Senator, who won't relish the deal. In the present setup the Senator has it all to himself. When he wants something in or out of the Courier he doesn't bother to ask Frey or me. He calls the city editor direct. The boys are all on his payroll. If Baird lets Frey sell, it will only be because Baird doesn't want to match the offer or keep his old friend from getting the high dollar."

I told Tush I was not interested. But I kept dreaming of what could be done with aggressive management. I talked it over with business and newspaper friends. In their opinion a real newspaper could never be developed in a suburb of Philadelphia. If a bridge were built, it would make the task still more difficult by further merging the identities of the two communities. All advised against it—all except Jill who urged, "Even if you have to pay a premium, locate where you want, which is all that counts."

I made the deal. On December 15, 1919, I paid $144,000 for Frey's 80 per cent of the Courier Company stock. This was on the basis of a $180,000 valuation for the concern which had $125,000 in tangible assets.

"You're paying fifty per cent more than it's worth for a bum bet," was the opinion of two of my advisers, Samuel D. Lit and Jacob D. Lit, heads of Lit Brothers, at that time Philadelphia's largest department store, which drew a considerable trade from South Jersey. Because they were Jill's uncles they were annoyed that their nephew-in-law was wasting his time and money on a "neighborhood sheet."

"If everything goes the way you have planned how much business do you think you can do?" Uncle Sam asked. He was a very positive character who wore his snow-white hair and mustache in the style of Mark Twain, to whom he bore a striking resemblance.

"A million dollars," was my answer.

"Nonsense," said Uncle Sam as he walked away.

But, despite their disapproval, Jill's uncles helped the Courier grow. They gave it a generous share of their advertising and told other merchants how their South Jersey business was increasing. It took five years for the Courier to reach the million-dollar goal I had predicted. When I retired in 1947 it was grossing three million dollars. It has recently been sold to the Gannett chain for more than five million, twenty-eight times the "high price" I paid in 1919.

Development of the Courier was not all plain sailing. During the first year my self-confidence and big ideas were under strain. When I met the staff I had a premonition of what I was in for. Tush was the only really capable man in the outfit. I would have to hire an adequate force to produce a better newspaper. This would cost money and entail losses until I could increase advertising income. But the paper was operating at a profit and I had reserve capital. It was not like the situation in Springfield, where I had only a few thousand to meet an already existing deficit. Here I had time to carry out my program in an orderly way.

But my resolve to take my time was shattered the third week. I crossed the ferry at the evening rush hour. Everyone was reading the screaming headlines in the Philadelphia papers about the latest escapade of the fabulous Grover Cleveland Bergdoll, heir to a large fortune and notorious draft-dodger of World War I.

A three-line squib at the bottom of page one was the Courier's coverage of this big story. "Why waste what little news space we have on a story to which the Philadelphia newspapers are giving full play?" was the managing editor's attitude. He told me my grandiose scheme of full news coverage was absurd. The sooner I realized that the only function of a Camden newspaper was to carry local news, the better for the Courier and all concerned.

I gave the managing editor notice, and took the train to Springfield. I had to recruit a ball team which would play the game my way. Within a month, I had half a dozen of my News-Record staff at work on the Courier—three in the newsroom, two in the advertising department, and my Springfield accountant, Alfred Neef. I had already sent for Elmer Pratt. Eventually twenty of my Springfield staff came to work in Camden. Counting wives and children, there were forty-eight former Springfielders living in South Jersey.

By this injection of new blood, the Courier was transformed into a lively newspaper. These Midwesterners were not afflicted with the defeatism of the Courier staff, resigned to publishing a second-rate sheet. My Springfield crew was accustomed to working faster, harder, and longer. After he had been in Camden a week, my Springfield advertising manager, Fred Willhite, came to my office one morning.

"What's ailing you, Boss?" he asked.

"Never felt better in my life. What are you driving at, Fred?"

"You're not getting to the office until eight-thirty. By the time you're through with the sales conference, it's nine-fifteen. The men don't make their first calls until nine-thirty. In Springfield you were at your desk before seven-thirty, and we hit the street not later than eight-thirty. That's an important hour to lose. You're not going soft on us, are you?"

I was fortunate in bringing my former city editor, Harry T. Saylor, to Camden as managing editor. He was that rare combination of a natural executive who commanded the loyalty of his staff, and a gifted writer who could turn out a serious editorial, a humorous column, or a thrilling news story with equal speed and facility. And sometimes he did all three in those early days at the Courier.

Son of an Illinois village storekeeper, who was the town's only freethinker, Harry's earliest ambition was to be a professional ballplayer. After he graduated from high school, he managed his semi-pro team. To get publicity he took to writing his own releases. He found it more remunerative to pound a typewriter than a horsehide ball. He drifted into sports writing. In 1916 he came to the Springfield News.

In time Harry became editor of all my newspapers—the Courier and the Morning Post of Camden, the Philadelphia Record, and the New York Post. He was well-balanced, never went off half-cocked or lost his sense of proportion. This does not mean that he lacked enthusiasm. No matter how hard the going, he always retained the zest for a good story which marks the difference between a great and a mediocre editor. The top man's enthusiasm is infectious. Harry's crew was always "rarin'" to go.

As soon as I had recruited a capable staff in Camden I cut out the political payola. I made the rule that no one on our payroll could be on any other, which put a crimp in Baird's direct control of our city desk.

All the talent which built the Courier was not imported. Camden supplied much excellent material and eventually the majority of the executives were local boys. One of our happiest local finds was Frank Ryan. When I bought the Courier, he had just completed his appenticeship in the composing room and was assistant make-up man. He could sling type the way a short-order cook tosses pancakes. One day, while I was watching him literally throw an extra together, he asked to see me. After he was through for the day, he came to my office.

"I want to be a reporter," he said. "I want to write."

"Glory be, Frank," I said. "You're the best make-up man we've got. You are a natural for that job. Why do you want to switch?"

"There's more future in the newsroom than in the composing room," was his answer.

"Frank, you've served a four-year apprenticeship to learn your trade. You're tops in the composing room. When Billy Wells retires, you'll be foreman. To help you get over your crazy idea, I'll give you a five-dollar raise. Go back to the composing room and help us beat the deadline." I should have known better but here I was echoing van Valkenburg when he tried to stop me from shifting from news to advertising!

Frank proved as stubborn as I had been. "I want to go into the newsroom," he persisted.

"But Frank, how do you know you can write?"

"I wrote sports for the Philadelphia papers when I was in baseball. I have some clippings here to show you."

"A cub gets fifteen dollars, half of what I am offering you in your present job."

"When can I go over to the newsroom?"

"As soon as Pratt releases you."

I notified Pratt and Saylor, who voiced their disgust that a first-class printer should be allowed to become a bum reporter. When I left the building late at night, I would often notice Frank pecking away at a typewriter. I prided myself on working longer hours than anyone else, but Ryan seemed intent on outdoing me. It was not long before Saylor admitted to me, "Maybe you didn't make a mistake in transferring young Ryan." In 1929, when Saylor became managing editor of the Philadelphia Record, he picked Ryan to succeed him on the Courier-Post newspapers. In 1947 Ryan inherited Saylor's title of editor, a position he held until his death in 1954. As an able executive, he commanded the loyalty of his crew; as a wise and conscientious editor, he held the respect of the community.

I was just completing this staff reorganization when I ran into an unexpected snag—a newsprint shortage. At Pop Gilman's advice I had stuck to the broker who had handled the Courier's newsprint for years. This broker advised against signing a contract for 1920 until prices came down from their World War I high. Meanwhile he would buy on the open market. The 1920 contract price was $100 a ton, double what I had been paying in Springfield. We thought the broker was sincere in his recommendation. Later we discovered that he was collecting double commissions from us and the paper mill, a criminal offense.

In February, 1920, the open-market price of newsprint began to soar. It went up $50 a ton between carloads. By May we were paying $270 a ton for the two tons a day we used—a premium of $340; $100,000 a year. I faced a loss of $75,000 on my first year's operation.

Talk about a frightened publisher. I had thought that my Springfield experience made me worry-proof. I discovered that the more you have, the more you fear. Pop Gilman could offer no immediate relief. He hoped he could help me after July first.

Two other small newspapers had accepted our broker's advice not to make contracts and were in the same fix as the Courier—the Philadelphia Gazette, an old established German-language newspaper, owned by Gus Mayer, and the Norristown (Pa.) Times-Herald, owned by Ralph Beaver Strassburger. Strassburger, Mayer, and I went to the paper mill in Watertown, New York, to plead for mercy.

Floyd Carlisle, president of the St. Regis Paper Company, was also president of the Watertown National Bank, where we met him. He proceeded to make short shrift of us. "Considering the difficulties under which we are working—shortage of wood, water, and paper—you should be glad to get any paper at all at any price," was his cold-as-ice answer to our plea.

I reminded him that some day the shoe might be on the other foot. A few years before, paper mills had been begging for tonnage. I had been in business long enough to see the pendulum swing. Here was his opportunity to sign long-term contracts with three well-established newspapers. My oratory had no effect.

"I'm going to turn you over to our sales manager," he said, to end the meeting. "As long as you have come all this way I want you to see the mill."

The sales manager had not checked with his boss. He used his regular customer's line for normal times when his object was to have a publisher sign a contract. Proudly he showed us the mountainous woodpile which he boasted contained a two-year supply, the new dam which insured plenty of water in spite of drought, told us of inexhaustible forest reserves. He completely contradicted everything Carlisle had said.

Fifteen years later, when Floyd Carlisle was president of Consolidated Edison, the great utility company which serves metropolitan New York, and I was publishing the New York Post, he asked to see me. I invited him to lunch. He wanted me to urge President Roosevelt to veto the Wheeler-Rayburn Bill, which the utilities had dubbed "The Death Sentence Act." I waited until after luncheon to remind him that we had met before. He had forgotten the incident. I recalled my last words on that occasion: "Some day the shoe may be on the other foot." Carlisle looked at his watch, said he had a two o'clock appointment, and left without finishing his coffee.

       *   *   *   *   *

On the train back from Watertown I was too worried to sleep. I made up my mind to go down fighting. I could think of only one way out: to make the Courier a two-cent paper.

"That's impossible," was Tush's reaction. "You don't know the people of Camden. They walk a mile to save a penny. We'll lose our circulation overnight. I don't care how much better you make the Courier, they'll gag on two cents."

"The less circulation, the better," was my answer. "Then we won't use so much newsprint."

"But, Dave, we'll lose advertising."

"Leave it to me. I'll keep the advertisers in line and hold some circulation by contests and stunts. We must do something, and do it right away."

"We must wait it out," was Tush's stand. "The newsprint market will come back to normal before the end of the year. Your friend Gilman may be able to help within three months."

"I'd rather take a chance on ruin now than suffer slow death. Perhaps the public won't take it so hard. We'll tell them on billboards and circulars that we're giving them a better newspaper."

The next morning, Caroline (Mrs. Tushingham) phoned that Tush was ill. I found him lying on a couch in the living room. He was like a man in a trance. He stared at me as though he did not comprehend what I was saying.

During the four months we had worked together, I had come to have real respect and liking for Tush. He was a hard worker, efficient and reliable. His charming personality was a buffer to my impatient, high-pressure tactics. I did not want to break up the team. While I was debating with myself the doctor arrived. He told me Tush had had similar attacks. "Whether they start from the stomach or the mind is like debating which came first, the chicken or the egg."

I decided not to give up my plan because Tush might have eaten something which did not agree with him. I phoned my executives to meet me that night in the office, and caught the next train for New York. I went to see Moe (Moses) Koenigsberg, manager of King Features Syndicate, agent for the Hearst newspapers. Koenigsberg was the King Momus of newspaperdom. Falstaffian in build and manner, a genius at newspaper promotion, more than any one man he guided the development of comic strips in the early twenties when syndicated features were just gathering the momentum which was to make them such a formidable factor in the forties. While he was in command he kept them free from sex, sadism, and crime, which later gave them a gamey flavor.

❖   ❖   ❖   ❖   ❖

Two years before, Moe had proven a friend. The Springfield Register had tried to rob the Springfield News-Record of "Revelations of a Wife," a soap opera serial by Adele Garrison (Mrs. Martin A. White). On Jill's suggestion, the Springfield News had bought this woman's page feature at its start in 1915, for fifteen dollars a week. When, by mistake, it was omitted one day, the News switchboard was tied up with complaints. A score of housewives, who could not get us on the phone, came to the office to protest. Tom Reis, publisher of the Register, heard of this and developed the obsession that "Revelations of a Wife" was the main cause of the News' circulation growth. Tom offered Moe double the price the News was paying. Moe said that was not the way he did business. Tom raised his offer to a hundred dollars a week. Moe was still adamant, but he did phone to ask whether we would release "Revelations" in return for other features on which the price tag was a hundred dollars. Jill was leaving for Philadelphia that day. Instead, she went to New York to see Moe, who insisted on taking her to lunch and telling her what a "human dynamo" I was. When Jill offered to increase our payment for "Revelations of a Wife," Moe said, "Let's leave those details for our salesman to handle the next time he's in Springfield. Dave has nothing to worry about. King Features never double-crosses a client." In his autobiography, Koenigsberg tells the sequel: "After Reis bought the News-Record he complained to me [Koenigsberg] one hundred thousand dollars of the purchase price was chargeable to my refusal to close a deal with him [Reis] for 'Revelations of a Wife.'"

❋   ❋   ❋   ❋   ❋

On my trip to New York in 1920, Koenigsberg listened to my tale of woe: "High-priced newsprint is ruining the Courier. The only solution is to add such good features we can go to two cents." Before the session was over, I had bought two pages of features, including a serialized novel, all for seventy-five dollars a week. For years syndicated salesmen used to kid me about my "crying towel raid on Koenigsberg."

By the time I reached my office that night, lugging a bulging package of feature publicity, I had worked myself into such a lather of enthusiasm it was infectious. With the slogan, *A Bigger and Better Newspaper,* my executives and I worked through the night preparing page ads, circulars, placards and billboards, experimenting with the layout of the new feature page, planning sensational news stories, subscription contests, pep talks for the newsboys who would make three quarters of a cent a copy instead of half a cent.

We broke the publicity on Friday and Saturday; went to two cents the following Monday—a blue Monday in every sense of the word, muggy and rainy. Bad weather was an omen of failure. I sat in my office pretending to work, afraid to go out on the streets and watch the newsstands.

Then into the gloom came good tidings. Panting with excitement, the circulation manager rushed into my office, shouting, "We put it over, we put it over. The boys are ordering more papers. Instead of going down, we'll be up a thousand or more." Quickly the news spread. Saylor, Pratt, Frank Kinsella, Alfred Neef, all the Springfield crew were in my office slapping each other's backs.

All this excitement over one cent! That is the way this must sound to the present generation, accustomed to five-cent and ten-cent newspapers. In forty years, many changes have come in our way of living and in the value of our money. In 1920 it took more guts to change from one cent to two cents than in 1960 from five to ten cents.

The two-cent paper went over much better than we had hoped. The best we had looked for was to hold even. Instead, circulation increased. The public wanted a better newspaper, and was willing to pay for it. We had underestimated the co-operation of the newsboys. There was another unexpected factor—status appeal. Camdenites did not want to be seen reading a penny paper when their neighbors were flaunting a better two-cent paper.

By the end of the year, the Post-Telegram followed our example and raised their price. But they had missed the boat. The Courier was established at two cents with 18,000 circulation, double that of its competitor.

No sooner was the two-cent price a sure success than Pop Gilman phoned to offer a newsprint contract at $110 a ton. He was also able to take care of the Times-Herald and the Gazette. Freed from dependence on the crooked broker, the three newspapers brought joint action. Rather than go to court the broker made a 50 per cent settlement of our claims. The Courier's share was $17,500. Pop gave a dinner to celebrate this happy conclusion. "May the worst always turn out for the best," was my toast. "Paying two hundred seventy dollars a ton appeared the worst that could happen. But if it had not been for that misfortune the Courier would never have raised its price."

The Courier's growing pains were not over. The new press was proving an awful lemon. We were cursed with a series of breakdowns. Every other week gears would fly into the air, so that the pressmen were afraid for their lives. It was a miracle no one was injured.

After each crash, experts would sit like medical consultants at the bedside of a dying patient. They assured me the press had run perfectly for many years in Toronto. It must be some fault in its re-erection or in its operation which was causing all our trouble.

Pratt became skeptical. He had a hunch the press was faulty in design and had never run satisfactorily. To get the lowdown I went myself to Toronto. I did not want to meet the high brass, so I hung around the back entrance to the newspaper plant and made friends with the paper handlers, who took time off to have a couple of beers with me. They introduced me to the foreman of the pressroom. A cadaverous Scotchman, it was going to be tough to get him to talk. With the pressman, who had run our press for many years, he met me after their run was off.

Both men were teetotalers, so we had our talk in a coffee shop. I did not let on I was the publisher. I explained myself as "the guy who's on the spot, responsible for getting the paper out." To my questions as to their experience with the press, they gave non-committal answers. Then I described the havoc the press was causing—gears flying into the air, endangering the lives of the press crew.

"You don't have to tell me," the veteran pressman interrupted. "I've been all through the same hell with that miserable hunk of junk." Elmer was right. The press had proved defective when it was first installed. It had only been used as an extra press, for peak loads, at half speed. The unique design of drive shafts and beveled gears had been abandoned on later models. Once the two men loosened up, they gave me all the dirt, plus their promise to say it on the witness stand, even if it cost them their jobs. I had sparked the craftsman's esprit de corps, which Kipling has dramatized, the mechanic's loyalty to good machinery, his loathing of bad.

At this point I told them I was the publisher, and promised to employ them if they were fired as a result of their testimony. I insisted upon putting this commitment in writing. On the table in the coffee shop I wrote duplicate letters in which I obligated myself and my corporation to protect them. The letter spelled out in detail "that said press had never run in a satisfactory manner, had frequently broken down because of fragmentation of the drive gears," etc., etc.

The copy of the letter, which they signed and I kept, recited, "The above is a correct statement of the information given by us." I had it in writing.

In New York the next morning, the president of the press company greeted me cordially. He was about to attend a meeting of his board of directors. Would I have lunch with them after the meeting?

I waited until coffee before I let them have it. I produced the signed statement. Of course, they expressed surprise and complete ignorance that the press had ever given trouble in Toronto, but they offered to credit me with the price of the press, the cost of its erection and all repairs plus damage to Courier circulation by breakdowns, against a new 64-page octuple at cost. We signed a contract that afternoon.

By the fall of 1920 I felt so confident my Camden venture would be a success we bought a home, our first after twelve years of marriage. It was in a suburb of Camden, Haddonfield, a Quaker village founded in 1701 by Elizabeth Haddon. An Englishwoman of wealth, she had followed William Penn to the new land. The house was on the King's Highway, originally constructed as a military road by British troops. Bullet marks on the old buildings along the street gave evidence of skirmishes between American and Hessian troops. A block away The Indian King Inn, where the colonial legislature met when the British occupied Trenton, is preserved as a State museum.

According to the records our spacious Georgian home was built in 1816 for "Master Farmer Roberts." Paneling, staircases, balustrades, were the work of master craftsmen. One of the exquisite fireplaces is now in my New York apartment. But in 1816 they knew nothing of insulation. Plaster was laid directly on brick so the house was cold and damp. It had a bad name in the community and was for sale below its worth. By putting up plasterboard walls inside the original walls, with an airspace between, this defect was cured.

*   *   *   *   *

One of our first house guests was Sidney Nyburg, the novelist. He insisted on visiting the home of Walt Whitman in Camden. I was not sure in which of the dilapidated houses on Mickle Street the Good Gray Poet had lived.

"Is this Walt Whitman's home?" I asked an old woman seated on the steps of one of them. She shook her head. To be helpful she shouted to her neighbors, "Anyone know a Mr. Whitman?" All within earshot shook their heads. Just then I noticed the old marble carriage block on which are chiseled the initials W.W. I had picked the right house.

How Sidney enjoyed this incident. During the rest of his visit he kept rubbing it in: "What an enlightened city the editor has chosen to serve. Whitman is the American poet who commands the greatest world-wide recognition. His work has been translated into more languages than those of any other American author. To that little house on Mickle Street came literary pilgrims from all parts of the globe. But Camden is too busy preserving soup to preserve this historic shrine."

It was hard to persuade the city government to buy Walt's humble home for $2,500, even harder to have them restore and maintain it. Jill took charge of the restoration. She hunted around until she found the original furniture and arranged it as it had been before. It belonged to a Mr. Fritzinger, a ward of Whitman's housekeeper, Mary O. Davis. He accepted Jill's offer to have the city replace the old furniture with new.

Jill insisted the custodian have some knowledge and appreciation of Whitman. Harry Bohlen, a Whitman enthusiast and something of a poet in his own right, was selected. A frail, self-effacing little man, when he quoted Whitman, which he could at great length, he seemed to grow in stature and dignity. Before the renovation was completed, he took up his residence in the Whitman

House. On our way home from the office, one Saturday afternoon, Jill and I stopped to see how the work was progressing. The place reeked of fresh paint. Harry looked ill.

"You can't sleep here with these fumes," Jill said. "Take a room in a hotel at our expense. Or better yet, come out to Haddonfield. David will bring you in Monday morning." When he overcame his shyness, Harry proved good company. He had a keen sense of humor. His worship of Whitman's writing did not prevent him from appreciating the poet's peculiarities. We spent a pleasant Sunday together. That night Harry suffered a heart attack from which he died the following Tuesday.

Despite the doctors' assurance that he would recover, Harry said he knew he was going to die. He told Jill the story of his life. Brought up a Catholic, he had become a freethinker. "Promise me you won't let a priest get to me?" he asked Jill. "I must prove a freethinker can die bravely." Bessie, my mother-in-law's nurse, a devout Catholic, noticed Catholic medals among Harry's effects. She telephoned her priest. When he arrived, I was in the living room with Harry's father and brother.

"Hurry, Father, there's no time to lose," urged Bessie, leading the priest upstairs. Jill stood on the stairs, arms outstretched, blocking his way.

"I gave my word to Harry no priest would attend him," said Jill. This altercation brought Bohlen Sr. and me into the hall.

"It's for you to decide," I put it up to Harry's father.

Just then the trained nurse appeared at the head of the stairs to tell us, "Mr. Bohlen is dead."

These incidents were embroidered by the superstitious. According to our cook, who claimed to be an authority on the subject, Whitman's ghost resented Bohlen's intrusion. When Bohlen fled to our home, the ghost pursued Bohlen, and prevented him from seeing a priest who could have saved Bohlen from the ghost's revenge. This was the usually accepted version.

Having installed a distinguished ghost, insulation, antique furniture, and old-fashioned gardens, Jill transformed the old house into a delightful home where we enjoyed many happy years. It was the scene of gay parties as well as of political conferences. A second daughter, Meredith, was added to the family in 1928, a second son, Jonathan, in 1930. In 1942 gas rationing compelled us to move to Philadelphia. I sold the house when I retired in 1947. If I had had my way, we would still be living there.

X

Camden Characters

So rapid was the growth of the Courier we had to enlarge our plant six times in seven years. We financed these expansions by the sale of 7 per cent preferred stock. That was before SEC. I wrote the stock prospectus and ads myself. We had no underwriters, no bankers, paid no commission. The stock was sold over the counter like sugar in a grocery store. In response to ads in the Courier our readers flocked into the office with checks and cash.

Our largest preferred stock subscribers were the two leading industrialists of the city—Eldridge R. Johnson, founder of the Victor Talking Machine Company, now operated by the Radio Corporation of America; and Dr. John T. Dorrance, owner of the Campbell Soup Company, both of whom I had first met through labor controversies.

Before I came to Camden, the two newspapers had a tacit understanding not to publish news of strikes or trade unions. After I took control, the Courier carried union notices and news. This shocked the conservative businessmen. Then one of Camden's factories had a strike, of which we gave a fair account. This was breaking a precedent. Word got around that I was a dangerous radical. Tush, my ambassador of peace and goodwill, could not cope with it. I ignored this tempest until cancellations of advertising contracts became serious. Then I went to the heads of the larger industries to explain my policy. I told them suppression and discrimination were not the proper tools with which to build sound labor relations. Refusal to publish labor news would not destroy unions or stop strikes. It would only force the unions to print their own inflammatory pamphlets and circulars.

Both Johnson and Dorrance saw my point. They passed the

word that they considered me a safe and sane publisher. Armed with their endorsements, Tushingham was able to stop the cabal and win back the canceled advertising.

Johnson was a huge man, always worrying about, and battling, overweight. He would start a meal by explaining that he was on a strict diet, "But don't let that keep you from ordering what you like," and end up by eating more than I did. On his large florid face was perched a tiny, incongruous waxed mustache. It created the effect of a dual personality which, in fact, he was. In his youth he had come to Camden from Wilmington, Delaware, as a machinist. He invented a stapling machine which brought him enough capital to start his own bicycle and machine shop. He designed a spring motor of uniform speed which was a marked improvement on the motor in Edison's phonograph. In those days we wound up our talking machines by hand. In 1894 Johnson started the Victor Talking Machine Company, which became the world leader in its field.

There was more to the man than his inventive genius and business ability. He had a real love of music, art, and literature. He was the first to engage Caruso and other great artists to make records. He gave generously to the University of Pennsylvania for the purchase of Grecian sculpture with which to enrich its museum, as well as to many charities. Because of this keen appreciation of art, the dog listening to its master's voice came to be the Victor trademark. On a visit to his London office, Johnson was shown the picture by Francis Barrand, noted English animal painter, of his dog "Nipper." The Edison Company had commissioned it, but for some unknown reason turned it down. The price was one hundred pounds.

"Those were the days when a hundred pounds was important money to my young company," Johnson told Jill and me. "I don't give myself credit for recognizing its unique appeal. We use it in every country in the world except in China, where the dog is looked upon as a scavenger, like the pig with us. But I did recognize it as a fine painting. I told Barrand that if he would paint out the Edison machine and substitute ours, I would take the picture at his price."

We were in Johnson's London office when he told this story. He took us into the board room to see the original. Over the years the paint had dried so that the outline of the Edison machine showed through that of the Victor.

Between 1923 and 1927 I met Johnson a number of times in London. On one occasion he invited us—Tom, then fourteen, Little Jill, eight, Jill and me—for a day's boating on the Thames. He gave Little Jill a beautifully illustrated edition of *Peter Pan*. On our way home we stopped to see Sir George Frampton's statue of Peter Pan in Kensington Gardens. Little Jill danced around the statue. She did not want to leave. It was growing late. Tom and I had to chase her through the garden paths. She took refuge in Johnson's arms.

"Don't let them take me away from Peter Pan," she pleaded.

"I'll bring Peter Pan to you," Johnson told Little Jill. "If you go home like a good little girl, I'll have a statue just like this one set up where you can see it every day."

A year later my daughter unveiled the replica of Peter Pan in Johnson Square, a few blocks from the Courier office. To provide a proper setting for the statue, Johnson also gave the city a fountain and other statuary which cost him $50,000. Surrounded by towering factories this monument to childhood fantasy is scarcely as appropriately placed as the original. But it was a valiant attempt to preserve the spell of a summer evening in Kensington Gardens and bring beauty into one corner of a drab factory town.

To more than fulfill his promise to Little Jill was characteristic of Johnson. He enjoyed surprising the solicitor for a charity by giving a greater amount than was asked. He would inquire, gruffly, "What do you expect me to give?" and then donate double the amount suggested. He offered to contribute $100,000 toward a building for the Camden Chamber of Commerce. I went to him with a plan for a modern hotel which Camden sorely needed. "You can kill two birds with one stone," I told him. "Help erect a modern hotel with appropriate quarters for the Chamber. Write them that while your offer still stands, you suggest they invest the hundred thousand in a community hotel with space for their organization."

"That's a good idea," Johnson said.

The next morning I received his letter for the Chamber of Commerce. With it was a second letter: "As you will notice, the $100,-000 is from the Victor Talking Machine Company for the benefit of the community in which it has grown and prospered. You neglected to ask for my personal subscription. Put me down for $50,000."

The next time I saw Johnson he told me I was "a lousy solicitor." "Don't you know enough to ask for more than you can get?" I was chairman of a committee which had to raise $1,500,000 for the new hotel. Johnson predicted, "With such a soft chairman the committee will never reach its goal and I will have to make up the difference." Without further help from him, we raised the money. The Walt Whitman Hotel proved a most useful and profitable civic enterprise.

❂   ❂   ❂   ❂   ❂

Dr. John T. Dorrance was as much below average height as Johnson was above it. A solemn and austere little man, he looked and acted like the senior deacon of an Episcopal church, which he was. And he never forgot it. I cannot remember his ever telling an off-color story or making any remark which could not be repeated in a young ladies' seminary. The son of a wealthy South Jersey family, when he graduated from M.I.T. he went to Heidelberg to take his Ph.D. in chemistry. He insisted on the handle to his name.

His uncles ran the small Campbell Preserving Company in Camden. Young Dorrance always stocked his yacht with plenty of preserves. Cooking was his hobby. One summer he experimented at the factory with condensed soup. It made a hit with his sailing companions. When Dorrance inherited the factory, condensed soup became its main product. He was a most scientific and thorough businessman. To perfect the herb flavoring of condensed soups, he went to Paris and worked as chef's helper in the leading restaurants. After finishing in the kitchen, he would don evening clothes and dine on the dishes he had helped to prepare. For years he used to get up at four in the morning to go to the Philadelphia produce market to buy the best vegetables.

When I first met him in 1920, he had developed his idea into a gigantic business. His ambition in life, as he frankly told me, was to become the richest man in the world. If he had lived to be seventy, he might well have achieved this goal. When he died at fifty-six, he had already accumulated $125,000,000. Like Henry Ford, he never contributed to charities. Another of his rules of life was that he never speculated on the stock market. He worked out business and financial problems on a mathematical basis. He would buy twenty million dollars' worth of government bonds to turn them over in a few weeks at a gain of a quarter of a percent. With gusto he would tell me of such a transaction. It was not the fifty thousand dollars which was important, but that he had made his profit with a minimum of risk. The three or four chauffeured automobiles which he maintained for his family's use were all marked in small gold letters, "Campbell Soup Co.," so they could be charged as business expense.

When his wife insisted on buying a palatial home on Philadelphia's fashionable Main Line, Dorrance objected because the Pennsylvania inheritance tax was three per cent higher than New Jersey's. Because his daughters were growing to marriageable age, Dorrance gave in. But he continued to maintain his New Jersey home, and made a point of sleeping in it two nights a week, so there would be no question that New Jersey was his legal residence.

That is how we became so well acquainted. His two-nights-a-week regime was lonely business. Dorrance was always trying to recruit friends to share his self-enforced absence from his family. One summer, when my family was in Europe, the two of us dined frequently together, and tried to get each other's very different points of view.

It was interesting to hear this devout pillar of the church explain why he felt justified in making no charitable contributions. It was his duty to devote himself exclusively to developing an industry which employed thousands, was the biggest buyer of produce from South Jersey farmers, and paid large taxes to the community. Dorrance did support projects in which I was interested, political campaigns, the community hotel, preferred stock of my newspapers. But each time he assured me he was breaking the rule of a lifetime because of personal friendship.

When he died in 1930 both the State of New Jersey and the Commonwealth of Pennsylvania claimed and collected inheritance taxes. This double taxation, one of the strangest miscarriages of justice in our legal history, cost his estate $12,000,000 more than if Dorrance had spent every night with his family. New Jersey used its windfall for relief of the unemployed—a State charity.

Although the offices of Johnson and Dorrance were within a block of each other, I do not remember that they ever met. They had nothing in common except their advertising agent, F. Wallis Armstrong. As advertising solicitor for the Courier, he wrote ads for Johnson's bicycle shop and Campbell's preserves. He left the Courier to give all his time to these two clients. He had hit the prize double of the advertising sweepstakes—the two largest accounts in the world in the 1920's. They paid him a million dollars a year in commissions. It was not all luck. Among his other clients were Whitman's Candies, Scott Paper, Philco, and Fels-Naptha. He branded their trademarks on the mass mind: the Victor Dog, the Campbell Kids, the Whitman Sampler Man, among others. Like most master hucksters, he was raucous and domineering. But his rather abrasive personality was leavened with a keen and impish sense of humor. When he and I happened to meet at lunch with Dorrance, he would whisper, "Watch me make the soup king lose his appetite."

"Jack (he was the only associate who did not use the Dr.)," he would say, after we sat down and were served the inevitable soup with which all Dorrance meals began, "Dave and I have a great idea which will preserve your name to posterity as well as increase your present popularity. Look out the window at that unkempt, weed-grown ferry plaza. You transform it into another St. Mark's Square, decorated with fountains and statuary, paved artistically with designs in different-colored stones. Dave will have the city commissioners change its name to Dorrance Plaza. It won't cost you more than a million."

Dorrance would lay down his soup spoon. He would look sad and hurt as he replied, "Wallis, I have no desire to preserve my name." The subject would be dropped, but Dorrance would scarcely nibble the other courses. The mere thought of spending a million dollars had ruined his appetite.

On his one visit to my office, Wallis gave vent to his sardonic humor. He recalled that, thirty years before, Tush had warned him not to give up his twelve-dollar-a-week job at the Courier for the uncertainty of writing ads for Johnson and Dorrance.

"If I had taken your advice, Tush," Wallis rubbed it in, "I'd be where you are."

"Tush is the most respected and popular man in this community," I interposed and brought the painful episode to a close.

With his great wealth, Wallis was able to indulge his hobby of breeding racehorses. Cavalcade, winner of the Derby and Belmont Stakes in 1934, and other great horses were foaled at his Meadowview Farm near Haddonfield. In justice to this remarkable character, he served for fifteen years on the New Jersey State Board of Control of Institutions, and gave a great deal of time and energy to improving conditions.

The King Midas complex can distort a man's character as terribly as alcohol. Men of great wealth are susceptible to this absurd affliction. Even my good and generous friend, Eldridge Johnson, was not immune. After he retired with more than forty million dollars, he was gripped by the obsession that a combination of income tax, inheritance tax and inflation would destroy his fortune. He worked himself into such a state that the sound of the word "tax" would make his face flush and the cords in his neck swell— even the mention of "carpet tacks" would produce this reaction. Our friendship was ended when I came out for Roosevelt, who, in Johnson's mind, was a fiend intent on destroying all wealth. After Roosevelt's election, he became a melancholic, shut himself off from everyone but his wife, son and attendants. This man, who had everything to make life worth while except peace of mind, spent his last days sitting alone, wringing his hands and bemoaning his fate. He died in 1945. His estate was not settled until after the death of his widow in January, 1961. It was valued at thirty-four million dollars.

Johnson, Dorrance, Armstrong, a strange triumvirate.

Within the half-mile radius of my office other interesting characters emerged from the industrial smog to achieve great wealth and national prominence. Two of them, Newton B. T. Roney and Senator David Baird, played such important parts in the development of the Courier they deserve a separate chapter.

XI

The Courier
Becomes a Monopoly

"As long as Baird is boss, Camden will never get to first base," Newt (Newton B. T.) Roney, son of the Courier's press foreman, told me soon after I came to town. A quiet, almost taciturn, individual, slight of build, diffident in manner, he spoke but seldom and then in a flat monotone. My first impression was negative. When I came to know him I realized the quiet man had a steel-trap mind.

Like Saylor, Newt had been a professional ball player. When a broken arm ended his athletic career he became a lawyer. His practice led him into building projects which were most successful. He planned a movie palace, profusely decorated as was then the vogue. He asked Baird's bank to finance it. Baird objected to "twenty-five thousand dollars of fancy work." After that turndown no other Camden bank would touch it. Newt sold his Camden properties in 1918 and transferred his attention to Miami Beach.

The Roney-Plaza, first of the large beach-front hotels, still stands as evidence of his vision. Before it, the better hotels were built away from the beach on the bay side or in Miami. Newt used to say, "Rodgers and Hammerstein discovered the South Pacific, but I discovered the South Atlantic. From the days of Ponce de León no one in Florida appreciated it until the Roney-Plaza built the first hotel cabanas in America."

From then on, the ocean front became Miami Beach's great asset. More clearly than anyone else Newt foresaw its future and became its leading operator. The newspapers estimated his wealth at five hundred million dollars at the height of the real estate boom. When it collapsed, in 1925, Newt was wiped out. Starting again, from scratch, he amassed another considerable fortune before he died in 1955.

Newt was no longer active in Camden when I came to know him in 1920, but he still felt he had a score to settle with Dave Baird. Characteristically, after that attack on Baird at our first meeting, Newt said nothing more on the subject for two years. He went out of his way to be friendly and helpful to the new publisher. The Roneys invited Jill and me to be their guests at Miami Beach in the winter of 1921. They were our guests when they came north in the summer. Newt enjoyed chess as much as I did and we spent considerable time together.

In June 1922 Newt asked me to lunch with him and Ed Kelleher, clerk of the New Jersey Supreme Court. Then Newt launched the plan which he must have had in mind when we first met. "Baird's one-man rule blocks all civic improvement. His only object is to run Camden as cheaply as possible and keep down the tax rate. To beat Baird at the polls is impossible as long as he controls the Democratic City Committee."

In New Jersey, as in many states, the minority party is entitled by law to a certain number of county commissioners and magistrates. To name these minority office holders the party in power keeps alive the pretense of a minority party. That was the plight of the Democratic City Committee, of which Patrick Harding, one of Baird's lieutenants, was chairman.

"Will the Courier back Ed Kelleher to displace Pat Harding?" That was the question Newt had been leading up to for two years.

I bought it. Newt provided a few thousand dollars; Ed, a natural politician, the strategy; and I, the publicity, the first publicity the local Democratic organization had had in a generation. Under Pat Harding the party avoided mention in the press.

We took Pat by surprise. Ed Kelleher was elected chairman. I was amazed at the response to the little space which the Courier gave Ed. Evidently there was more latent opposition to Baird than I had realized. But control of the City Committee meant nothing in itself. There were no ward organizations with which the party could operate at the coming municipal election.

"How much will it cost to build up a real party?" I asked.

"I can do it for ten thousand dollars," said Ed, "and I can raise half of it in small donations."

"Dave, I'm good for twenty-five hundred if you are," said Newt.

That was the beginning of the opposition to the Baird machine in the election of 1922 for mayor and councilmen. The campaign opened with a personal attack on me because of Courier editorials and news stories favoring extension of Broadway, Camden's main stem, to the bridge plaza at a cost of $250,000. According to the Post-Telegram, "Stern, the carpet-bagger, is intent on ruining the city where he has so recently arrived. If Stern had his way, families would be driven from their homes, tax-paying properties destroyed, and the city bankrupted by squandering a fortune on a useless street."

Ed Kelleher dug up the tax returns on Baird's lumberyard and other real estate, worth more than $2,000,000, but assessed for only $630,000. This underassessment cost the city $40,000 a year, double the interest and amortization on a $250,000 bond issue for extending Broadway.

Without opposition or criticism for so many years, Baird did not know how to take it. He demanded a retraction. His properties were assessed for $680,000, not $630,000. We printed his letter on the front page. Camden was losing $39,000 a year, not $40,000. This controversy awakened political interest in a city which had not had a municipal contest in twenty-five years. The public was enjoying the fracas. The city was alive with parades and rallies. Our circulation was mounting.

Then the anvil chorus started. "Disinterested" friends warned that Baird was allowing me the rope with which to hang myself. After election I would be finished. Philadelphia advertisers joined the chorus. Baird had powerful connections across the river. This campaign of *Schrecklichkeit* did not make me pull my editorial punches, but I did caution Saylor to lean over backward in presenting election news fairly. Saylor addressed identical letters, asking six questions about their future policies, to Victor King, the Democratic candidate for Mayor, and Acting Mayor Frank Van Hart, the Republican candidate. King's prompt reply, which Saylor wrote, was a strong campaign document. When Van Hart refused to answer, it created a bad impression. I could not understand why an experienced politician should make this mistake. After the election I learned what had happened. To present the letter to Van Hart, Saylor had chosen Walter McLoon, a rough, hard-drinking reporter who had been carrying on a one-man feud with Van Hart. Without knocking, McLoon busted into Van Hart's office, slammed the letter on his desk, and shouted, "Here, Big Shot, is something you've got to answer." Van Hart was so angry he told McLoon, "I don't have to answer, and I won't. I'll stand on my record."

To my surprise King won the election by eight hundred votes. But it was a Pyrrhic victory. Baird retained a majority in the City Council. Without the Council, the mayor was a figurehead. Newt and Ed insisted we press on to complete victory by calling for a referendum election on commission government. If we won, we would have a chance to elect a majority of the five commissioners.

It was customary for the Mayor of Camden to deliver an annual printed message to the City Council when it convened on New Year's Day. Traditionally, this message had been a few pages of generalities without facts, figures, or definite proposals. We decided Mayor King's message would be different. It should launch our campaign for commission government.

I hired an expert from the Bureau of Municipal Research to make a comparison of city services and costs in Camden and other American cities of its size. He worked for a month in my office and uncovered a mass of startling data.

At the Christmas Eve office party, I said I was going to take Christmas week off. I shut myself up in a third-floor room of my home with a suitcaseful of the expert's reports. The message had to be in print by New Year's Eve, which meant working against time. But an indictment of municipal mismanagement, documented with authority for every statement, was on the councilmen's desks on New Year's morning.

Camden's cost per mile for street cleaning was much higher than the average for other cities. The reason was obvious. The payroll listed almost as many supervisors as street cleaners. The

Police and Fire Departments were similarly top-heavy. Only in the Health and Hygiene Department was Camden more economical than its sister cities. But, without visiting nurses or adequate health services, Camden had a higher infant mortality rate than other communities. The women of Camden, recently enfranchised, made this their issue. During the final days of the campaign, their speakers were accusing the Baird machine of murdering babies.

At the referendum election of March, 1923, commission government won overwhelmingly. In May, all of our five commissioners were elected. The Baird machine's twenty-five-year hold on the city of Camden was broken.

The day after the election of city commissioners, Newt Roney left for Miami Beach, his mission accomplished. He never again took an active interest in Camden politics. Ed Kelleher went south with Newt for a much-needed rest. Starting from scratch, Ed had organized one hundred divisions in thirteen wards, recruited workers to get out the votes, and watchers to see that the votes were counted.

Newt and Ed left me a more difficult job than I had anticipated. Because of their unexpected victory, the five commissioners were feeling their oats. None of them had had any experience in city government. Their first clash arose in dividing the city departments among themselves. When they could not agree, they came to my office at 10 A.M. I pretended an engagement, and ducked. When I returned, at eleven, they were still there. Mel Middleton, an investment banker, the obvious man to handle the city's finances, wanted the Police and Fire Departments. This staid, middle-aged banker was a fire buff. Like Mayor La Guardia he had a yen to follow the fire engines. We had to promise him an honorary fire-chief badge, an alarm signal in his home, and a siren for his car, before he would accept the Finance Department. There were other equally absurd differences to be ironed out. We sent out for lunch and then for supper. It was 10 P.M. before this silly business was settled.

To keep the five commissioners functioning without friction was a full-time job. Jill, Harry and Elmer kept complaining I was a politician, not a publisher. With characteristic sarcasm, whenever

Elmer came to my office he prefaced what he had to say with, "If I'm not intruding on city business."

On Ed's return from Miami Beach I was glad to leave town. With our two children Jill and I went to Europe for six weeks. When we returned in September, the fat was in the fire. Split into two factions, the commissioners were intent on cutting each other's throats. This is an example of the weakness in reform government. When the reformers win they assume the fight is won and give no thought to strengthening the party organization for the next election. The "old pros," win or lose, work 365 days a year. The breach in the Camden City Commission was never entirely healed. But, in spite of the friction, there was much real accomplishment.

The commissioners engaged a city planning engineer to connect Camden's traffic arteries with the new bridge which was to be completed in 1926. They first offered the job to Ralph Modjeski, chief engineer of the Delaware River Bridge. Modjeski said it would not be ethical for him to take it or to recommend a particular city planner. Instead, he gave us a list of six engineers with whom he could work. He urged us to go to Baltimore the next day. "You will find all six of them at the City Planning Engineers Convention."

Victor King, Mel Middleton and I took a suite at the Belvedere, headquarters for the convention. We invited Modjeski's six nominees to a cocktail party. This proved a mistake. One engineer said he would be glad to come to Camden to survey the situation. Immediately the others accused him of unethical conduct, of soliciting business. Verbal bricks flew thick and fast. Victor and Mel looked as embarrassed as if they had walked into the bridal suite. One of the six did not take part in the altercation. A handsome giant of a man, six foot six, he stood on the sidelines with a quizzical smile.

"In the midst of battle, despite shot and shell, you smile," I said.

"Even a city planner can have a sense of humor," he replied.

That was the start of my friendship with Charles W. Leavitt, a rare combination of engineer, artist, and diplomat. On recommendations of the States of New York and New Jersey, for which he had done much work, Camden engaged him. It took some arguing to have the commissioners agree to his retainer of fifty thousand dollars. The Post-Telegram raised the usual howl, "Dave Stern is so drunk with power he is bankrupting the city." And many of our Democratic leaders said it was a waste of money. It turned out to be the best fifty thousand dollars Camden ever spent. Leavitt not only gave Camden a plan of bridge approaches including the extension of Broadway and the Admiral Wilson and Crescent Boulevards, but he laid out the Cooper River Parkway, one of Camden County's great assets.

Philadelphia did not employ a city planner. When Leavitt offered his services, Mayor W. Freeling Kendrick's answer was, "A captain of traffic police, with a flair for engineering, solves our traffic problems." A year later Philadelphia built an underpass at its end of the bridge which blocked the rapid transit facilities of the bridge. Three years later this underpass had to be torn out and reconstructed at an additional cost of three million dollars. It took Philadelphia twenty years to complete the first unit of its bridge approach highways.

As there was no first-class hotel in Camden—the Walt Whitman had not been completed—Leavitt made his headquarters in my home at Haddonfield. A civic face-lifting operation, such as he proposed, is bound to raise opposition. Together we would attend a round of sectional meetings. With long experience in such problems, Leavitt employed tact, wit and charm to smooth the way for the new zoning ordinance. When we finally reached home I would be worn out, but Leavitt would sit up far into the night working at his drawing board. Eldridge Johnson, who shared my enthusiasm for Leavitt's work, was especially interested in the parkway, for which he donated a boathouse and other recreational facilities. I brought together Johnson, Leavitt, Modjeski, and Paul Cret, architect for the bridge, at several interesting dinners. Modjeski, son of the famous tragedienne Mme. Helena Modjeska, was a mathematician and artist as well as a bridge engineer. He would have been as handsome as his mother if it had not been for his bulging, oversize forehead. Cret, head of the University of Pennsylvania School of Architecture, has left many masterpieces—the chapel at Valley Forge, the Pan-American Building, Folger Shakespeare

Library in Washington, and others. A graduate of the Sorbonne, he was as ebullient as Modjeski was restrained.

I wish I had a recording of the debate between Modjeski and Cret, at one of the dinners, on the meaning of beauty. Modjeski insisted that the great steel cable towers, which he had designed, were beautiful in themselves. Cret wanted to cover the steel with granite facing, for which there was no engineering need.

"Only the functional is beautiful," was Modjeski's creed. "A false wall is false beauty." Johnson, Leavitt and I agreed that Cret riddled this theory and won the argument. But Modjeski won out with the bridge commission—Cret's plan would have cost a million dollars. And Modjeski's theory has prevailed with all the suspension bridges which have since been built. I admit their steel towers, silhouetted against the sky, have an austere beauty. But "only the functional is beautiful" is a false premise which has blighted much modern architecture. The United Nations skyscraper is a glaring example.

᪥   ᪥   ᪥   ᪥   ᪥

As the Delaware River bridge neared completion in 1926 a real estate boom developed in Camden. Speculators overflowed the offices onto a curb market where a milling, excited crowd traded options. The fever spread. Philadelphia and New York friends wanted my advice about getting in on this bonanza. One of them was Arthur Brisbane, editor of the Hearst newspapers. The Courier ran his column "Today," America's most widely syndicated feature. He spent a Saturday morning looking over the territory. After a hearty lunch at which he drank a quart of champagne, he sat down at my typewriter and pounded out his Sunday column. A photographer fired a flash powder close to his face. (The electric flash bulb had not been invented.) Arthur never missed a stroke on the typewriter. When he read over his ten pages of copy he made one pencil correction. He was the most technically skillful newspaper man I have ever encountered. Hearst paid him five thousand dollars a week, the highest salary for an editor, before or since. Arthur was a compulsive real estate speculator. When Hearst was asked why he did not retire, he answered, "I've got to keep working to bail Arthur out of his bum real estate deals."

During this hysteria, Newt Roney kept sending me Miami newspapers loaded with real estate advertising. "Why don't you get Camden to follow suit?" he wrote. Camden realtors used small classified ads. To insert a ten-inch ad was to splurge. In charge of this department was an import from Springfield, George Keary. I had discovered him when he signed up more rural route subscriptions than any other solicitor. His early training had been handling publicity for a quack doctor and a carnival. His only trouble was that he oversold. George would hypnotize an advertiser into buying too much space and sour the account.

"If I could get one real estate office to break loose with page ads, the rest would follow the leader," George told me.

"Here's a way to break the log jam," I suggested. "Give some young realtor a five-thousand-dollar credit for ten pages. If it doesn't pay, we'll cancel the debt."

A few days later George brought to my office a handsome boy. Bob Tucker was twenty-four but looked younger. When he had been mustered out of the Army his father had given him five hundred dollars for college expenses. Unfortunately, the old man handed it to Bob in cash. After a week's fling Bob woke up in Camden, broke and ashamed to go home. He took a job selling lots. When he had saved enough he opened his own office "down at the ferry plaza where I have the first shot at the land-hungry prospects." In spite of his youth I gave him credit for ten page ads, prepared by Keary in his best carnival style. Within a few weeks we were deluged with real estate advertising. Many days we ran to press capacity, sixty-four pages. Our advertising department was crowded with realtors begging for more space than we had to sell.

Bob Tucker led the procession of speculators. He opened offices in other cities. In New York he rented the second floor of the Times Square Building. Magazines ran stories about "Camden's Wonder Boy." To celebrate his sudden success he invited his clients to a mammoth party in New York. It required two Pullman trains, plentifully stocked with bootleg liquor, to transport a thousand guests from Philadelphia and Camden to New York.

A week before this shindig I heard rumors that the boom was tottering. By the night of the big party I knew it was busted. I was slated to deliver an after-dinner eulogy on "Camden's Wonder Boy." That ride from Camden to New York with a trainload of drunks was as uncomfortable as the trip from Salt Lake City to Caliente with a bunch of hoboes, eighteen years before. My audience was too full of liquor to pay attention to my warning that, while South Jersey had a great future, it would take years for it to build up.

The Camden boom withered as quickly as the one at Miami Beach. The next time I saw Bob he was selling haberdashery. Fortunately, I had kept clear of this frenzy of speculation. Outside of my home and my business I never owned any South Jersey real estate. But the boom did affect me in one way. The Courier made so much money during those four fat months I raised the salaries of all my executives.

❊   ❊   ❊   ❊   ❊

Convincing the city commissioners they should employ a capable Superintendent of Health was harder than persuading them to engage a city planner. Camden had never had a city planner, so there were no local candidates for the post. But Superintendent of Health, at six thousand dollars a year, had always been the sinecure of a practicing physician who handled it on the side. All five commissioners had family doctors who wanted this cushy appointment. After much argument Mayor King was authorized to write to the American Medical Association for a list of qualified physicians. We found we could not get an experienced man for six thousand dollars. It was only after I threatened to tell the public the Commission was going back on its campaign promise to improve public health service that the salary was increased to ten thousand dollars. Dr. Arthur L. Stone, who was selected, proved so efficient he was retained by subsequent administrations until his death. He brought Camden's health rating from the bottom to near the top of the heap for cities of its class.

But when he first took office he raised a storm from which I had a hard time protecting him. On his order, the police roped off several blocks of a slum section in which smallpox cases had been reported. A vaccination station was set up in a vacant store. To get out of the police net you had to show a vaccination certificate. The opposition made the most of these "Russian Communist" tactics, even though it prevented a smallpox epidemic.

In the three years between the election of anti-Baird city commissioners in 1923 and the opening of the bridge in 1926, Camden was under the strain of many changes and much excitement—political upheaval, real estate boom and collapse, alteration of the city map with new thoroughfares, and new zoning. Considering that the community had stood still for a generation under one-man rule, the reaction was remarkably favorable. But a bitter, conservative minority kept repeating that "carpetbagger Stern is ruining the town." David Baird, Jr., son of the deposed boss, was the leader and spokesman of these irreconcilables. His father did not share his animosity. In spite of our political battles old Senator Baird and I maintained cordial personal relations. Whenever he heard I was going on a trip he used to come to see me and give me a box of fine cigars. As he was too old to negotiate the stairs to my office I would go down and visit with him in his limousine, parked in front of the Courier building.

When I came to Camden, "Uncle Dave" was eighty but still vigorous and sovereign of Camden and South Jersey. He might have sat as a model for Thomas Nast's cartoons of the oversize political boss. It was hard to draw a line where his barrel-chest sloped into his belly. His sandy-gray eyebrows, as prominent as those of John L. Lewis, matched a handle-bar mustache. His years in America had not entirely dulled the edge of his County Derry accent. This Protestant Irishman had immigrated to America when he was seventeen. His first job was in a Pocono Mountain lumber camp. He floated into Camden on a lumber raft in 1870, and stayed to establish a profitable lumberyard which supplied Camden's rapidly growing factories. The lumberjacks Uncle Dave brought to Camden proved tougher than the native roustabouts. His customers, the factory owners, turned to Uncle Dave on election days for strong-arm squads to insure that Camden remained safely and sanely Republican.

Gradually, Uncle Dave took over the political organization. As reward for his services to the party, in 1917, he was appointed to a vacancy in the United States Senate and, in 1918, he was elected to complete the unexpired term. His business and financial success kept pace with his political power and prestige. In 1922 he became chairman of the Board of the Camden First National Bank, of which Morse Archer was president. Archer's fear that Baird would turn it into a "political bank" proved unfounded. "The old man has never even suggested anything off color," Archer told me after they had worked together several years.

You knew, when you talked to Uncle Dave, that he was a man of shrewdness and ability and honesty within the bounds of his world—a world of things exactly as they are and no nonsense, sir, about changing it. He wanted "his town" as it was, an industrial center without zoning or planning, without parks or embellishments which would raise the tax rate and "drive business away." He strenuously opposed votes for women, but when the Nineteenth Amendment was enacted, he cultivated the "women vote" with a homely blarney which was disarming. Jill attended his first meeting with the victorious suffragettes. He opened his short talk with: "Ladies, I were ag'in you, but now I'm for you, and if there is anything this old man can do, I'm at your service."

"Really he didn't say anything," Jill reported. "But the women cheered and clapped as though he had. He's a remarkable man. I can't help liking him."

Senator Baird took his triple defeat, in the three city elections of 1922 and 1923, with good grace. He still controlled Camden County, and while we had several skirmishes on that score, by 1925 acrimony had died down. Then a Courier editorial on the extension of Broadway fanned it anew. My proposal that the city's mainstem be cut through to the bridge plaza had marked my first clash with Baird, who declared it a useless waste of money. After the street was constructed, I made every effort to justify the city's investment by bringing substantial new buildings to the thoroughfare. As chief money raiser and president of the Walt Whitman Hotel Corporation I was able to locate it at the corner of Cooper Street and the new Broadway. This led John B. Wilson, a local financier, to erect the city's first skyscraper office building on the opposite corner. Then I persuaded my friend Jules Mastbaum, owner of a large theater chain, to build a motion-picture palace next to the Walt Whitman Hotel.

I shall never forget the opening of that theater. All of Camden's VIPs were there. Jill and my children had seats in the front row. Jules and Jimmy Walker, Mayor of New York, drove up from Atlantic City. A most colorful personality, Jules loved to play practical jokes. He would go to great pains to fool and discomfit a friend. When they met me in the lobby both Jules and Jimmy pretended that they were drunk, which was not too difficult as they had a good start.

"Now I've got my chance to tell Camden what a double-crossing, no-good son-of-a-bitch you are," was Jules' greeting.

"What in hell are you talking about?" I was startled.

"You know well enough." Jules' face was grim.

"Do you know what's biting him?" I turned to Jimmy.

"Ask your conscience, young man." Walker's scowl was more sinister than Jules'.

I rushed over to John McGurk, president of the theater company. "You've got to keep Jules off the platform," I told McGurk. "He's crazy drunk. He'll disgrace all of us."

McGurk hurried over to Jules. After a few minutes' talk he came back to me and shrugged his shoulders. "I can't do anything with him," McGurk said.

"I'll have the police arrest him as drunk and disorderly," I proposed in desperation.

"Won't do any good, Dave." John's face was solemn. "Walker will say it if Jules don't, and you can't arrest the Mayor of New York."

I did not have the nerve to take my seat with Jill. In a cold sweat I stood in the rear.

"I built this theater because my friend Dave Stern asked me to," was the opening of Jules' speech. He went on to recount how much I had done for Camden. Walker echoed his fulsome eulogy. At the party after the ceremonies, Jules and Jimmy had so much fun kidding me I had to forgive them. "The way you turned green in the lobby proves you've a hell of a guilty conscience," was their refrain.

Within two years of completion of the new street, these improvements and others assured the city a tax return of 20 per cent on its investment. Then, to crown the vindication of my judgment, the Camden First National announced it would erect a palatial bank building on the new thoroughfare. Senator Baird, largest stockholder of the bank and chairman of its board, presided at the meeting which decided to make this move. In the Courier editorial congratulating the bank on this wise and progressive enterprise, we said it was an admission by Baird that he had been wrong, the Courier right, about the extension of Broadway. It was a feather in my cap and I could not help crowing.

This editorial infuriated David Baird, Jr. He took it as a personal attack on his father, whom he worshiped. Dave Jr. was so emotional and high-strung that when he became angered his voice would break and tears would come to his eyes. He was very different from his suave, even-tempered father. I had been his sworn enemy since Mayor King's first message to the Council, which he knew I had written, revealed the Baird machine's misrule. Dave asked Congressman Frank Patterson, publisher of the Post-Telegram, to answer the Courier editorial. When Patterson, an easygoing veteran politician, told Dave to calm down and forget it, Dave was so worked up he bought the Post-Telegram for $250,000. Dave went about town declaring he was going to drive "that Jew carpetbagger out of Camden." He boasted that he had hired a publisher "so much smarter than Stern the Courier will fold within a year." He had picked an unusually able newspaperman, Pierrepont Isham Prentice, whom I later employed as telegraph editor of the Philadelphia Record. Prentice left me to become publisher of Time Magazine.

Prentice's considerable skill was offset by Dave's insistence on tiresome tirades against the Courier and its publisher. As in Springfield, my competition knocked me to success. Only once did Dave and Prentice catch me off guard. I gave a dinner for the heads of the forty-six local governments in the county, mayors of cities and boroughs, chairmen of township commissions.

Most of them had never met one another before. They found many problems of mutual interest. "You're letting your sewage flow to the Delaware by gravity, while across the street we're pumping ours over a telegraph pole," is the way one official expressed it. It was unanimously agreed that so much had been gained at this get-together that they should form an association and meet once a month. I was so enthusiastic I wrote an editorial on the advantages of local government consolidations. I went so far as to suggest that as the county became more populous, it might be well to merge all local governments into a unified county administration.

Dave Jr. took this as a conspiracy to break his father's control of the county. His opposition found popular response. Community pride was affronted by my proposal of consolidations. Haddonfield, founded in 1701, did not want to be identified with adjacent Haddon Heights, founded in 1889. In every corner of the county similar chauvinism attacked the Courier. I had stirred up a hornet's nest, and abandoned the project. As far as I know, the heads of local governments, whom I had brought together at that most interesting dinner, never met again.

I have regretted that, in spite of Dave Jr., I did not go on with the idea. Multiplicity of local governments is a great weakness of the American system. In the United States there are 3,100 counties, 100,000 local taxing authorities. Our 140 metropolitan centers are subdivided into 15,000 local governments. This labyrinth of authorities not only wastes billions of dollars but handicaps regional planning to provide for our rapidly shifting population.

In horse-and-buggy days, small local units of government were necessary. The fifty-mile length of Camden County was a day's journey. Today a motorcycle policeman can negotiate it in forty minutes. Telephone, automobile and concrete highway have made larger units of administration logical and convenient. But local pride preserves the old, wasteful and confusing arrangement.

Within two miles of my home in Haddonfield were five small high schools and as many police chiefs, resplendent in gold braid. In my editorial I had mentioned that regional high schools for two thousand pupils would provide better education at less cost. This proved a particularly abrasive suggestion. The local high school was the community's center and pride. "You want to do away with Haddonfield High's football team, which won the county championship?" an irate neighbor asked me. I was the most unpopular man in the village.

❋   ❋   ❋   ❋   ❋

To get ahead of the Courier, Dave Jr. spent so much on circulation promotion he ended his first year as publisher of the Post-Telegram with a loss of $250,000. I was not surprised when I received word that his father wanted to see me.

"In spite of all this battling, you're putting on weight," was Senator Baird's greeting. "My boy, it's time we ended this nonsense."

"Senator, we haven't answered back," I said. "We're hoping young Dave will calm down."

"Yes, you've been smart about that," Baird admitted. "Smarter than Dave. It's time he stopped trying to run a newspaper. He lost a lot of money last year. I want you to buy his paper at a fair price. He paid Frank Patterson two hundred fifty thousand."

"Senator, you're a wise man," I replied. "You have me sized up as the softie I am. The longer Dave goes on the way he's behaving, the surer we are the Post-Telegram will fold and we won't have to pay anything. But you know I won't take advantage of the situation. I'll pay three hundred thousand."

"It's a deal." The Senator held out his hand. We sent for our attorneys to draft an agreement. Highly elated, I returned to my office and called the meeting of my editorial executives described at the beginning of this book.

Everything was to turn out just the opposite of what I foresaw that day. Now that I had a monopoly I thought my worries were ended. They would have been—if I had not become bored, bought other newspapers and kept under strain until I retired, twenty-one years later. I thought I would gain political power. Instead I lost it. As the only newspaper publisher, I had to be careful not to misuse my position and needlessly offend any faction.

So that its staff should not be thrown out of work, the Post-

Telegram was continued as the Morning Post. The two papers, with a combined circulation of 35,000, which grew over the years to 80,000, were most profitable. But all the excitement and fight had been taken out of the operation. When the city commissioners staged another brawl, the Courier and Post stayed neutral. Because of this intraparty strife, the Republicans won control of the City Commission in 1927. Earlier in that year, Senator Baird had died and Dave Jr. had stepped into his shoes as head of the party. He made the Republican campaign a personal attack on me. On the last day of that contest, Saylor happened to be in my office when blaring horns drew us to the window. We were being serenaded by a procession of autos carrying placards, DOWN WITH BOSS STERN.

"The signs should read DOWN WITH SUCKER STERN," I told Harry. "Half my time has been spent trying to keep those five opera singing commissioners of ours in tune. And the other half apologizing for them in the paper."

"I hope you've learned your lesson," said Harry. But I had not. In Philadelphia a few years later, I was in a similar political turmoil.

The Republican victory afforded me a not unwelcome respite from political responsibility. I could devote full time to publishing. While I had been engrossed with civic business my staff had to get along without me. They did so remarkably well that now I felt like a fifth wheel. The only outlet for my energies was to expand and improve an operation which was already running smoothly.

When I ran out of ideas for improvements I hired experts to show us where we could do better. These masterminds exasperated me. Even though we were functioning efficiently and profitably they recommended major and disrupting changes in every department. There was one exception. Jacob Omansky had made a much publicized record for himself as circulation manager of Stars and Stripes during World War I. After he was discharged from service he organized a circulation survey and consulting service. To advertise this business he issued a monthly bulletin of promotion stunts being used throughout the United States. It was so well written and arranged I hired him to make a survey of our circulation department.

After two weeks' study he came to my office. "It's a well-run operation," he said. "I found nothing radically wrong. My report contains suggestions for only minor changes."

"What kind of expert are you?" I asked. "All the others tell me everything we're doing is wrong."

"If you feel this report is not worth the thousand-dollar fee, forget it." Jake was offended.

"If, after examination, a doctor says you are in good health, he is not entitled to his fee—is that the logic?" I bantered. "Of course we'll give you your check. I wish you would come home to dinner with me."

Why was I so lucky as to invite Jake to my home? He was an unimpressive man who talked slowly, pedantically, like a school teacher. Was I merely trying to make amends for my misunderstood humor, or, in spite of his negative personality, had I sensed his extraordinary ability and character?

Jill and I found him charming. Self-educated, he was an omnivorous reader with a love of literature and art. We sat up so late becoming acquainted, Jake spent the night.

Driving in to the office the next morning, he confirmed what I already had been thinking: "The Courier-Post has reached the point of diminishing returns. You can force its growth, but it will cost more than you can get out of it. If you're too young to take it easy, buy another newspaper."

"If I ever do," I replied, "I hope you join me."

He did, the following year on the Philadelphia Record.

XII

In Spite of Tolstoy

On a pleasant afternoon in the spring of 1928 I visited Eldridge Johnson at his home in Moorestown, another old Quaker borough near Haddonfield. In 1926 he had sold the Victor Talking Machine Company for forty million dollars and retired.

Johnson suggested we sit in his bedroom. I knew what that meant because I had been there before. The most conspicuous object in this room was a big vault. It guarded not money but brandies, wines, and cigars.

"I want you to try one of these 1922 Romeo and Juliets," said Johnson, after he had mastered the combination and thrown back the steel door. "The best tobacco year since 1918. Taste this old brandy."

We sat looking out over the shallow valley which stretches to the east from Moorestown. The peach and apple orchards formed a carpet of pink and white. It was a pleasant background for fine cigars and rare brandy.

"What more could a man want than to take his ease with a friend on an afternoon like this?" asked Johnson.

"I want something more," I answered. "The Philadelphia Record is for sale. I want to buy it. Your friend, Levi Rue, is chairman of the Board of Trustees of the Wanamaker estate, which owns the Record. I want you to tell Rue of our work together in city planning and park development. I could be a constructive force in Philadelphia which is held back by stupid machine rule as Camden was until I dislodged Baird. Remember Leavitt's experience when he offered to plan Philadelphia's bridge approaches. You can get me the best price on the Record."

"So you're not content," mused Johnson. "You can't relax. Man is a funny animal! You've worked hard and fought hard for eight years. Now that you've won, you can enjoy your home and family, travel, and see the world. Aren't you making enough money?"

"Yes," I replied. "I have no complaint on that score."

"I was looking forward to meeting you in England this summer," Johnson continued. "Tell me why you want to complicate your life."

"I've made good as a small-town publisher. I'd like to be in the major league."

"Ego, ego, ego," interrupted Johnson. "Man's greatest strength and weakness." All afternoon we argued. As the shadows lengthened and the evening haze turned the vivid color of the valley into soft pastel shades, Johnson said, "I'll see Rue, make a deal for you, and invest any amount you need, on one condition." He walked over to a bookcase and took out a volume of short stories by Tolstoy.

"My only condition is that you stay home tonight and read this story, 'Does a Man Need Much Land?' Don't read it now. Wait until after dinner. Sleep on it. Phone me tomorrow morning. If you're still of the same mind, I'll see Rue."

Tolstoy tells the story of a kulak, a wealthy Russian peasant, obsessed with a desire to own more land. He hears that the Tartars, far out on the steppes, are giving away land. With a great ox train to carry his family and worldly goods, he makes a journey of many weeks. Finally he reaches the Tartar chief, who tells him he can have all the land he is able to walk around between sunrise and sunset. At dawn, the old farmer looks over the vast expanse of virgin soil. He starts to walk, then breaks into a jog trot. Toward sunset, he is still some distance from his starting point. To get there before the sun dips below the horizon he has to run. He reaches his goal only to fall dead. He is buried on the spot. So six feet of land is all he needs.

The next morning I phoned Johnson. "In spite of Tolstoy's warning, I want to buy the Record. That peasant was in his sixties. I'm forty-two."

"In other words, you have lost your sense of proportion sooner than the peasant," was Johnson's rejoinder. "But since you've carried out your promise, I'll carry out mine."

My decision to buy the Record was not on sudden impulse. Before I visited Johnson I had been considering the project for two years. The idea was put in my head, shortly after I had bought the Post-Telegram, by Al (Albert M.) Greenfield. Al, nicknamed "The Egg" because of his completely bald dome-shaped head, was a financial meteor in Philadelphia's conservative banking and business atmosphere. Starting from scratch, twenty years before, he had built up the leading real estate firm, become president of the city's fastest-growing bank and investment company, and amassed a considerable personal fortune. In his phenomenally rapid rise to wealth and power, Al had made as many enemies as friends. He was the shrewdest wheeler-dealer in Philadelphia. The older men he had outsmarted were jealous and vented their spleen. But Al, blessed with a rhinoceros hide, and not disturbed by such attacks, was riding high.

To discuss his plan that I join him in buying the Record, Al asked me to dine with him on election night, November, 1926. After dinner we went to Mayor Kendrick's office to hear the election returns. Al was given warm greetings by the politicians assembled there, including Bill (William S.) Vare, the Republican boss. After we left, I said to Al, "If I came to Philadelphia, my first job would be to attack your friends and you would be in the doghouse. Thanks for your offer but it wouldn't work."

        ❄   ❄   ❄   ❄   ❄

"Why haven't you bought the Record?" I asked Al when I met him a year later.

"I am not interested without you," he replied.

"Frankly, Al," I said, "I'm thinking of buying it myself but I won't step in if you are still in the picture."

"For the good of Philadelphia"—he was vehement—"buy the Record with or without me. If I can be of any help in financing or in any other way, I am at your service."

The Philadelphia Record was established in 1870 by Philadelphia Democrats who had had no party newspaper since the Civil War. One of the founders was Robert Singerly, the son of an investment banker. His main occupation had been breeding race horses. He became impatient with the pinchpenny policies of his associates and bought them out in 1877. He proved an able publisher. In the nineties the Record claimed the largest circulation in Philadelphia—188,000. Singerly built what was, for that time, a palatial newspaper plant, the first skyscraper in Philadelphia, all of eight stories high.

Singerly was not the man to stick to one last. He became obsessed with the idea of turning old newsprint into new, a process which has never proved commercially successful. To remove ink discoloration completely, so much bleach has to be used that the tensile strength of the paper is destroyed. Newsprint made from old newspapers is either an unpleasant brown or white, and too weak for the web to hold on rotary presses. Singerly would not admit defeat. He wrecked his own fortune and two banks before he committed suicide in 1902. The court appointed as receiver for the Record George H. Earle II, who put Singerly's secretary, Michael H. Hanson, in charge as general manager. This was the Mike Hanson who had taken a friendly interest in me when I worked for the Record in 1910.

The Record prospered under Hanson. The other nine dailies were Republican as were the majority of Philadelphians. But the Record had a following of citizens who wanted to read the other side.

In 1905, by order of the bankruptcy court, the Record was sold at public auction for a million dollars to Tom Wanamaker, son of John Wanamaker, Philadelphia's leading merchant. Hanson continued as general manager. Although Tom Wanamaker was a Republican, he did not interfere with the Record's editorial policy. After Tom Wanamaker's death in 1915, his brother Rodman came into control. Rodman's only interest was in dividends. Hanson was allowed no money for plant improvements or promotion. Frustrated by this shortsighted policy, he resigned in 1920 to become general manager of the Paul Block newspapers.

After Hanson left, the Record went downhill. Its circulation dwindled to less than 100,000. The Rodman Wanamaker estate offered to sell it for $3,500,000. Early in 1928 the Record was suspended by the Audit Bureau of Circulations for falsifying its net-paid figures. Advertisers deserted it. When the Record went into the red, the trustees of the estate went into a panic. Eldridge Johnson was able to bring the price down to $1,750,000—half the original asking figure. This included the equity in the Record Building, conservatively valued at $500,000, making the net cost for the newspaper $1,250,000.

In booming 1928 it was as easy to sell securities as pink lemonade at a circus. The stock issue of the new Record Company was over-subscribed. When I started to explain the financial plan many friends cut me short with, "Dave, I don't want details. Where do I sign and for how much?" This plan called for sale of 350,000 shares of common stock at one dollar a share, 17,500 shares of preferred at $100. The Courier-Post Company was buying 175,000 shares of common and control so that, as parent company, it could support its subsidiary. With the proceeds of this stock, $2,100,000, plus sale of the equity in the building for $500,000, the Record Company would have $2,600,000. After paying the $1,750,000 purchase price, there would be $850,000 for working capital and for a new plant, which was essential because modern presses could not be fitted into the old building. The forty-year-old Record presses turned out an odd-sized, inconvenient page and were ready for the junk heap.

I had intended to sell the Record Building immediately, subject to occupancy until we moved. Al Greenfield advised me to postpone the sale until we vacated, or could set the exact date on which we would be out. "The property will bring a higher price if it is not subject to indefinite occupancy," he advised. "Real estate values are soaring. Next year I believe I can get seven hundred and fifty thousand for your equity instead of the half million you're now asking. Meanwhile my bank will advance you what you need for the new plant." Neither of us foresaw what was going to happen in 1929.

❊   ❊   ❊   ❊   ❊

I went to Philadelphia alone to take over the Record on June 10, 1928. Until I had sized up the situation I did not want to disrupt either the Record or the Courier-Post staffs by transfer of executives or by hirings and firings. I took the title of treasurer, which office happened to be vacant. When Rowe Stewart, the publisher, introduced me to the department heads I told them that most of my time would be occupied with a new plant. "I may come to your office to ask questions," I said, "but not to interfere."

For a month I stuck to this policy of saying nothing while watching news and other matters mishandled or neglected. Sharing this ordeal with me was Hank Eaton. I wanted him to become editor of the Record. He said he was too old but he did consent to spend a month in Philadelphia observing and advising me on reorganization of the news and editorial departments. Later he became a director of the Record Company and gave a couple of days a month to supervision until his death in 1941.

In the twenty years since Hank had given me my first job on the Ledger, we, and this "we" includes our wives, had become close friends. When the Curtis-Martin Company launched the Evening Ledger in 1914, Hank, then managing editor of the Public Ledger, P. H. Whaley, chief editorial writer, and Ben K. Raleigh, city editor, had been transferred to the new paper. An immediate success, its circulation passed 200,000 within the first year. One factor in this rapid growth was a campaign against a crooked political deal on the Broad Street subway. Just when the Evening Ledger had this multi-million steal blocked, Jack (John C.) Martin, the publisher, ordered a complete about-face. City Council passed the enabling ordinance without a whimper from the Evening Ledger. Eaton, Whaley and Raleigh were thinking of resigning when Martin, up against a newsprint shortage, ordered news space cut in half. Eaton said it would ruin the paper and refused to obey. That afternoon he learned Martin had cut the press run from 250,000 to 200,000. The three editors were so let down they resigned, as did M'liss (Eleanor Kinsella), the Ledger's leading columnist.

Their remarkable job on the Evening Ledger was well known and they were offered good positions. But they wanted to work together. They conceived the idea of a Washington newsletter service. That was in 1919 when I returned to Philadelphia from Springfield. Because I had sold two newspapers at a profit, they looked on me as a business brain and wanted my opinion of their project. I told them to forget it. Fortunately, they did not take my advice. The Whaley-Eaton Service, pioneer of newsletters, earned comfortable fortunes for the three of them. Ben Raleigh and M'liss, who was to become Mrs. Raleigh, took charge of the foreign correspondence and made their headquarters in Paris. The Raleighs did such brilliant work that Whaley-Eaton added a weekly foreign letter to its service. In 1932, Ben was deported by the French government for reporting that the Bank of France was falsifying its statements while it issued billions of paper francs. Within a few weeks the government fell, the new premier admitted the truth of Ben's story and Ben was welcomed back to Paris with flying colors.

*　　*　　*　　*　　*

Hank had agreed with me that we should devote a month to observation before making any changes. But at the end of three weeks, he received a tip on a secret meeting to refinance the transit system. It was a sequel to the crooked subway deal which he had fought ten years before—only this was a bigger steal. The city was to buy subways and surface lines for $250,000,000. We estimated $75,000,000 as a fair valuation. Like an old fire horse who hears the alarm, Hank had to get back in harness.

The meeting of bankers, city, and transit officials was to take place early Sunday morning in the office of General W. W. Atterbury, president of the Pennsylvania Railroad, at the old Broad Street Station, since torn down.

"Early Sunday morning is a give-away in itself," said Hank. "If they were not up to some skulduggery, they wouldn't pick the day and time when they would be least likely to be observed." We sent for the city editor and instructed him to surround Broad Street Station with reporters and photographers. "And don't neglect the back entrances or freight elevators," was Hank's parting suggestion.

A few minutes later the managing editor asked to see us.

"I owe it to the Record to tell you this sort of thing just isn't done in Philadelphia," he said.

"What sort of thing?" I feigned naïve surprise.

"Baiting the president of the Pennsylvania Railroad," he explained. "I've been working in Philadelphia for twenty years. I have never known the Record or any other newspaper to treat Pennsy's top brass with anything but respect. I don't think you realize how powerful the railroad is and how dangerous such a story might be."

"I ought to know," I told the managing editor. "I lost my first job because I insulted the Pennsy, and Mr. Eaton, here, was the city editor who gave me thirty seconds to resign before he fired me. That was twenty years ago, just before you came to Philadelphia. So it has been done before, and I'm going to take the calculated risk of being a second offender."

As expected, our reporters were refused admittance to the meeting. To escape reporters and photographers, the leading citizens left via a freight elevator. Thanks to Hank's foresight our boys caught the VIPs trying to avoid recognition, some of them covering their faces like criminals caught in the act. It was a beautiful start of a long battle.

The refinancing of the transit system dragged through the courts for seven years. Finally the capitalization was fixed at $83,-000,000, only 10 per cent more than the Record's original figure of $75,000,000. We had saved Philadelphia $167,000,000 of debt—$10,000,000 annual interest and amortization for twenty years. But it was too complicated a story to hold public interest. There were long pauses between court hearings and decisions, appeals and counterappeals. By the time victory was achieved in 1935, everyone had forgotten that the Record had started the fight in 1928. I never worked harder on a story, nor accomplished more definite public benefit. But there was little or no public appreciation.

In contrast to the lack of interest in this transit campaign was the intense reaction to the Record's attack on Pennsylvania's Sunday blue laws, which ran at the same time.

Pre-Revolutionary laws forbade movies, professional sports or any form of entertainment for which an admission was charged, on the Sabbath. "Dead as a Sunday in Philadelphia" was a vaudeville joke. Over the weekend hotels were empty, trains to New York and Atlantic City crowded, as travelers, as well as many citizens, fled the city. Hotel and amusement interests figured this exodus cost them ten million dollars a year. The Record denounced the Sunday laws as undemocratic. The wealthy could go out of town to avoid them while the average citizen was deprived of his free choice as to how he spent his day off. When our statement that 80 per cent of the population wanted Sunday movies and sports was questioned, the Record sent reply postcards to the million registered voters.

More than 75 per cent of the reply cards were returned and 90 per cent of them were in favor of Sunday sports and movies. The Sabbatarians had urged their adherents to ignore this wicked poll and not mail the reply cards. So they contended that the 25 per cent who had failed to vote were on their side. But even accepting this obviously erroneous assumption, the poll proved that at least 67 per cent of the electorate wanted Sunday movies and baseball. This gave the State legislature courage to grant local option on Sunday laws to cities and counties. In the Philadelphia referendum more than 75 per cent of the votes were for a liberalized Sunday.

When I initiated this campaign I anticipated attack by religious groups. So I had adverse comments on the reply cards and in letters brought to my office. The baskets on a large table soon overflowed. "In trying to break down the Christian Sabbath you are enemies of the nation"; "As allies of the rum interests and cohorts of the Devil you are deceiving no intelligent person" were typical of the more restrained phrases. The Sabbatarians were certainly hot under the collar.

A few years later, in 1936, I had another lesson in the dangers of the controversial which involves religion. A Record editorial described the followers of Franco in the Spanish revolution as "a motley collection of Monarchists, Fascists and hired riffraff. It would be a great tragedy for the world and for Spain if the republic succumbs to their attack." I was reflecting the view of my friend Claude Bowers, eminent historian, who served as ambassador to Spain from 1933 to 1939.

The editorial had appeared on a Friday. The following Sunday morning I was awakened by a phone call from Irv (Irwin) Orner, Record circulation director. The Record had been denounced from Catholic pulpits and members of that church had been forbidden to read it. Priests had driven our newsboys from their stands at the entrance of churches where Catholics customarily bought their Sunday papers after attending mass. Irv estimated Sunday sales would be cut twenty-five thousand. Already the switchboard was clogged with orders to stop delivery of the daily Record.

A slap in the face by a friend would have been no more of a shock than Irv's message. Because I bitterly resented religious prejudice I had gone all out in support of Jack Kelly, a Catholic, for Mayor of Philadelphia in 1935, and of Al Smith for President in 1928. Many of my executives were Catholics. As the only Democratic newspaper in Philadelphia the Record had a large percentage of Catholic readers. Why had none of our friends in the Church given us some warning? A few days later the city was blanketed with pamphlets which proclaimed that "J. David Stern applauds murder of priests and rape of nuns." J. J. O'Malley, chief magistrate of Philadelphia, of whose conduct the Record had been highly critical, boasted to Tip (Timothy P.) O'Neil, our city editor, "I paid for it." Evidently our political enemies had had advance information of the boycott.

When I reached my office Sunday forenoon my executives were already meeting with Matt (Matthew H.) McCloskey, Jr., a Democratic leader and close friend of Cardinal Dougherty, Archbishop of Philadelphia. I was furious at what I considered an outrageous injustice. I wanted to fight it out. But all my associates agreed with Matt that it would be foolish and futile.

"You can't win an argument with a priest" was the way Matt put it. "Give me any kind of a letter to the Cardinal and I'll get him to call off the dogs."

Against my better judgment I wrote the Cardinal that no offense to his church had been intended. I had taken it for granted that my letter was a personal one. The following week it was published on the front page of the Catholic Standard and Times, official weekly of the diocese, with a gracious acceptance of my explanation by the Cardinal which made my "explanation" into an apology. In retrospect, it may have been the expedient course, but at the time I felt completely humiliated. It was a year before the Record recovered the circulation it had lost.

This incident had more than local significance. According to Claude Bowers it was the failure of the world's democracies to support the Spanish government which forced it to turn to Russia for supplies and assistance. As a consequence the Communist element in the government gained control.

"When I came to Madrid in 1933," Claude told me, "the Communists carried no more weight in politics than they did in other European democracies. It was only after France, Great Britain and the United States gave the Spanish government the cold shoulder that the Communists became dominant. Washington paid no attention to my reports and recommendations. Because the other democracies failed to support the Spanish democracy, Hitler and Mussolini jumped to the conclusion that the free world had gone soft and lacked the stamina to stem fascism. That is why Hitler thought Great Britain would not fight the invasion of Poland."

Of course there were two sides to the picture. Spanish liberals fell into the fatal error of making a united front with Communists who forced the government into extreme measures. Instead of standing for religious liberty, the government banished all priests, confiscated church property, allowed mobs to murder and pillage church property. But back of it all was the absurd aloofness of the great powers, and ours in particular. For my lack of courage in this chain of events I share the blame with my fellow capon publishers.

❖   ❖   ❖   ❖   ❖

As in every trade, there are tricks in arousing public interest. Occasionally I resorted to what Saylor called the "upchuck method" because it was calculated to turn a reader's stomach at breakfast. The Record ran a series of stories and editorials on an overcrowded tuberculosis pavilion at the Philadelphia General Hospital, where conditions were disgusting. In this antiquated building beds were so close together the nurses could not service the patients who "were dying like flies because they cannot get proper air or sunlight," as one physician described it. But the public appeared indifferent until I changed the caption and lead on an editorial. "Philadelphia—Well-Dressed but with a Running Sore" I wrote for the head and then went on to describe the City of Brotherly Love as a well-dressed old gentleman who had just appropriated millions for a new art museum. But the effect of all these fine feathers was destroyed by a horrible running sore—the tuberculosis pavilion which I described in nauseating detail.

The response was immediate. Mayor Mackey called for a public hearing at the hospital, which he hoped would refute the Record's charges, and at first the hospital staff testified his way. But when they called the superintendent of nurses, a brave woman, she spoke up: "The Record understates the case. Conditions are horrible and inhuman."

Within the week the City Council appropriated three million dollars for a new tuberculosis pavilion. The "running sore" was too much for Philadelphia to take with its breakfast.

✻   ✻   ✻   ✻   ✻

After our scoop on the transit meeting in General Atterbury's office, Hank Eaton and I agreed that the Record needed a new managing editor. I sent for Harry Saylor, my old reliable. The effect of his leadership was immediate. Jill came over to run the woman's page and the book page. I recruited Elmer Pratt to help me with the new plant. My nephew, David Stern Loeb, was drafted from Camden to take charge of production, and later to become business manager. Gradually the two staffs became intermingled. Another important addition was Jake Omansky. He agreed to make his office at the Record, but insisted he would act only as a consultant while he continued his circulation promotion service. It was a year before I persuaded him to sell his business and give us full time as general manager.

I found a suitable building for the new plant at the corner of Broad and Wood Streets. Its ten floors, 70 by 350 feet, provided five times the space of the old Record Building. If I was lucky in my choice of a building, I was even more fortunate in my landlord, Colonel Louis J. Kolb. He became so interested in his new tenant that he bought stock in the Record Company and later in its subsidiary, the New York Post Company. He served as vice president and director of both corporations until his death in 1941.

The son of a German immigrant, Kolb had started work in a lumberyard. He decided there was more opportunity in baking. His energy and ingenuity built up the leading bakery in Philadelphia. He had retired in 1926 after organizing the General Baking Company. His avocation was the collecting of objects of art, historical documents, and curios. The private dwelling at Eighteenth and Chestnut which he used as his office was filled with a collection which outdid Ripley's.

In his younger days when he had difficulty getting in to see a certain financier, he had besieged him much as I had George Ochs. One day he pulled out a trick watch which so fascinated the financier's secretary she persuaded her boss to see Kolb. He got the loan. After that experience, he became a walking curiosity shop. He often interrupted directors' meetings to display his gadgets.

Louis Kolb was a black Republican. To him, Roosevelt and the New Deal were anathema, but he never tried to influence my editorial policy. He got a kick out of shocking his conservative friends at the Union League Club in Philadelphia and the Bankers Club in New York by serving as vice president of those "terrible radical newspapers." Back of his conservatism was a streak of liberalism. He wanted the other side of the tracks to have its say. The Record was the only New Deal newspaper in Philadelphia; the Post the only one in New York.

The Record moved to its new home in September, 1929. Transferring a newspaper from one plant to another is a nerve-racking ordeal. Thanks to Elmer Pratt, it was accomplished without missing an edition. And once we were in the larger, efficiently planned quarters, we realized how great had been the handicap of the cramped helter-skelter arrangement in the old building. The Record was pulling out of the red while the Courier-Post's profits were holding steady. I saw fair sailing ahead.

Then came an unexpected blow that knocked me dizzy. The stock market crashed in October, 1929. Real estate values fell as precipitously as securities. Overnight the $500,000 equity in the Record Building evaporated. I had counted on this $500,000 to pay for the new presses.

Al Greenfield, whose advice was partly responsible for the fix in which I found myself, came to the rescue. "Nothing to get excited about," he kept reassuring me. "Bankers' Security Corporation [affiliate of Bankers' Trust Company of Philadelphia] will give the Record a long-term loan."

I had just about recovered my equilibrium from this body blow when I was jolted by a sock to the chin which nearly floored me for the count. In January 1930, the Bankers' Trust Company of Philadelphia, the Record's chief depository, closed. Our working balance of $350,000 was frozen. Accounts in other banks totaled $30,000 and we had a $40,000 payroll to meet at the end of the week. Bankers' Trust was the first of the Philadelphia banks to fold. Later we became quite used to the phenomenon.

It was a rainy Monday morning when word came that Al's bank had failed to open its doors. A phone call to Camden confirmed what I already knew. They had no surplus cash. Frank Murphy, my secretary, cut off all phone calls and callers. I sat in my back office, trying to figure what to do. To be explicit, I sat in my private bathroom. My bowels were loose from fear.

That luxurious lavatory saved the Record from extinction. In renovating the Kolb building for the new tenant, the contractor went all out on the president's suite. The large bathroom was a tasteful blending of gray marble, tile, and porcelain. To the other equipment had been added a barber's chair which I found the most comfortable place to take a nap. No matter how low his morale or how upset his innards, a man could not utterly despair in such a convenient and pleasant room.

Tolstoy's story, which Eldridge Johnson had had me read before buying the Record, haunted me. If the good Lord let me wriggle out of this fix, I would never tempt fortune again. I did wriggle out. But four years later I bought the New York Post. "The burnt fool's bandaged finger goes wobbling back to the fire" is one of the fundamental truths which Kipling lists in *Gods of the Copy Book Maxims*.

My bathroom reverie was interrupted when Frank, disregarding my order, announced Pop Gilman. A check on Bankers' Trust of Philadelphia to the Gilman Paper Company for $125,000 had bounced.

"Pop, we're busted," I said. "I had three hundred and fifty thousand in the Bankers' Trust. Now I haven't fifty thousand in all my bank accounts in Philadelphia and Camden. I don't know how I can meet the payroll at the end of the week. We'll have to shut down."

"You'll do nothing of the sort," Pop said as he put his arms around me. "Your friends will back you. Give me your note for this check and forget about it. You can have all the newsprint you need and we'll send you fifty thousand cash tomorrow. That will meet your first payroll. Get busy; go to work. Get your big advertisers to pay in advance."

Pop turned the tide. I called an executive conference. My associates filed into my office prepared to hear the worst. Thanks to Pop, I met them with a smiling face and concrete plans to hurdle the crisis. In response to a phone call the head of one department store had readily agreed to send me $25,000 advance payment on his account.

"Here we go again," I told my executives. "In Springfield we used to collect cash in advance from advertisers to meet the payroll. Now we have to go begging again. It's a challenge. We'll meet it."

We did. But for a few months it was touch and go. Our larger advertisers helped us with immediate cash and our suppliers followed Gilman's example by allowing long-term credit. We stopped promotion which slowed up development. But the momentum of a year and a half's hard work kept circulation and advertising growing in spite of the depression.

After my executive conference, I went to see Al. He was as cool as a cucumber. He told me he was six million dollars in debt on personal guarantees of real estate mortgages and bonds. In the last days he had poured into the Bankers' Trust all the cash of his real estate business and other enterprises, as well as his personal accounts and those of his family. He had the guts and ability to make a marvelous comeback.

Eventually the receivers of Bankers' Trust of Philadelphia paid off 75 per cent of its deposits, which proved that it had been solvent and never should have been closed. The other Philadelphia bankers had resented the rapid growth of Al's bank. In the fall of 1929, they had persuaded him to take over and save from closing a string of suburban banks. They promised their support. When he needed it, they turned thumbs down.

❋   ❋   ❋   ❋   ❋

While we were pulling out of our financial difficulties, a New York newspaper broker walked into my office to ask, "Have you any Record stock for sale?"

"That's a strange question. Why do you ask?"

He represented Ralph Beaver Strassburger, publisher of the Norristown Times-Herald, whom I had helped to get out of a newsprint gouge ten years before. On condition that he have first option on the Philadelphia Inquirer if it were ever offered for sale, Strassburger had bought $500,000 of its preferred stock in 1929.

Under the able management of James Elverson and his son, James Jr., the Inquirer had won the lead in the Philadelphia morning field. Elverson Sr. left the paper to his son and daughter. The daughter had married Jules Patenôtre, the French Ambassador to the United States, and lived abroad. When her brother died in 1929 Mme. Patenôtre became sole owner of the Inquirer. She sent her son, Raimond Patenôtre, a French journalist, to take charge. His closest American friend was Strassburger, who maintained a home in Paris and a racehorse breeding-farm near Deauville.

Soon after their arrival in Philadelphia Jill and I gave a dinner party for the Raimond Patenôtres. They were a gay young couple more interested in having fun than in newspaper publishing. It was not long before they found Philadelphia tedious. Disregarding his commitment to Strassburger, Patenôtre sold the Inquirer for nine million dollars to the Curtis-Martin Corporation, owners of the Public Ledger, Evening Ledger and the New York Post. To avoid U. S. taxes Patenôtre chartered a plane, took Jack Martin, president of Curtis-Martin, and their lawyers, to Canada where the agreements were signed and the checks passed. It did not work. After twenty years of litigation the Patenôtres had to pay the government several million in back taxes and interest.

Strassburger's preferred stock was called and paid off by Curtis-

Martin, but he was furious that his option had been ignored. In revenge, he wanted to help the Record take first place in the morning field. When this *deus ex machina* flew in the window, it was hard for me to keep a poker face. My tongue was hanging out for more capital. I told Strassburger's representative that there was no stock for sale. "But," I was careful to add, "the Board of Directors might consider a new issue to obtain additional capital for more rapid development."

We agreed to issue 15,000 shares of common stock, of which Strassburger was to buy 10,000 shares and the Courier-Post Company 5,000. After going over our books Strassburger's accountants fixed a fair price at $33 a share. This was the stock we had issued at one dollar two years before.

Strassburger was elected a Record director. He proved a volatile member of the Board. After a few months, his original enthusiasm changed to impatient criticism that we were not making faster progress. He was to settle for his stock in four quarterly installments. After paying two installments, he went off to Europe and forgot about the remainder. Then we learned that Strassburger and Jack Martin had been discussing the sale of the Record to the Curtis-Martin Corporation. The Board of Directors demanded Strassburger's resignation.

❋   ❋   ❋   ❋   ❋

The year 1930 was hectic. It started with the closing of the Bankers' Trust. It ended on an equally sour note. As I was leaving my office New Year's Eve, I was stopped in the hall by my financial editor, Harry E. Kalodner.

"I would like to see you in your office," he said.

"Can't it wait until next year? I am late for a New Year's Eve party."

"Mr. Stern, this is urgent and important."

We walked back to my office.

"I have just been offered a thousand dollars for a list of your creditors so Strassburger can throw the Record into bankruptcy," Kalodner told me.

The New Year's Eve party was forgotten. At a hastily called

conference with my attorneys, Charles E. Fox and Jerome J. Rothschild, we decided not to reveal our knowledge of the plot. Kalodner went back to his contact to suggest our head book-keeper, Joseph V. Minon, as a source of information.

We led the conspirators on to numerous meetings where dicta-phones were planted. Frank M. Murphy, my secretary, transcribed hundreds of pages of incriminating conversation. Strassburger's operators asked Charles Gilman, Pop's younger son and vice presi-dent of the Gilman Paper Company, to meet Jack Martin and Charles Tyler of the Curtis-Martin newspapers. At our request, Gil-man kept the appointment and was offered a long-term newsprint contract. He was to start bankruptcy proceedings against the Rec-ord for the balance of $75,000 we still owed on the check that bounced when Bankers' Trust closed.

I wanted Strassburger arrested, but we had done our detective work so well counsel feared we might be accused of acting as *agents provocateurs*. The lawyers worked out a compromise. Strass-burger paid up the $165,000 balance he owed on his stock sub-scription and gave me a ten-year voting trust of his stock.

Harry Kalodner, who revealed the Strassburger plot, played an important part in the development of the Record. He had a fine legal mind and a real love for the law. Like many other veterans, when he came back from service in World War I, he had found it difficult to build a law practice. He returned to newspaper work at which he had earned his way through law school. He handled our successful battle against the attempt to have the city buy the transit system for $250,000,000. He made newspaper history when the press was denied access to a stockholders' meeting of the Phil-adelphia Rapid Transit Company. He rushed to a broker's office, bought a share of PRT stock, then induced the transfer agent to issue a new certificate in his name. Armed with this document, he made his way into the meeting in time to get an exclusive story.

When George H. Earle III ran for Governor in 1934, I asked Harry to help George through the first weeks of his campaign. I never got Harry back. George issued an ultimatum that he would quit the race if Harry was not released for the rest of the cam-paign and to be his secretary if he won the governorship. George made Harry Secretary of Revenue in charge of the finances of the Commonwealth. Harry did a marvelous job revamping the tax laws. Later, George appointed Harry to a vacancy on the Court of Common Pleas of Philadelphia. Due to an unfortunate speech by George, Harry was defeated for election to the permanent term. Then President Roosevelt named Harry a U. S. District Judge. His performance on the bench was so outstanding that President Truman promoted him to the Court of Appeals, where he is now serving with distinction.

XIII

The Record
Backs Roosevelt

"That winds it up." I was dismissing our editorial writers. "But wait, we haven't given Hugh a chance to sound off on the Governor of New York." It was the end of a conference at the Record in January, 1932. In Harry Saylor's absence I had been presiding and I was joshing Hugh Sutherland, who had been repeatedly urging us to switch our support from Al Smith to Roosevelt for the Democratic Presidential nomination.

"Some day I'll have the small satisfaction of saying, 'I told you so,'" Hugh said after the others had left. An imposing individual with the look of a zealot on his thin, long face, Hugh was a dynamic talker as well as writer. As editor of the Philadelphia North American he had won national recognition for his World War I editorials, which had been reprinted in book form. When the North American folded we had welcomed him as a potent addition to our editorial board.

"I hear Roosevelt is in such bad health he could not function as President," I said, knowing it would get a rise out of Hugh—and it did.

"That's a damned lie." Hugh barked with more than accustomed heat. "The utility lobby spreads that vile propaganda. Because he's winning his fight for lower rates, they hate Roosevelt's guts. His legs may be crippled but not his fine mind and brave heart. His liberal platform and the Record's editorial policies are dead ringers for each other. You two think alike. It's the logical move for the Record to support the liberal wing of the party. And I'm telling you for the steenth time, the brown derby is washed up. If you have any doubts about Roosevelt's competence go up to Albany and see for yourself, as I have suggested before."

"Hugh, to end the argument, this time I'll take you up." I said, "You make arrangements. Any time next week." That is how I first came to meet Franklin D. Roosevelt in February, 1932.

Saylor and I had agreed that the Record should support Smith in 1932, as it had in 1928. Smith still held a large and loyal following in Pennsylvania who wanted him to have another try at the Presidency. We resented one of Sutherland's arguments, "You can't elect a Catholic."

My several meetings with Smith had impressed me that he was sincere and able. But there was one chink in the Happy Warrior's armor which worried me. He insisted on overplaying the role of the uncouth tough guy from the sidewalks of New York—just as I had overplayed the roustabout when out West with Dan Renear. Smith cocked his brown derby at one angle, his cigar at another, deliberately mispronounced words and was always dragging his humble upbringing into the conversation.

The day before my talk with Sutherland, I had spent an hour with Smith in his New York office, discussing ways by which we could strengthen Democratic county organizations in Pennsylvania. In the 1928 campaign the Record had sent to Democratic county chairmen 250,000 pamphlets, which had not been distributed in many counties for lack of local party machinery. Smith lolled back in his chair, smoking a cigar. The ashes fell on his vest. He cussed as he brushed them off and spit in the big spittoon. I would not have remembered this trivial incident if he had not repeated it three times. His clothes were a motley of ashes and saliva.

"Governor, how do you rate Grover Cleveland as a politician?" I asked.

"One of the greatest," was his answer.

"Is it true that he electioneered in the Bowery wearing high silk hat, white tie, and tails?"

"So they say, but that was fifty years ago. They wouldn't stand for that kind of la-di-da today. Now you've got to level with the voter."

My hint had fallen on deaf ears. I did not have the nerve to be more explicit. It was that session with Smith which impelled me to take Sutherland's advice and meet Roosevelt. Smith's affectation, rather than his religion, had lost him the Presidency in 1928.

The moment I met him, I was captivated by Roosevelt's charm. He was a truly handsome man, so vital and robust above the waist you forgot his infirmity. He wanted to hear all about the problems of publishing a liberal newspaper in a rock-ribbed Republican stronghold like Philadelphia. He insisted on an account of my earlier career. He had a knack for turning the conversation to the other fellow's interests. He said he envied me, that he had always wanted to be a newspaper publisher. Then he expressed admiration for my editorial campaign against overcapitalization of the transit system, against a city wage tax which had sparked a march of 18,000 on City Hall, and against Philadelphia's Sunday blue laws. His secretaries had briefed him well on just what I would like to hear. It dawned on me that our talk was running in reverse; instead of my finding out about him, he was exploring me.

Finally I said, "Governor, let's talk about the coming convention. That's what I came up here for."

"Well, Dave, just what do you want to know?"

"To be perfectly frank, Governor, I came up here to check the utility lobby's propaganda that you're soft in the head."

Roosevelt roared with laughter. "Just stick around, Dave, and find out," he said. Perhaps that challenge set the pace for the conversation at luncheon. The other two guests were the president and general counsel of one of America's largest railroads. The talk turned to railroad financing. Governor Roosevelt quoted a string of figures on the bonded indebtedness per mile of various railroad systems. The railroad president questioned Roosevelt's figures, but his general counsel said, "I think the Governor is right."

All through luncheon Roosevelt rattled off figures. He had a more accurate knowledge of railroad financing than the railroad men, and they admitted it. His photographic memory for statistics was amazing.

"I just clipped a piece from the Boston Transcript which proves my point," was the President's greeting a year later when I came to the White House to protest lowering the gold content of the dollar. "It shows the change in the prices of ten commodities in ten years." He rang for Miss LeHand and asked her to bring him the clipping. She returned to say she could not find it.

"I remember the figures well enough." He jotted the twenty figures on a desk pad. As he was finishing, Miss LeHand returned. She had found the clipping. When we checked, the President had made a mistake in only one of the twenty figures. Number-minded people are often lacking in human understanding. Roosevelt was a rare exception. Once I complained that it was hard to arouse the public in a crusade for lower electric rates because the saving to the small householder was less than ten dollars a year.

"I licked that one with my waffle iron campaign in 1930," was his answer. "I had a big canvas on which were painted a waffle iron, a toaster, a washing machine, an electric refrigerator. Instead of quoting dollar savings, I told the housewives that, when rates were reduced, they could use all these appliances without increasing their monthly bills. That did the trick."

❅   ❅   ❅   ❅   ❅

As I was leaving after my first meeting with Governor Roosevelt in February, 1932, he said, "Your trip here shows you are conscientious about your political commitments. You should follow Al Smith's slogan and look at the record, my record, not your Record. I want you and your associates to be convinced I am delivering the goods. I'll ask Sam Rosenman, my personal counsel, to go to Philadelphia with a complete record of my campaign promises and those I have fulfilled in my four years as Governor. You will find my batting average is better than seventy-five per cent."

A few days later, Sam Rosenman arrived at the Record with the documentary evidence. Governor Roosevelt had failed in only one major objective—unemployment insurance. And he had missed it by a very close vote in the legislature.

After Rosenman's visit, Saylor and I shared Sutherland's enthusiasm. We published a series of editorials, which were widely reprinted, giving a detailed account of Governor Roosevelt's remarkable achievements. We were the first and, I believe, the only metropolitan newspaper which came out for Franklin Roosevelt before the 1932 Democratic Convention.

During the preconvention campaign I went to Albany three more times. Roosevelt realized that the government must undertake immediate, direct, strong measures to help the unemployed and break the depression. But he talked about balancing the Federal budget. Roosevelt was an economic conservative. He was also a humanitarian and, fortunately for this nation, his humanitarianism outweighed his conservatism. I put it up to him, "If you have to choose between letting a man starve and unbalancing the budget, which shall it be?"

"I wish the issue could be that clear, which it is not, but if it were, I would unbalance the budget," was his answer. This conflict, between his financial conservatism and his humane compulsion to help the underdog, persisted through the first years of his administration.

The day after President Roosevelt took office I said to him, "Would you like to know the first thing I would do if I were President?"

"And what would President Stern do?" F.D.R. mocked my over-eagerness to give advice.

"I would send for John Maynard Keynes," was my answer. "He's the greatest economist of our time. He advocates deficit spending to counteract depression."

"In this country we have no use for Keynes," was Roosevelt's reply.

This was literally true. Among American financiers and statesmen, Keynes, who questioned the gold standard, was anathema. In the spring of that eventful 1932, because of my series of editorials on the Federal fiscal policy, or lack of it, I had been asked to testify before the Senate Finance Committee. When I quoted Keynes I was interrupted by the chairman, Smoot of Ute (Senator Reed Smoot of Utah). "We don't mention that man's name in this committee," he shouted with as much heat as if I had insulted the dignity of the Senate by using a four-letter word.

I was careful not to utter the abrasive name when I lunched with President Hoover the next day, but I expounded Keynesian economics for two hours. I tried to persuade Hoover to embargo gold, which was running out of our country like water through a sluice. The President had the power to issue such an edict without consulting Congress. He gave me a courteous hearing. But at the end I felt I had been pouring water on a duck's back. The President repeated what he had said when we sat down to lunch, "I must restore confidence to the businessman. All the measures you have proposed would confuse and frighten him."

Hoover and Smoot were typical of Washington in those days— and it is not so very different today. I talked to leaders of both parties and found their minds closed. Many of them were ignorant of even the rudiments of economics. Deficit spending meant to them "a resort to printing-press money." To tell them that our principal medium of exchange was bank credit, that volume and velocity (bank clearings) of bank credit, rather than gold, controlled the value of money was like trying to tell a child, "There ain't no Santa Claus." They did not want to hear it or believe it.

Characteristic of that kind of "thinking" was a story in the American Banker, the only daily financial newspaper in those days. GOD'S DECREE FIXES GOLD AS PERMANENT SYMBOL OF MONEY was the headline of the lead story on November 28, 1931. " 'God has decreed that gold is always to be the symbol of money as is evidenced by the manner in which gold supply has kept pace with the world's growth,' said George R. James, member of the Federal Reserve Board," the first paragraph read. After a column of such twaddle, studded with gems such as, "If people kept in close touch with God's laws, there would be fewer economic disasters," the story came to a fitting climax: "After serving for eight years on the Federal Reserve Board Mr. James has just been appointed for ten years more by President Hoover." Who says brains and ability are not recognized in the Federal service?

During the period 1931 to 1933, I ran a series of editorials urging that we "fight the depression as we fought the war." "A gold embargo was used by President Wilson to make the world safe for democracy. Let us use it now to make America safe for Americans." "We must reduce the value of the dollar to a normal level before we can have normal business" and "The stronger the dollar the weaker the nation" were phrases I kept repeating. They had no effect on the Hoover Administration. Soon after he took office, President Roosevelt did embargo gold—prohibiting its export from this country. But in those first days of his Administration, he was toying with the idea that he could raise farm prices and bring down the swollen value of the dollar by reducing its gold content.

❖   ❖   ❖   ❖   ❖

This ancient and utterly fallacious theory had recently received new impetus. It was sparked by a bizarre combination of an ingenious professor of sociology, a skillful college carpenter, and an enterprising manufacturer of office appliances. Dr. Irving Fisher of Yale kept his data on index cards which he spread on his desk when he prepared a lecture or wrote a book. His desk was so large that many of the cards were out of range of his bifocals. At his suggestion the carpenter built a panel of slots to hold a hundred cards. It proved so convenient that the carpenter was kept busy making similar contraptions for other members of the faculty. When James H. Rand, Jr., head of Remington Rand, Inc., saw it he realized its possibilities and started the Visible Index Company. Dr. Fisher's share of the profits was three million dollars. This suddenly acquired wealth made him, in the opinion of the faculty, as well as his own, an authority on money. Fisher started the Stable Money League. The gold content of the dollar was to be varied so as to hold its purchasing power at a constant level. My boyhood friend, Ralph Wescott, was managing director of the League, so I kept in touch with its progress. I was astounded by the rapidity of its growth, by the number and quality of the thousands who joined. One of Fisher's disciples was Dr. George F. Warren, Professor of Agricultural Economics at Cornell, and a friend of both Franklin Roosevelt and Henry Morgenthau, Jr., who had adjoining farms in Dutchess County, New York. They often consulted Dr. Warren on farming problems. He gave such good advice that the two gentlemen farmers considered him a brilliant man, which he was, in his field. The plight of the farmers drove agricultural leaders to clutch at straws. Crop prices were not only 40 per cent below parity but they were below a bare subsistence level for a majority of farmers.

In the farm belt crackpot relief plans were more abundant than weeds.

On the other side of the picture, Wall Street was warning the President that deficit government spending would bring on a wild inflation such as had afflicted France and Germany. So Roosevelt fell for Warren's panacea. I predicted that reduction of the gold content of the dollar would have only a temporary effect and that within a month prices would fall to their previous level. I understated the case. It took only two weeks after devaluation before commodity prices were back to their previous low. Then, finally, on April 8th, President Roosevelt publicly admitted that some inflation of credit by government spending was necessary. I think the most telling argument that I used was a statement by the Rt. Honorable Montagu Norman, Governor of the Bank of England: "We know little of inflation and deflation, but one thing we do know is that it is harder to control deflation than inflation."

"You've got to make your choice between Scylla and Charybdis," I told the President. "There's no way to navigate in between."

During this contention I earned my title as "Administration hair shirt." "Here's Dave the hair shirt, come to denounce the Warren plan" was the President's usual greeting. I wonder now at his forbearance and patience with my strident criticism of his plan both in his office and in editorials which expressed my "bitter disappointment" in the course he was steering. I was furious that my hero was falling for this crackpot scheme. I must have been a pain in the neck to the White House Secretariat, as well as to the President. In going over my correspondence with F.D.R. at the Hyde Park library, I came across a warning to the Secretary of Treasury, hastily scribbled by Marvin H. McIntyre, "that hairshirt Dave is due in town tomorrow," and advising the Secretary to read and prepare himself on my latest letter to the President, which was attached, before I arrived.

After devaluation proved futile, I never mentioned the subject again and neither did Roosevelt. But when I bought the New York Post, in his letter of congratulation he wrote, "There are times when a 'hair shirt' is a good thing for an administration. I always welcome honest and constructive criticism, and you are one of the people upon whom I can count to get honest convictions."

Other than slowing up effective measures to relieve the depression, devaluation had no immediate effect on the national economy. Of course this increase in the price of gold cost Uncle Sam, the biggest buyer of the metal, countless billions. But this loss will not reveal itself until the uselessness of gold, other than for jewelry and plugging teeth, is generally acknowledged. Such is the inertia of human thinking, that it will be a long time before that happens. It took three hundred years before all astronomers were willing to accept the startling idea of Copernicus and Galileo that the earth revolves around the sun. The Ptolemaic system that the sun circles around the earth was being taught at Harvard until 1822.

Meanwhile we are stimulating the mining of a worthless metal, especially in South Africa, where the native miners are sorely puzzled: "Why white man dig gold out of one hole in ground, carry it across ocean to bury in another [Fort Knox]?" The gold fetish will persist longer than most fallacies because world finance did not suddenly go off the gold standard; it gradually slid off over a long period of years. The use of credit money began in the Middle Ages when goldsmiths issued receipts for the metal deposited with them. Exchange of these receipts was more convenient and less expensive than transporting bullion under armed guard. Since then credit in banks grew out of all proportion to the gold coverage and became the controlling factor in the price equation. To the mathematics of the situation is added an emotional factor. People, especially people with money, fight the idea that their dollars are an abstraction represented only by entries on the books of a bank. They want to be sure that their bank credits can be changed into something they can put in their pockets, and even if they are presently allowed only pieces of paper, that there is a gold backing for those paper notes in Fort Knox.

Not so long ago many parts of the country fought shy of paper money. When I hocked my furniture to bring my family back East from Seattle in 1909, I cashed a check for three hundred dollars at a large Seattle bank. The teller shoved fifteen double eagles (twenty-dollar gold pieces) through the window. When I put them in my pocket they were so heavy I asked for paper money. The teller had none in his cage. When he returned from the vault he said, "I'm ashamed to hand you these bills, they're so worn and torn. If you can come back this afternoon, I'll have clean money for you."

The gold fetish dies slowly. As long as it is dominant we cannot hope for clear thinking or stabilization of the dollar. We will continue to be afflicted with a succession of booms and depressions just as cities used to be ravaged by periodic epidemics until they accepted the rules of hygiene. It was fifty years after doctors had discovered the connection between typhoid and polluted water until cities got around to cleaning up or chlorinating their water supplies. Recently there have been hopeful signs that conservative financiers are awakening to the absurdity of the present thinking. Within another generation our money may be rationalized and stabilized.

As further evidence of Roosevelt's conservative thinking on financial problems, he threatened to veto the Glass-Steagall bill which established Federal Deposit Insurance, protecting all bank deposits up to $5,000, later to $10,000. When I ran several editorials in support of his bill, Senator Carter Glass of Virginia asked me to urge the President to sign it.

On this mission I took with me Dr. Luther Harr, who had just resigned as Professor of Banking at the Wharton School of the University of Pennsylvania to become treasurer of the Record and Courier-Post companies. After we had our say, the President turned on us. "You want me to socialize the banking system. Federal insurance would wipe out the difference between the good banker and the bad banker. With his deposit insured the depositor would go to the nearest, most convenient bank. He would give no consideration to the safety of the bank. Uncle Sam would really be the banker on whom the depositor relied."

A few days later Senator Joseph F. Guffey of Pennsylvania reported to me that the President had seemed annoyed by my visit and had asked him, "Why does Dave Stern bring a crank like Harr to see me?" But the President was finally persuaded to sign the bill as an emergency measure which would pull cash out of mattresses where it had been hidden by many citizens, frightened by the bank closings. He told me that he had signed it "against principle as an expedient." F.D.I.C. turned out to be one of the most constructive laws of his administration. Today conservative bankers would not want it rescinded.

It was just a year after the unfortunate experiment in reducing the gold content of the dollar that Roosevelt greeted me one morning with, "I've just invited Keynes to visit us."

"A wise move, Mr. President," was all I said. I did not voice what was in my mind. If he had taken my advice a year ago, he would have saved time and billions in licking the depression, and he would have avoided that devaluation blunder.

*   *   *   *   *

On my preconvention visits to Albany in 1932, Governor Roosevelt and I had little time for basic issues. Most of our talks were confined to practical politics. As I was leaving his office on my last trip, a week before the convention, the Governor called me back.

"I almost forgot an important story," he said. "John O'Donnell has just come over to our camp. He controls six delegates." O'Donnell was chairman of the Philadelphia Democratic City Committee, as well as a Philadelphia County commissioner. He had journeyed to New York to see Al Smith. Through an oversight he was kept waiting for hours. Taking offense, John walked over to Roosevelt's headquarters. Jim (James A.) Farley, campaign manager, lost no time in pledging John to the Roosevelt cause. When the Smith camp learned of this defection, Frank I-Am-The-Law Hague, boss of Jersey City and campaign manager for Al Smith, went to Philadelphia to see John. The more Hague argued, the more adamant John became.

In his exasperation, Hague asked O'Donnell if he might use his phone to call General William Wallace Atterbury, president of the Pennsylvania Railroad and Republican National Committeeman. Frank asked Atterbury to intercede with John.

"Dave, if you can put that story over," Governor Roosevelt said, "if you can show the absurdity of Frank Hague trying to have Atterbury, a Republican leader, order delegates to vote for Al Smith, it will be a knockout at the Convention. Assign a good reporter who'll handle O'Donnell tactfully, so he'll stand pat on the story. Send five thousand copies of the Record to Jim Farley at the Congress Hotel in Chicago. It will be a great help. I see the headline: TRIPLE PLAY, HAGUE TO ATTERBURY TO O'DONNELL." Roosevelt often talked like a newspaperman. He would outline a story in city editor style and end with, "I see a headline." He never forgot that he had been managing editor of the Harvard Crimson. "If you had stuck to the newspaper game," I used to say, "you might have gotten somewhere."

Instead of entrusting the mission to a reporter, I went to see John O'Donnell and wrote a story which made it quite obvious the conservative wing of the Democratic Party, backing Al Smith, and the reactionary Old Guard of the G.O.P. were as alike as two peas in a pod. During the Harding, Coolidge, and Hoover administrations, conservatives had kept the Democratic Party going in Republican states such as Pennsylvania. Some of the big industrialists contributed to both parties to insure that no matter which side won, the national Administration would be safely conservative. That was the background of the triple play of Hague to Atterbury to O'Donnell.

*   *   *   *   *

As business friends had warned me ten years before, when the Courier bucked the Baird machine, they now predicted dire consequences if the Record supported "that socialist Roosevelt." William L. Nevin, meeting me on a train to New York, said, "Dave, don't you know that the Bolshevik Governor of New York has paresis, not polio? You're trying to put a madman in the White House." I am not proud that I walked away without answering him. Nevin was lawyer for the Wanamaker estate and head of the John Wanamaker department store, our largest advertiser, which had been treating the Record very generously. This incident explains why so few newspapers supported Roosevelt either before or after the Convention. For a publisher to come out for Roosevelt before the Convention was dangerous business. Those of us who did, cherish the title FRBC (for Roosevelt before the Convention).

Roosevelt's victory in 1932 came from the grass roots. His genius as an orator and as a politician won delegates and voters. He convinced them that something could be done about unemployment, apple sellers at every corner, lengthening queues at soup kitchens —and that he was the man to do it. The conservatives did not seem to realize that continuance of intense depression was building up radicalism and endangering democracy. If Roosevelt had not become President in 1932, this country would be afflicted today, as France and Italy are, with a substantial Communist Party and a Communist bloc in Congress.

Before the 1932 Convention the Record was the principal newspaper voice for the liberal theory. I have to hand it to my loyal Board of Directors. Conservatives like Louis Kolb, Al Greenfield, Maurice Weyl, and Samuel Fels never tried to influence my editorial policy. I told them I had been through political battles in New Brunswick and Camden, and knew what I was doing. If the Record was to win a following, it must prove itself under fire. While reassuring my directors, I was well aware of the risk I was taking. If Smith won the nomination, the Record would be branded as a radical sheet which had tried to destroy the American way of life.

I have listed Sam Fels among the conservatives, but only in the sense that he was an economic conservative like President Roosevelt. I think Sam's conservatism was a reaction to the extreme liberalism of his brother Joe, a socialist and single taxer. Sam was most liberal and charitable in helping the underprivileged. He invested $100,000 in the Record, "because I have been impressed by your good work in Camden—especially in city planning," he told me. He had a quick, keen mind which enabled him to build up the Fels-Naptha Company into one of the most profitable soap concerns in the country.

Of all the Record's directors Sam Fels took the greatest interest in the details of the business. At least once a month he would spend an afternoon at the plant. His special concern was with the mechanical processes, the clearness of our printing, the color and finish of newsprint, the reproduction of halftones. A little wisp of a man with a Vandyke beard and old-fashioned clothes, he looked as if he had stepped out of a seventeenth-century Spanish portrait. Because his eyesight was failing, I enlarged the body type to satisfy his complaint that the Record was hard to read. As usual, Sam was right. This innovation was subsequently adopted by most newspapers. After spending several hours going around the plant he would come back to my office to ply me with questions. I never saw him relax except when we played chess. But with all his nervous tension, Sam was blessed with a wry sense of humor. When business was very bad, the question came up as to whether the company should continue its one million dollars' insurance on my life. "Even though our president looks so confoundedly healthy," said Sam, "I move we maintain the insurance."

Needling me was a favorite sport of my directors. Most caustic critic was my cousin, Maurice N. Weyl, secretary-treasurer of the company. He had as brilliant a mind as his brother, Dr. Walter E. Weyl, the economist. On or off the stage I have never met Maurice's equal at mental arithmetic. "When I couldn't sleep last night I raised seventeen to the seventeenth power," he once told me. On the death of my uncle and guardian, Edward Stern, Maurice had become president of Edward Stern & Company, a large job-printing plant. Uncle Ed was a kindly man with an irascible temper of which Maurice and I bore the brunt. Maurice, ten years my senior, would come to my rescue when the old man was too hard on me. That was the beginning of our friendship. He became a stockholder and officer of the Courier-Post Company and the Record Company. He was always my staunch supporter, but that did not prevent his ribbing me at directors' meetings.

I could take this joshing from my directors because, as majority stockholder, I was in control. When an argument became too heated, Kolb would end it with, "We might as well vote his way before Dave gets down on the floor and kicks and screams until we give in."

Except when Strassburger was an abrasive member of the Board, those directors' meetings were a lot of fun. Louis Kolb originated the custom of matching Sam and the other three non-salaried directors for their twenty-dollar fees. The four salaried directors did not receive fees. The meeting could not proceed until one of the five won the hundred dollars and Kolb had displayed his latest pocket curio.

❋   ❋   ❋   ❋   ❋

When the news came that Roosevelt had been nominated by the Democratic Convention, a celebration started in my back office. There was a pantry, well-stocked with bootleg liquor. It began as an office party but as the night wore on, friends dropped in to congratulate us. I was surprised to find how many men of affairs had been in secret accord with the Record's editorial policy but had not dared to reveal their sympathy. One of these visitors was Al Greenfield, a staunch Republican and personal friend of President Hoover.

"Al, don't tell me you've come over to our camp?" I said in greeting him.

"No, I won't say that yet," he replied. "It would give you a swelled head. I dropped in to congratulate you on picking the right horse. I admit I'm thinking it over. The Hoover Administration has us in an awfully tight fix. Perhaps your theory of spending our way out of the depression is right."

I was feeling on top of the world when I went home that night. But the next morning Saylor and Sutherland brought me down to earth. The Pennsylvania State Democratic leaders, who had been for Smith, were declaring they would not work for a Bolshevik candidate. We did not know in how many states similar defections were taking place. Without party organization Roosevelt could not win the election.

John O'Donnell came to see me. He did not seem very happy about the victory of his candidate. Bill Vare, Republican boss, had given him hell for throwing six delegates to Roosevelt. When I suggested a statement denouncing the Vare machine, John was very frank about it. "Dave, I can't do that to my old friend who has kept me on the payroll for so many years. Vare has been paying the rent of Democratic headquarters. I can't bite the hand that's fed me."

I was completely stymied as to how we could get a Roosevelt campaign going in Philadelphia and Pennsylvania. Then the State leaders had the decency to resign and turn the Democratic State Committee over to Roosevelt men. Joseph F. Guffey, later to become U.S. Senator, David Lawrence, now Governor, and Warren Van Dyke, who had just been elected chairman of the State Committee, the new party leaders, arrived together in my office.

Joe Guffey came from a family of liberal Democrats who had kept the party alive in western Pennsylvania during the lean patronage-bereft years of Republican administrations. His grandfather, uncle, and father had been active in politics. It may have been a case of prenatal influences but Joe looked like a Roman senator. I used to tell him that if he would wear a toga, I could get him a job in Hollywood. Joe had lived, thought, and studied politics from his early youth. He had a prodigious memory for details of political history. Like a baseball fan who remembers the record of every league player, Joe could tell you who received how many votes in every one of Pennsylvania's sixty-seven counties in any year. Dave Lawrence and Warren Van Dyke were of the same turn of mind. But Dave was more of the worrying type with a perpetual frown on his deeply lined face. Warren, a rotund, cherubic little man, was an expert on election law, an indefatigable detail man. The three were masters at the game of politics.

Their first meeting in my office had a gloomy beginning. They needed at least $100,000 to finance any kind of campaign and had no idea where they could get it.

"We're lucky if national headquarters allots us ten thousand dollars," Dave Lawrence said. "They may write Pennsylvania off as a bad bet and give us nothing."

During the past four years the party machinery had deteriorated. In many sections the Democratic county committees had gone out of existence. But now at least I had sincere, intelligent men to work with. I told them a personal contribution of $1,000 was my limit, but the Record would supply a million copies of a four-page campaign newspaper which would save them a $30,000 printing bill. I phoned Al Greenfield and told him what was going on in my office. Al hated to be left out of anything. He came over to tell us he would raise $25,000. By dinnertime enthusiasm had replaced gloom.

A few days later Joe Guffey phoned me from Pittsburgh: "Dave, a miracle—a ten-thousand-dollar contribution from the Main Line." Philadelphia's oldest and wealthiest suburban section lies along the main line of the Pennsylvania Railroad and is inhabited by old families, strictly Republican. If Joe had received a snowball from hell, he could not have been more surprised.

"It's from George H. Earle III," Joe continued. "He lives in Haverford. I haven't been able to reach him on the phone. Do you know him?"

"I have never met him," I replied. "But I know his family."

"Get him on the phone. Tell him I'd like to meet him the next time I'm in Philadelphia. Take him to lunch. Find out what's cooking. Maybe some of those black Republicans are changing their color. Maybe he can give us some good prospects."

When I reached Earle he invited me to lunch at the Racquet Club. He could give me no prospects for campaign contributions. As far as he knew he was the lone Democrat in his circle. He had been excommunicated by Main Line society. His brother Ralph would not speak to him.

George H. Earle III was the son of the George H. Earle II who, as receiver, had run the Record at the turn of the century. In his youth George III had been an athlete, a nine-goal polo player who had had most of his bones broken in the course of his reckless riding. In World War I he received the Navy Cross. When the torpedo boat he was commanding caught fire, he went below to fight the blaze and suffered burns which nearly cost him his life. While he was an outdoorsman with a passion for fishing and hunting, he was well-read in the classics and economics. As vice president of the Pennsylvania Sugar Refining Company, which his father had founded, he became an expert on commodity prices. Convinced that the Hoover Administration's policies would ruin the national economy, he sold sugar short and made a killing. "My ten-thousand-dollar contribution to the Roosevelt campaign is a tithing," he told me. "A tenth of my profit from bad government which I owe to the cause of good government."

George and I found ourselves in agreement on economic as well as political issues. We both accepted Keynes' theory that, in depression, a government should spend more than its income. We both enjoyed chess and played a game after lunch. I hope I am never called to account for the times we kept VIPs waiting in his office or mine while we finished a game!

He had a brilliant mind which was usually hidden by an attitude of quizzical indifference. I figured this pose was his armor against the ultraconservative, stuffy atmosphere in which he lived. I figured wrong. I learned too late that this nonchalant air was not a pose but the key to his character: George was incapable of taking himself or anyone else seriously. He could get worked up in a cause but before long he would become bored and unconcerned.

George had peculiar eyes, so heavily lidded they appeared closed until he was aroused. Then, with light blue eyes ablaze, he could talk eloquently and forcefully. A stocky, heavily muscled athlete in his youth, now that he had lost interest in sports he had put on so much weight that he walked with a peculiar lumbering gait. We nicknamed him "the man who walks like a bear."

George recalled my Uncle Simon Muhr and my Uncle Simon Stern, who had been manager of the Finance Company of Pennsylvania, the Earle family bank. He told me that his father's last words to him were, "Take this ring to Simon Muhr now." On his deathbed his father handed him a diamond ring. A few months before his father had admired a ring Simon Muhr was wearing, and offered to buy it. Uncle Simon had refused to sell but insisted, "If you like it, wear it." George Earle II must have feared that if he died in possession of the ring, his friend's title to it might be questioned. When George returned from his errand his father was dead.

During the Presidential campaign George and I saw a great deal of each other. Jill and I became friends of his gracious and beautiful wife, Huberta, and their four handsome sons. I have never known a man more bountifully blessed or one more indifferent to his blessings.

XIV

Earle for Governor

Jill and I invited the Earles and a few other friends to hear the 1932 Presidential election returns at the Record. When Roosevelt's victory was assured, my office suite became overcrowded with band-wagon hitchhikers. It was impossible to prevent such intrusions. Guarding the door to my offices was the exclusive prerogative of Uncle George, the Record's last link with Singerly. Born a slave on the Singerly estate in Maryland, he had served as Singerly's valet and office receptionist. He had continued in the latter capacity through all the changes in ownership. The formalities of a bygone age were preserved by this dignified old gentleman. Over ninety, he was becoming feeble. His eyesight was so bad he poured Scotch and bourbon into the same decanter. But neither Frank Murphy nor I dared interfere with Uncle George. When he opened the door with a stately bow, Tom, Dick, or Harry went in.

I was disappointed that we had not carried Pennsylvania, but Joe Guffey, Dave Lawrence and Warren Van Dyke had done a remarkable job with little time and less money. Reprints of Record stories and editorials, circulated throughout the state, had helped. All the Pennsylvania newspapers, except the Record, three small upstate dailies, and a dozen weeklies, had supported Hoover. Recognition of what had been accomplished came in wires from the President-elect and Jim Farley.

Roosevelt won New Jersey. Hague had been true to his preconvention pledge to support whoever was nominated. The Camden Courier and the Camden Post had retained their political potency. They supported a split ticket—Roosevelt for President and Wolverton, Republican, for Congressman in the First District (Camden, Salem, and Gloucester Counties). Hague protested that we were weakening our support of Roosevelt. He used the same argument as Governor Lowden's campaign manager when he prevailed on me to come out for Hughes in 1916, "The voters won't split their tickets." But I could not let Charles (Charles A.) Wolverton down. I had urged him to run against Frank Patterson in 1924 when I was fighting the Baird machine. He had proved an able Congressman, served as chairman of the Committee on Interstate and Foreign Commerce, and was re-elected until he retired in 1956. My hunch that the voters would "split their tickets" was vindicated. Both Roosevelt and Wolverton received substantial majorities.

A few weeks after election the Pennsylvania Democratic leaders were again in my office. No time should be lost in organizing Philadelphia. "With all the dirt you've got on the Vare machine you can win the row offices," was their refrain. They were talking about the election in November, 1933, of controller, city treasurer, registrar of wills and coroner. Except for the controller, who audited finances, these offices had only routine duties and were of little public interest. Their political importance was in the three hundred jobs they controlled. I was reluctant to use the Record's heavy artillery on this minor target. It would be difficult to arouse public interest.

"If we win this election, we're set for Governor and Senator in 1934," Dave Lawrence argued. "If we let it slide we kiss the 1934 election goodbye." I was persuaded to get into this purely political battle. But I served notice that I could not work with John O'Donnell. Both President Roosevelt and Jim Farley insisted that we were under obligation to John and could not dump him. "That has to be our position," Joe Guffey said. "We can't help it if you jump the traces."

Finding a man to replace O'Donnell was a problem. "Why don't you pick a man like that as party leader?" Jill asked one night. "He's good-looking, popular, successful, and a great athlete." She was referring to the late Jack (John B.) Kelly. He had just left our table in a restaurant where we were dining with Queenie Smith, the musical comedy star, and her husband Bob Garland, the New York critic.

"For many reasons," I explained. "Jack's a successful businessman and in Philadelphia a businessman shuns the Democratic Party like poison ivy. Besides, he knows nothing about practical politics." Like so many of Jill's suggestions, I rejected it at first but the more I thought about it the better I liked it.

Jack Kelly was a handsome man who had kept himself in perfect trim since winning four Olympic sculling championships. Because of his ready wit Jack often served as toastmaster at public banquets. He was active in athletic organizations. Head of a large bricklaying business, he carried a gold card of life membership in the Bricklayers Union where he had served his apprenticeship. His wife had been physical instructress at a girls' high school. Two of their children were to win international note: John Jr., who equaled his father's rowing record, and Grace, film star and Princess of Monaco.

It was no surprise when Jack turned down my suggestion that he become active in politics. "Most of our business is with the big industries and they're all Republicans," he explained. Jack had just asked me to join the Penn Athletic Club, of which he was president. He wanted to show me over the luxurious new clubhouse. I accepted his invitation to dinner on condition that, after a tour of the club, he would let me show him the Record plant. I arranged for a meeting of New Deal Democrats in my office that night. When we walked in on this meeting Jack was greeted with loud acclaim and the request that he preside. While Jack was protesting, I disappeared. When I returned, a half hour later, my Machiavellian scheme had worked. Jack was presiding. He had been infected with the virus!

Before the night was over he agreed to head the movement to oust O'Donnell and rejuvenate the Democratic City Committee. Jack took to politics like a duck to water. He brought into the party organization young businessmen and lawyers who worked hard under his skillful leadership, among them Matt McCloskey, Jr., now treasurer of the Democratic National Committee. The Record helped whip up public interest in what was usually a routine by-election. Jack and Matt had built an effective Democratic organization. But they were battling a long-established and corrupt machine which had 20,000 city employees to man the polls.

"If it weren't for the zero wards we'd have it in the bag," Jack complained a few days before the election. "Zero wards" were so called because they often returned a unanimous vote for the Republican ticket, zero for the Democratic. "I wish there were some way to stop the plug-uglies from scaring the voters and giving assistance." An incapacitated (blind or paralyzed) voter could request assistance in filling out his ballot. In zero wards, when a Republican precinct captain was not sure of a voter, the man would be told, "You need assistance."

"Suppose we had a bunch of United States Deputy Marshals around the polls," I suggested. "Wouldn't that throw the fear of God into them; wouldn't that slow them up? The chief investigator for the Senate Committee on Privileges and Elections happens to be in town. My friend Jimmie (Senator James F.) Byrnes is chairman. Perhaps we can get their permission to swear in a hundred husky deputy marshals."

Senator Byrnes agreed to co-operate on condition that there was no objection by the United States Attorney in Philadelphia. Unfortunately that official was an elderly conservative. He objected to the Federal government investigating a local election where no Federal offices were involved. The night before election a heated debate was staged in my back office. Jack and Matt were reinforced by their best legal talent. But we could not budge the old man. In the course of the argument so much whisky was consumed that the United States Attorney fell sound asleep. Although he weighed two hundred pounds, Jack picked him up as gently as a baby, stretched him out on the floor behind the davenport, placed a pillow under his head and a blanket over him.

"Doesn't he look sweet," said Jack, after completing this kindly act. "Now we can swear in the deputies." Looking like a football squad, they were waiting in the hall. Jack had selected the huskiest athletes he knew. As each man was sworn in by the chief investigator he was handed a king-size yellow badge and a notebook. UNITED STATES DEPUTY MARSHAL was printed on the badges in letters big enough to be read from across the street. The instructions were, "Don't talk, don't get into an argument or interfere. Just keep writing in your notebook."

It worked. If two-headed elephants had invaded the polls the Republican workers could not have been more shocked or scared. The usual Republican majorities in the zero wards were cut in half. The Democrats won all the row offices.

✿   ✿   ✿   ✿   ✿

George Earle made as favorable an impression on Roosevelt as he had on me. The President appointed him minister to Austria. Before he left for Vienna I had George's permission to present his name for Governor. I ran into opposition from the State leaders. We were all agreed on Guffey for Senator. Joe wanted as his running mate Warren Van Dyke, chairman of the State Committee, a capable man, but unknown in Philadelphia. I argued that we should run a member of a well-known Philadelphia family. Earle's great-grandfather, Thomas Earle, was known as "the father of the Constitution." He had presided at the convention which revised the Pennsylvania Constitution in 1838. Both Earle's father and grandfather had been prominent in civic affairs. Philadelphians had grown up thinking of Democrats as small fry. We needed an aristocrat to change the picture. Roosevelt, with his Harvard accent and family background, had proven a potent vote-getter. Earle could do the same. Jack Kelly agreed with me as did President Roosevelt and Jim Farley.

Guffey and Lawrence admitted George had brains, personality, and position. At first their only objection was his political inexperience. Then they brought up George's reputation as a playboy. They argued we would be taking a chance by placing a man of his type in the Governor's chair. But when Jim Farley sent word that the President agreed with me, Joe and Dave gave in. I cabled George to come home.

On his arrival I hit another road block. "How much can we count on from George Earle and his rich family?" State headquarters wanted to know. George's answer was, "Nothing." Beneficiary of a substantial trust, he always lived beyond his means. In Vienna he had splurged himself into debt. Like his father, he loved to buy and give jewelry to his friends. When he was elected Governor he presented me with a platinum dress watch and chain as a memento of the occasion. Both watch and chain were so encrusted with diamonds I could not wear them. I had the diamonds made into a necklace for my wife, and the watch, *sans* gems, is most useful. "Never look a gift horse in the mouth" is a good adage. I mention this incident to illustrate that George was an overgenerous, impulsive spender.

His brother Ralph, as prudent as George was not, had become very wealthy. But Ralph, who felt that George had disgraced the family by becoming a Democrat, made a substantial campaign contribution to the Republicans, and persuaded his mother to do the same. At the very end of the campaign she did make a contribution of $25,000 to George's campaign but when I saw her, the stately old grandame was adamant. She was of the same vintage as President Roosevelt's mother, and as handsome. The two dowagers reminded me of the hen clucking as the duckling she has hatched swims away. They both used the same words in describing the deviation of their sons from conservatism: "I don't know where my son picked up his strange ideas." In the case of Mrs. Sara Roosevelt, it was an impersonal remark. In the case of Mrs. Earle, it was directed pointedly at me. She had just observed, "Though your name is Stern, you look like a Muhr, a most unusual family." I read her thought: "That eccentric Simon Muhr's nephew is getting my son messed up in politics."

When Guffey and Lawrence heard that Earle could promise no substantial campaign contribution, they became sarcastic. "Your silk-stocking candidate wants a free ride. This should be a warning to you how naïve he is. When you first asked him whether he would run, a man with any experience in politics would have told you he could not raise any money."

They issued an ultimatum. The campaign would cost more than $500,000. They pledged themselves to raise $250,000. Unless I could show them a sure $250,000 from Philadelphia, they would enter Warren Van Dyke's name in the primary. As they controlled the Democratic county committees outside Philadelphia, they held the trump card. I could not offer much of an argument against them. George's nonchalant manner when he had told me, "Dave, I can't put up a cent," had shocked me. I could not raise $250,000. I was stymied.

Huberta Earle saved the day. A wealthy friend, who had enjoyed the Earles' hospitality in Vienna, would make a campaign contribution of $250,000 if her husband received an ambassadorship. After all, wasn't he fully qualified for a diplomatic post? He was listed as one of the ten best-dressed men in America. Handsome, charming, an ornament to any social gathering, he came of a distinguished family. If he ever expressed an idea on foreign relations, it was not my privilege to hear it, but he did turn out to be a useful member of the diplomatic corps and served in many key posts during and after the war.

Jim Farley, who had become my closest friend in the Roosevelt Administration, endorsed the deal. The check was passed in the penthouse on top of the New York Post Building. Jim Farley and Joe Guffey were there to assure the lady that the commitment would be fulfilled. The two principals, the governor-in-the-making and the ambassador-to-be, were not present. They were represented by their wives who appeared as cool as if they were old hands at political deals. At lunch we men were rather lame in making polite conversation. The ladies broke the ice by frankly discussing the subject at issue. Then came a male chorus on the double public benefit to be achieved by breaking the G.O.P.'s deadening stranglehold on Pennsylvania and, at the same time, injecting into our diplomatic service a cultured gentleman, educated abroad, fluent in French and German. After all this fine talk the ambassadress-to-be insisted on a private conference with Huberta and me. Before she would hand over her check I had to give my personal guarantee that I would return the money if her husband were not appointed.

With Philadelphia's share of the campaign fund in hand, Joe Guffey and Dave Lawrence accepted George Earle as the organization candidate. He was nominated in the primaries and elected the first Democratic Governor of Pennsylvania in forty years. Joe Guffey was elected U.S. Senator. George proved a brilliant and tireless campaigner, trigger-minded and adroit in answering hecklers. Joe and Dave kept telling me, "We underestimated George. He's a wow. He's Presidential caliber."

At the time I was proud of my part in this train of events. I was fighting on the side of the angels to overcome the evil of Republican misrule. Of course, I realized that bartering diplomatic posts for campaign contributions is a vile custom which weakens and demeans our diplomatic service. My conscience was anesthetized by the old moral painkiller "accepted practice." Of course Congress should end this practice by requiring a minimum of five years' service in the State Department as a condition precedent to ambassadorship. But both parties seem reluctant to cut off this source of revenue.

When Governor Earle took office in 1935, I was so occupied with the newly acquired New York Post I could spare no time to help him get his administration started. Fortunately, I had an able understudy in Harry Kalodner, the Governor's secretary and closest adviser. As long as Harry was in Harrisburg, he protected George from the grafters.

But the grafters found a way to get the watchdog out of Harrisburg. Harry had always preferred law to journalism or politics. When a vacancy occurred on the Philadelphia bench in 1936 the Governor appointed Harry. I did my best to block this but I heard of it too late.

When Harry left Harrisburg, I knew what would happen and it did. The spoilsmen took over. George Earle was personally honest. But he was always the playboy. He just could not take his job seriously. His interest aroused in a project, he could be brilliant and forceful, but he would not keep at it to see it through.

In the late summer of 1936 I went to Harrisburg for a political conference. Huberta and the children were away, so we sat down to a stag dinner of sixteen at the Executive Mansion. George had a trick of flicking a drop of water from a spoon into the eye of a guest. After the Governor had made a few bull's-eyes, we all started trying our hands at the game.

Drops of water grew to teaspoonsful, to tablespoonsful, to gobletsful. Attorney General Charles J. Margiotti chased Secretary of Revenue Kalodner around the room with a pitcherful. Harry fell and cut his forehead. After he had received first aid we settled down to the business for which we had assembled. I had a hell of a good time, tinctured with foreboding that some day we would have to pay for all this nonsense.

In spite of such horseplay the Earle administration achieved an outstanding record of liberal and progressive legislature—accomplished in spite of a Republican legislature largely through the force of personality and adroitness of the Governor. The graft-ridden, inhuman county poorhouses, which had been a crying disgrace to the State, were abolished. In their stead a Department of Public Assistance was established with all employees strictly on the merit system. The law, which has become a model for many other states, was written by a distinguished committee, headed by Herbert F. Goodrich, then Dean of the University of Pennsylvania Law School and now a U.S. judge. This legislation provided for direct grants to the aged, blind, widowed mothers, and unemployed. The first director of this Department of Public Assistance was a nonpolitical appointment—Bob (Robert L.) Johnson, later to become Chancellor of Temple University. As the law specified, Bob selected the personnel of his department strictly on merit. He paid no attention to pleas of the legislators to take care of the political hacks who had been running the county poor farms, now out of their jobs. Bob was not overtactful in turning down these requests. The opposition to him became so bitter and intense that, after a year, the Governor was compelled to accept his resignation. But Bob had established the department on a high, nonpolitical plane which has been more or less maintained ever since. This and many other reforms, including the abolishing of child labor and the extension of workmen's compensation to include occupational diseases such as silicosis, from which so many miners suffered, were accomplished.

When Earle took office the State government was broke. Here is where Kalodner's genius for tax legislation revealed itself. The immediate emergency of an empty treasury was met by issuing tax anticipation notes. Pennsylvania was the pioneer State to impose a cigarette tax. Exemption of manufacturing corporations from capital stock tax was repealed. A gross receipts tax on utilities was another long-delayed tax reform.

Earle found his progressive plans stymied by a provision in the State Constitution of 1838 which his great-grandfather had masterminded. It imposed a debt limit of a million dollars, which, back in 1838, had been a colossal sum. Earle was faced with urgent necessity of building hospitals for the insane, penal institutions, teachers' colleges, and enlarging State colleges, which had been allowed to deteriorate under pinchpenny Republican administrations. Closing the county poor farms placed an additional burden on State hospitals which must provide for those immates who were incapable of self-care. Immediate action was imperative. To change the Constitution would require two years.

Harry Kalodner came to the rescue. He devised a State Authority which could build and lease to the State. The State Constitution did not prohibit the State from making long-term leases and the Authority could borrow on these leases. "Only a Philadelphia lawyer could have thought it up," I said when Harry told me of his device to bypass the Constitution.

So remarkable were the accomplishments of the Earle administration during its first eighteen months that, at the Democratic National Convention held in Philadelphia, July, 1936, there was much talk of George Earle as the logical successor to Roosevelt in 1940.

❋ ❋ ❋ ❋ ❋

Turning Pennsylvania, Republican stronghold, Democratic was not my only interest. During those early years on the Record I was continually working myself into a lather on public causes. One of these crusades had its inception on a bleak February afternoon of 1933. I was looking out of my office window at Broad Street, bereft of pedestrians because of the icy winds. Up the street came a small parade, three hundred men and women buffeting the chill blasts and carrying banners protesting Hitler's persecution of Jews. The men's long beards, the women's *sheitels*, showed they were orthodox Eastern European Jews. I felt ashamed that I was in my warm office instead of in the ranks of that feeble protest. How little the children and grandchildren of German-Jewish immigrants had bestirred themselves in behalf of their afflicted coreligionists. I had just heard that Samuel Untermyer, prominent New York lawyer, was organizing an anti-Nazi league. The next morning I was in his office. "How can I help?" I asked.

"Three jobs for you." Sam, a bantamweight bundle of nerves, talked and acted like chain lightning. "First get the big Philadelphia stores to boycott German goods. Second, organize a public protest meeting with prominent non-Jewish speakers. Third, raise money. That third job is especially important for you because this afternoon our board will elect you secretary-treasurer."

I organized a protest rally in the Hammerstein Opera House with speeches by Governor Gifford Pinchot and others. An overflow crowd listened to the speeches on loudspeakers. The make-up of that audience depressed me. A third were Christians, of whom the majority were Friends. Jews of Eastern European stock, Russian, Polish, Roumanian, Hungarian, made up the rest of the audience. Except for Sam Fels, Jerry Rothschild, and myself, there were no Jews of German ancestry in the auditorium.

Philadelphia merchants followed the pattern of the audience at the rally. Stores owned by gentiles were more ready to boycott German imports than stores owned by Jews of German ancestry. Sam Untermyer was having the same experience in New York. When Macy's would not co-operate he fumed against the Strauses, who controlled the "world's largest store." New York newspapers would not print a line of his attacks on their largest advertiser. At his request I printed them in the Record and he circulated thousands of reprints. That was in the summer of 1933. In December I bought the New York Post and found myself in the doghouse with New York's leading advertiser.

XV

The New York Post

"Curtis Bok is on the phone." Al Greenfield waked me.

"Tell him I'll call back."

"Here he is, Curtis," Al said and shoved the phone into my hand.

"The New York Post closes today," was Bok's message. "Dave, you still have time to save a great newspaper."

"Thanks for calling, Curtis, but no thanks for offering to put the dying baby on my doorstep." I was in no mood for a rescue operation that morning in November, 1933. After a hilarious party at Doc (Dr. A.S.W.) Rosenbach's New York gallery, Al and I had spent what was left of the night at a New York hotel. Up at his usual time, indefatigable Al had called his office to say where he could be reached, and had been "thoughtful" enough to tell his secretary to notify my office.

"I've arranged that you need give us no cash," Curtis persisted, "and we are including the million-dollar equity in the building."

"Sorry, Curtis, the answer is still no."

As I was hanging up, Al stayed my hand. "Do me a favor," he whispered. "Ask for half an hour to think it over and call back."

"I'll raise a million for you," Al said as I left the phone.

"Not enough. To pull the Post out of the red will take at least three million. It's losing twenty-five thousand a week."

"We'll raise three million." Al was as persistent as Curtis.

"Must you keep repeating what we've gone over before and decided?" My two friends' intense concern with my affairs was getting on my nerves, which were already on edge from the night before.

❖   ❖   ❖   ❖   ❖

I should explain why the ultraconservative trustees of the Cyrus H. K. Curtis estate were offering the New York Post on a silver platter to a liberal New Deal publisher. In the 1920's Cyrus Curtis, whom I remember as a very small and very solemn individual with a full white beard, was the most successful magazine publisher in the United States, if not in the world. The Saturday Evening Post, Ladies' Home Journal, and other magazines had brought him a large fortune. He had a happy faculty of picking the right editors and then giving them complete independence. One of these was Edward William Bok, editor of the Ladies' Home Journal, who married his publisher's only child, Mary Louise Curtis. The Boks had two sons, the elder of whom, Curtis Bok, had phoned me.

Late in life, after the death of his first wife, Cyrus Curtis married a widow who had a married daughter. Curtis took a great liking to his step-son-in-law, Jack (John C.) Martin, a salesman of heavy machinery in the Middle West. Curtis persuaded the Martins to make their home with him. But when he tried to make a place for Jack in the Curtis Publishing Company, he ran into family friction.

To show his daughter, grandsons, and executives that he did not need them to give Jack an opening, Curtis formed the Curtis-Martin Company, with Jack as president, and proceeded to buy all the newspapers in Philadelphia except the Record, the Bulletin, and the News. His first move was to purchase the Philadelphia Public Ledger, to which the Evening Ledger was added a few years later. Then the Press, the North American and the Inquirer were acquired and merged into one morning newspaper, the Philadelphia Inquirer-Ledger. This telescoping of four newspapers into one caused much resentment, not only from thousands of newspaper employees who lost their jobs, but also from readers of the defunct newspapers.

Meanwhile, not satisfied with the purchase of four morning and Sunday newspapers in Philadelphia, plus the establishment of the Evening Ledger, the Curtis-Martin Company bought the New York Post in 1926. Curtis invested $42,000,000 in these enterprises of which only $13,000,000 was recovered by the Curtis estate when it sold the Inquirer, the last of its newspaper properties, to M. L. Annenberg, in 1938.

Upon the death of Curtis in June, 1933, the trustees of his estate came into control of the Curtis-Martin Company. When they learned that the New York Post was losing $1,250,000 a year, double what the Inquirer-Ledger was earning, they insisted Jack sell the Post. He could not find a buyer. The best deal he could make was with the other New York newspapers for a $250,000 nuisance value payment on suspension of publication. Sale of machinery and equipment would net $500,000 more, $750,000 in all, for the $13,000,000 Curtis had sunk in the Post. The trustees did not want to keep on shelling out $4,000 a day, throwing good money after bad, to preserve a property which had no sales value. They were all for accepting the $250,000 and stopping publication —all except Curtis Bok.

"We must not let another newspaper die on our doorstep," he declared. "The New York Post has the most distinguished history of any newspaper in America. We owe it to the memory of my grandfather to pass it into competent hands."

Reluctantly his fellow trustees gave Curtis a month to find another solution. He got in touch with me. We had become friends during the 1932 Presidential campaign. Like George Earle, he was one of a few young men of wealthy Philadelphia families who came over to the liberal camp. An able lawyer and effective campaign orator, he was an enthusiastic worker for Roosevelt although his political activity cost him his position as Assistant District Attorney of Philadelphia. Governor Earle appointed him to a vacancy on the Orphans' Court (equivalent of Surrogate's Court in other states). From that post he advanced to President Judge of a Court of Common Pleas, and, in 1958, to the Supreme Court of Pennsylvania. He is a tall, thin man with the solemn air of a Trappist monk which conceals the keen sense of humor evident in the sparkling books he has written.

Curtis had come to my office a month before his phone call to New York. He was carrying a book. He opened the conversation by saying, "If you haven't already read this, I wish you could stay home tonight and wade into it." He was repeating Eldridge Johnson's technique. The book was Allan Nevins' brilliant and scholarly *The Evening Post, A Century of Journalism*.

"I especially want you to read pages one hundred sixty-four and five, where I have placed this marker," Curtis continued. "William Cullen Bryant, editor of the Post for fifty years, was the first champion of trade unionism in this country. If it had not been for his editorials in 1836, the movement might never have gotten under way in this country." Then Curtis read an editorial protesting the fining of twenty-one tailors because they had met to form a union: " 'Strike the right of associating for the sale of labor from the privilege of a freeman, and you may as well bind him to a master, or ascribe him to the soil. If this is not slavery, we have forgotten its definition.' "

Curtis put the book down. "Dave, as the champion of trade unionism, you are carrying on the crusade which Bryant started almost a century ago."

"Curtis, what's on your mind?" I asked. Then he told me, in detail, the Post situation.

"I understand why Jack can't find a buyer," I explained to Curtis. "It would take a smart publisher at least three years to put the Post on a paying basis and cost four or five million dollars. Who wants to risk that kind of money these days? [In October 1933 the nation was still suffering from depression jitters.] Better forget the sentiment and take the seven hundred and fifty thousand before you waste any more money."

"But, Dave, think what you'd have if you did put it over," Curtis countered. "The newspaper with the most distinguished history and reputation in America. And you are the publisher to maintain that reputation."

"Very complimentary, Curtis, but compliments won't meet payrolls."

Curtis kept after me until I agreed to talk it over with my associates. At parting I said, "If I did take it on, I would need every dollar of cash I could raise. All I could give the Curtis estate would be preferred stock."

"That is going to be hard," Curtis replied, "but if you'll save the Post, I'll undertake to make such an arrangement."

Talking it over did not solve my dilemma. My friends and associates divided into two camps. Jill, Al Greenfield, Jake Omansky, and F.D.R. urged me to make the deal. The President expressed himself much as Curtis Bok: "The Post is an historic institution. You must preserve it." He assured me of his full support. Jake Omansky felt that we had a great opportunity to ride the rising tide of liberalism. Jill said, "You've taken chances before. Why be afraid of this one?" Al Greenfield predicted a wave of prosperity starting in 1934.

Pop Gilman, Harry Saylor, Louis Kolb and Sam Fels agreed with me that we should not jeopardize our growing success in Philadelphia. I invited both sides to dinner at my home. After listening to what everyone had to say, I made what I thought was, and should have been, the final decision: "We're not ready to go to New York. We're not yet firmly established in Philadelphia. When we took on Philadelphia, the Courier-Post was entrenched in Camden. Three years from now the Record may be in as safe a position in Philadelphia. Until then we cannot divide our strength."

The next day I called Curtis Bok to tell him that we had definitely decided to decline his offer. But still Curtis refused to take no for an answer. "I've persuaded the trustees to waive any cash payment," he persisted. "You'll get the equity in the building which you can sell to an insurance company and lease from them. That ought to give you another million dollars in ready cash."

"Curtis, I'm deeply appreciative of all you've done," I replied, "but the answer is still no." I thought the matter was finished business, which brings me back to that fateful message from Curtis to my hotel room in New York: "The New York Post closes today."

The moment I hung up the phone with, "I'll call you back in half an hour," Al went to work on me. He is a consummate salesman. He painted the picture of a knight in shining armor, fighting for the New Deal, planting his standard on the pinnacle, New York. I was unmoved. Finally, in disgust, he said, "As for me, I would rather fall off the top rung than never climb the ladder."

That taunt got me. At three that afternoon, we met Jack Martin in Al's New York office. Martin had with him his lawyer who had arranged payment by the other New York newspapers of $250,000 on suspension of the Post. Martin was to meet with the representatives of the publishers at four that afternoon. By five o'clock we

had made a deal. Jack's lawyer called up the waiting newspapermen at the other meeting to tell them the suspension was off. On
December 15, 1933, I became publisher of the New York Post.

Then began the hardest six years of my life. Forgotten was Tolstoy's story of the peasant who craved more land, forgotten the
bank closings of 1930 when I swore I would never tempt fate again.
The genes of Grandmother Muhr were dominant.

I paid no cash for the Post. Instead, I gave the trustees of the
Cyrus H. K. Curtis estate $1,500,000 in second preferred stock,
subordinate to $1,000,000 of first preferred representing the work-
ing capital with which we started.

Lawyers for the Curtis estate were co-operative. They insisted
on only one vexing condition. The New York Post Company's
books were to be closed as of December 15th. I did not have to
take possession until January 1st. But the loss for the balance of
the year—$4,000 a publication day—would be on me. The idea of
paying $50,000 for losses by the old management griped me. I
managed to squeeze two months of legal work and financing into
two weeks. I had to have $1,000,000 cash in the new company by
December 15th. Louis Kolb, Pop Gilman, Sam Untermyer, Bill
(William) Fox, the moving picture magnate, and Al Greenfield
took most of the issue.

During the hectic two weeks between signing the contracts
and taking over the Post, into my office walked Ralph Strassburger flying a flag of truce. He had heard of the Post deal. He
apologized for the way he had behaved about his investment in
the Record, blamed it on bad advice. To show his change of heart,
he offered to invest in the new venture. Like a chess player under
time pressure, I made a mistake. I accepted his check for $200,000.
Within three years, Ralph was back at his old trick of staging a
proxy fight to gain control.

While I was occupied with lawyers and financing, Jake Omansky prepared our New York Post plan. It showed how we could
cut the Post's operating loss in half. The Record and Courier-Post,
which were acquiring the majority common stock of the new company, could finance this loss while we developed circulation and
advertising. It looked good on paper.

My first day as publisher of the Post was strenuous. The many important decisions to be made had to be postponed when Steve Early, White House press secretary, phoned to forbid publication of President Roosevelt's letter of congratulation. A four-column cut of this letter was already in the center of the front page make-up.

"It's too personal and intimate" said Steve. "It will get us in bad with the other New York newspaper publishers."

"You're already in bad with all of them except Joe [Joseph M. Patterson, publisher of the New York Daily News]," was my retort. "And now you want to get in bad with me."

"That stuff about the hair shirt won't be understood," Steve persisted. "It's a private joke between the President and you." Steve had happened into the President's office earlier in the year while I was vehemently denouncing the Warren plan. When I left the President, Steve was waiting to warn me, "You're riding the boss too hard." The hair shirt incident irritated Steve more than it did Roosevelt.

It took an hour on the phone before Marvin McIntyre, my special friend on the White House staff, persuaded the President to reverse Steve. There were hundreds of other congratulatory messages, including cables from Geoffrey Dawson of the London Times and William Percival Crozier of the Manchester Guardian. Mayor Fiorello H. LaGuardia wrote, "I look to Dave Stern for encouragement, inspiration and counsel." Earlier in the year I had arranged for Fiorello to write a daily political column for the Record, but my plan to turn the Little Flower into a syndicated columnist was abandoned when he decided to run for Mayor on the Fusion ticket. He was one of the most colorful, exciting, fighting liberals I have ever had the happiness of knowing.

"Don't work yourself to death. Affectionate regards," was the message from Wee Willie (William H.) Woodin, Secretary of the Treasury. He had borne the brunt of my criticism of the Administration's monetary policies.

Reading these messages of good will made me feel very cheerful when I left the office to keep a luncheon appointment with Bernie (Bernard F.) Gimbel, head of the department store chain.

Bernie and I had grown up together, or rather we started growing together. Bernie kept on growing to become a football star at Penn and intercollegiate heavyweight boxing champion. According to psychoanalytical jargon, this gross injustice caused a trauma. During our college days, whenever I became sufficiently drunk, I went looking for Bernie to beat him up, to his great embarrassment. As he expressed it, "If I ever hit you, you'd fall apart and I would be indicted for murder." He used to drag me back to my room, throw me on the bed and sit on me until I calmed down while he threatened, "The next time I'm going to let you have it." He never did, thank God. His Philadelphia store had been very fair to my Camden newspapers and to the Record. When I got into a fight with his Philadelphia manager, he resolved the controversy by changing managers. I was hoping that the Post would enjoy the same favored treatment.

"Dave, the people across the street are sore as a boiled owl," Bernie told me. "I don't know how you can cure it. That smart Sam Untermyer and his Nazi boycott got you into this fix with Macy's. Let him figure a way out. We'll increase our advertising but Macy's is the leader and most of the merchants play follow-the-leader."

So everyone was not so friendly. My cheerfulness of the morning evaporated. When I returned to my new office and the grim business of cutting down expenses at the Post, Jake was waiting for me with a long list of measures to reduce the daily loss of four thousand dollars. We had already made the first economy move by changing the format from tabloid to standard size, so that features, art, cartoons, and promotion ads would be interchangeable with the Record and Camden newspapers. The second item on Jake's list was "Cut financial tables." It had been Jack Martin's pride that the Post ran more complete and accurate stock and commodity reports than any other newspaper in New York. This required twenty tabulators plus extra compositors and additional newsprint. Jake was for dropping all financial news except a one-column market review as the Daily News and the Mirror were doing. Looking back, I think he was right. I was afraid of such a drastic cut. We compromised by reducing our financial coverage to that of the other evening newspapers at a saving of a thousand dollars a day.

There were two repercussions to this reduction of financial reports, one funny, the other not so funny. So accurate and reliable were the Post's tables, the New York morning newspapers reset from them. When, without warning, the Post cut its tables, the morning papers were thrown into a panic. Suddenly they had to do for themselves the job which the Post had been doing for them. The not so funny effect was that our circulation dropped from 60,000 to 40,000. Brokerage houses had been buying the Post in bulk and using its tables in their statistical departments.

It was not long before we overcame this initial setback. We were giving New York a forceful liberal newspaper such as it had not had since the World was absorbed by the Telegram. By the fall of 1934, the Post's circulation passed the 100,000 mark. While our vigorous news and editorial policies were factors, I give equal credit to Jake Omansky's genius in promotion. Our funds were so limited I could allow him no appropriations. So Jake proceeded to make his operations self-liquidating by collecting weekly fees from puzzle contestants, and charging enough extra for "special de luxe" editions to cover the expenses of book distributions. He literally pulled the Post up by its bookstraps.

Webster's Unabridged Dictionary in two volumes was Jake's first promotion. He had found the plates of a 1908 edition in a junk yard. He phoned William H. Stevenson, editor of the London Herald, to ask if he could lend us anyone for a few months to give us the know-how. For years the Herald had been making a success of its book distributions. Stevenson said his son, John, who had worked in their promotion department, happened to be in New York. Jake lost no time in hiring the young man. The first time I met him was when he brought me proof of the initial dictionary ad—a double spread (two pages) crowded with three thousand words of small type proclaiming the advantages of an unabridged lexicon. "Where's the price, the ninety-three cents for each volume, and the twenty-four coupons' requirement?" I asked. John pointed to them, buried in fine print at the bottom right-hand corner.

"That's the first thing a reader wants to know," I said.

"That's the last thing we want him to find out," John replied. "We must develop desire before spelling out the conditions."

"It doesn't make sense to me," I said. "If I saw an ad like this, I'd be so annoyed at not finding the price I wouldn't read all that fine type."

"It's the way we do it in London," John replied in his clipped British accent.

"I bet New Yorkers won't have the patience of Londoners. But the only way to find out is to try it."

After John left, I phoned Jake, "He's only a schoolboy."

"He says he's twenty-one," Jake replied. "He's damned clever."

"I doubt if he's eighteen," I told Jake. "You're taking an awful chance letting a child run a hundred-thousand-dollar project." In recent years, John, who has amassed a fortune as head of the Greystone Press, has confessed that he was nineteen when we first met.

The unabridged dictionary was a tremendous success. Jake and John went on from that great start to distribute millions of books, complete sets of Shakespeare, Mark Twain, Robert Louis Stevenson, Balzac, Victor Hugo, Dickens, Dumas, Joseph Conrad, and others. They "practically gave away" these sets at cost. But enough readers wanted de luxe editions, on which we made a profit, to pay promotion and handling expenses.

Building evening circulation in New York is difficult. New Yorkers buy their evening papers at newsstands. Fewer than 15 per cent are home-delivered. So it was impractical to sign up a reader for a subscription as in other cities. To obtain a set of books, one hundred coupons clipped from the Post had to accompany the order. It was Jake's idea that if we could get a family to read the Post for three months, the habit would hold them. The Post's mounting circulation proved his theory correct.

When Jake proposed sets of Balzac and Conrad, I warned that he was going over the ceiling of popular appeal. His reply was to quote my slogan at editorial conferences: "Anyone who edits down to the American public is a sucker." When, against my advice, he put out a portfolio of reproductions of Van Gogh paintings and it went over big, I stopped prompting. He did finally go over the ceiling with a ten-volume set of the Oxford Dictionary. I think that was the only failure in scores of book and art promotions.

At the same time he was distributing books and art, Jake was running puzzle contests. Again he showed his knack for finding brilliant youngsters. Paul Sarazen, head of our puzzle department, was the impresario of this strange business which later grew to national importance. I am not proud of my part in getting it started. When we began to collect weekly cash fees from contestants, the Post Office Department objected. We could have met this objection by omitting contest publicity from our mail edition. But Jake felt that if we let the Post Office ruling stand, we would be skating on thin ice.

I went to see Jim Farley, the Postmaster General. He called in his legal department. After a lengthy conference, Jim ordered the rule changed so that the Post could not only collect coupons from contestants but also cash payments. Thus, the puzzle department, like the book department, paid its own way.

Of all Jake's stunts, the most ingenious was an advertising promotion. With his weekly puzzle answer, a contestant had to enclose an advertisement clipped from the Post to which was attached a sales slip showing he had purchased the article advertised. Our advertising volume took a sudden bound.

While Jake was doing such a great job, I was not performing so well with the news and editorial departments for which I was responsible. I had to spend half my time in Philadelphia, so that I could not give the full supervision which is so essential at the start. The day I took over, Harry B. Nason, Jr., the managing editor, said, "I want to stick with you. But, frankly, all my experience has been on conservative newspapers. You ought to get an editor who talks your language."

I engaged Ernest Gruening, an ardent New Dealer who had earned a national reputation as a courageous liberal. He had won my admiration for the single-handed fight he had waged against the utilities as editor and publisher of the Portland (Maine) Evening News, 1927 to 1932. He was editor of the Nation when I persuaded him to resign and join me. Ernest and I were in com-

plete accord on editorial policies. I found him a brilliant and forceful writer. But he was handicapped by lack of metropolitan newspaper experience. He gave us an editorial page of which I was
proud. But he found it difficult to co-ordinate handling of the
news with editorial policy. If I could have given full time to the
job, Ernest would eventually have caught on to the wider scope of
his duties.

When Secretary of the Interior Harold Ickes wanted Gruening
as Director of Territories and Island Possessions, Ernest and I
agreed it would be a wise move. After his three months' service
with the Post, we parted the best of friends. Although under no
legal obligation to do so, I handed him a check for five thousand
dollars. Ernest went on to become Governor of Alaska Territory.
He is now senior U. S. Senator of the new State.

Time magazine injected a sour note into this incident. It explained that Gruening and I could not get along because Gruening
was of German-Jewish ancestry while I was a Russian Jew. Until
I read this article I had not known that Ernest was Jewish. I was
sore at Harry (Henry R.) Luce, who professed to be my friend
and had sent his younger brother to serve his newspaper apprenticeship at the Record. But I decided to ignore the story. Without
telling me, an elderly cousin took it upon herself to write to Time.
She gave a genealogical table of my German-Jewish ancestry for
three generations and berated Time for its insult. Again I decided
that any statement by me would only magnify this nonsense. But
the comedy of errors persisted. A syndicated editorial column appeared in a score of Jewish weeklies denouncing me as a racial
snob who had insulted all non-German Jews. I threw the many
letters I received into the wastebasket. Not all of them were in-
sulting. A few commended me for pride of ancestry. On what thin
gruel small souls feed!

After Gruening left I brought my wheel horse, Harry Saylor, to
New York. He pulled me out of my difficulties at the Post, as he
had, six years before, at the Record. This gave me more time for
Philadelphia, where the Earle-for-Governor and Guffey-for-Senator
campaign was waxing hot and heavy. Bill (William F.) Hawkes,
another of the Springfield News-Record imports, took Saylor's

place as managing editor of the Record in charge of the news department. My son came over from Camden to Philadelphia to be general manager. Tush and Frank Ryan were doing an excellent job in Camden. I had efficient organizations in the three cities. When Earle and Guffey won I saw smooth sailing ahead. I had forgotten the trouble amateur politicians had given me in Camden ten years before.

XVI

Political Vendettas

Except that they don't shoot each other, politicians can be as bitter and stupid in their feuds as Kentucky mountaineers. Usually it is the amateur liberal reformer who jumps the traces and starts an intra-party war. The professional politician wants to keep the party together, so that he can earn a living.

The dozen of us in my back office election night, November, 1934—Uncle George had died and Frank Murphy controlled the door—were mostly amateurs. We had worked together and were friends. While we awaited the outcome of the gubernatorial contest, we relieved the tension with whiskey, all of us except George Earle, who was on the water wagon. He was furiously chewing gum. Every time Harry Kalodner brought returns from the newsroom George would pop another stick in his mouth, which was so full he looked as though he had the mumps. I was worrying that he would choke himself when Harry announced Earle was elected. Instead of congratulating George, my first reaction was, "For God's sake, George, spit out that gum."

Then began a celebration which, like a Polish wedding, lasted three days. Starting from scratch, after Roosevelt's election in 1932, we had captured the Keystone State, stronghold of Republicanism. Earle was the first Democratic Governor of Pennsylvania in forty years. "Jack Kelly for Mayor in 1935" was the slogan at this victory party. While no formal action was taken by the Democratic City Committee at the time, Jack was nominated by acclaim.

One of the "friends" in my back office election night was Sam (S. Davis) Wilson, City Controller. I had helped to elect him in 1933. Our paths had crossed in 1908 when Sam, as investigator for the Law and Order Society, had dug up the criminal record of

Leonard White, the school janitor whom I had interviewed as a cub reporter for the Public Ledger. But we did not meet until 1928. Then Sam was chief investigator for City Controller WillB Hadley (not a typographical error; twins were named WillA and WillB). The newspapers had dubbed Sam "WillB's man of mystery." How he acquired that title is beyond me. He was more eager for personal publicity and better able to attain it than anyone else in City Hall. He had a knack of dramatizing his work. If he ferreted out the padded expense account of one city employee, he would tell the reporters he had unearthed a colossal conspiracy to bankrupt the city. Fearless and indefatigable, a shark at accounting, he was a born inquisitor. He started his career at nineteen by uncovering a graft scandal high up in the State government of New Hampshire. In the course of his hectic career he had held his own in many physical encounters, had even killed a man in self-defense, for which he was exonerated. A heavy-set muscular man with the sharp features of a zealot, he was a rabble-rousing campaign orator.

I found Sam good company. He could give me more gossip about who was paying whom than my city editor. Sam liked his whiskey straight, as I did. He used to drop into my office late in the afternoon, "to spill the dirt and kill a quart."

When he was elected City Controller Sam proceeded to manufacture news at a prodigious rate. As a friend of the publisher, the Record gave him full play, so that he made the front page at least once a week. I should have realized that the Record was building up a Frankenstein's monster.

In May of 1935, Jack Kelly and I were discussing his coming campaign when Sam barged into my office and, without any preliminaries, announced: "I'm the logical candidate for Mayor."

"You know we've all agreed on Jack," was my surprised reply.

"There's never been any action by the City Committee," Sam retorted.

"If Sam wants it so much, I'll step aside," said Jack, always the good sport.

"That's a wise decision, Jack," said Sam. "A Catholic can't be elected in this town."

"Who in hell says a Catholic can't be elected?" I exploded.

"That's a damned insult to Americanism. Jack, it's your duty to lay that ghost."

"If that's the way you feel about it," Sam said, "you can count me out of the Democratic Party." He left as abruptly as he had entered.

We did not appreciate the significance of his words until the next day when Jerry (Jerome J.) Louchheim, who had succeeded Bill Vare as boss of the Republican machine, announced that S. Davis Wilson was his candidate for Mayor. Jerry was head of Philadelphia's largest construction company, builders of the Delaware River bridge and the city's subway system.

Now Jerry was getting even with me for having blocked him in the mayoralty election of 1931, when he had wanted to run George Biles, one of his engineers. The Record put up such a barrage against contractor-boss rule that he abandoned his plan and ran Hampy (J. Hampton) Moore, a respectable political hack. We had made the public aware of the highway robbery in which the Republican machine was indulging. Against any old-line machine candidate Kelly was a sure winner. Unfortunately we had publicized City Controller Wilson as a champion of honest government. He was the only candidate who could split the anti-machine vote. Jerry had pulled a slick political trick.

To say that I was furious is an understatement. I lost my temper. I made the same mistake which my competitors had made in Springfield and Camden. I knocked Sam too often and too hard. "Sutler Sam, the camp follower, travels with whichever army offers him the high dollar" was the theme of editorials and news articles which delved into "S. Devious Wilson's" past.

Sam won the election by 46,000 votes out of 700,000. Jack Kelly was in my office election night. I could see that he was taking it very hard.

"Jack, it was all my fault," I said. "I knocked the son-of-a-bitch too hard."

A few days later I heard that Jack and his friends were blaming me for his defeat. When I faced him with this his answer was, "Dave, you said it yourself election night right here in this office." Our warm friendship started to cool.

At this time another factor arose to widen the breach. The State was doing a lot of building and Jack's friend, Matt McCloskey, Jr., was getting most of the contracts. Jack had brought Matt into the Earle campaign; Matt had played an active and prominent part. He was a combination of opposites; his prematurely snow-white hair gave him a distinguished appearance which contrasted with his jolly, happy-go-lucky personality; intensely religious, he enjoyed telling ribald jokes. Starting as a cost accountant for a builder, it was not long before he was on his own and developed one of the leading construction companies in the nation.

Matt's work for the State was most embarrassing to the Record, which had attacked Vare and Louchheim as contractor-bosses. "Now the shoe is on the other foot," the Republican newspapers repeated every time McCloskey was awarded another State contract. The situation was making the Record look ridiculous. I told Matt so. Matt insisted that he was winning contracts "on the up-and-up," because his efficient organization put in low bids. Subsequent events have proven this true. Matt has received as many big contracts from Republican administrations as from Democratic. I told Matt that a contractor, like a judge, should not be active in politics. It undermined public confidence in government. I insisted that he make the choice between politics and public works. Matt said he would give up politics and signed a statement to that effect in my office.

Both George Earle and Jack Kelly were furious that I had talked their friend Matt out of the party. They complained that I had acted in a highhanded way, that I should have called a party conference. They said that Al Greenfield was using his political "in" to feather his own nest. Al had been chief money raiser for the party. He had asked the Governor for only one appointment— State motion picture censor. I thought he wanted to take care of a friend. I was not smart enough to catch the play: Al's real estate firm and insurance agency were representing the big theater chains.

This quarrel grew into a feud which split the party wide open. Senator Guffey stood with me. Secretary of State Dave Lawrence sided with the Governor and Jack Kelly. It culminated in the bitter primary battle of 1940 when George, Jack, and Dave tried to block Guffey's re-nomination.

Meanwhile Matt, over whom the storm had started, went blithely on his way, friendly to both factions and doing more and more work for the State and Federal governments. Every time we met he thanked me for having relieved him of wasting time and money in politics. After I retired Matt again became active in the Democratic Party and served as treasurer of the Democratic National Committee.

A week after election, Sam Wilson walked into my office. "Have you got a drink for a thirsty mayor?" was his greeting. My first impulse was to shout, "Get the hell out," but I was curious to hear what he had to say. After a few drinks Sam unburdened himself. "I just can't stomach those reactionary sons-of-bitches. I don't belong in their camp." The Mayor became a regular visitor. Jerry Louchheim did not get too much satisfaction from electing Sam.

A truce in the Pennsylvania Democratic feud was declared for the 1936 Presidential election. Roosevelt could charm the lion and lamb into pulling together. He even made me bury the hatchet with Frank Hague, with whom we had been feuding for ten years.

At the Presidential elections of 1936, 1940, 1944, Frank came to see me. His opening remark, delivered in a hoarse whisper, was always the same: "Dave, we've got to forget everything and elect him." The old reprobate would roll his eyes to heaven and utter these words so sanctimoniously, it sounded as though he were referring to the Deity rather than the President. This preliminary ceremony over, he would get down to practical politics. I could not help admiring Frank's efficiency. He never referred to a memo; he carried in his head the special causes and irritations of every minority group in the State. He knew who was the key man in each situation. It was I who was taking notes from him. The efficiency of professional politicians like Hague appealed to Roosevelt, the master politician. He appreciated expert, painstaking craftsmanship. With fuss and fury, liberal reformers work terrifically, then forget about preserving the political organization they have built up. The professional keeps on the job every day in the year. President Roosevelt was wise in refusing to purge corrupt bosses who were on his side. If he had adopted the policy I urged, he could not have achieved the great good for the nation which he did.

Immediately after his 1932 election, I had asked Roosevelt to give me three appointments in New Jersey—U. S. Attorney in Trenton, U. S. Marshal, and District Director of Internal Revenue —so that an anti-Hague Democratic organization could be established. "We've got to get rid of Hague," I told Roosevelt, "if we want to build a decent party in New Jersey."

"The President should not become involved in a State factional fight," the President replied. "If Frank is so terrible, you ought to have no trouble driving him out. But as long as he's National Committeeman from New Jersey, I must recognize him as party leader." The President took the same stand on Boss Pendergast of Missouri, Kelly of Illinois, and other leaders of corrupt local machines. I reminded him that he had started his political career fighting Tammany in the New York State Senate.

"What was proper for a State Senator does not apply to the President," was his answer.

Taking the President's challenge, "If Frank is so terrible, you ought to have no trouble driving him out," the New York Post launched a series of articles exposing the corruption of the Hague machine. Frank blew his top. He was not used to criticism. The North Jersey newspapers had long ago given up the struggle. "I-Am-The-Law" was so mad, he ordered his police to stop the sale of the New York Post on streets and newsstands of Jersey City. He denounced me as a "Communist." By coincidence, on the same day he delivered this attack, a Communist meeting in Philadelphia thundered from the left that "Dave Stern is a reactionary fascist." A Latin poet has written that he who walks in the crown of the road makes himself a target for mud from the gutters on both sides.

The Post obtained a preliminary injunction from the United States District Court in Trenton to prevent interference with its sale in Jersey City. Before the papers could be served, Hague, on the advice of his lawyers, had reversed his impulsive order to the police. I was never able to dislodge Hague. Big business in North Jersey found it more convenient to pay tribute than to fight him.

The newspapers and local leaders were properly scared of his ruthless retaliatory tactics.

* * * * *

Early in the 1936 campaign the President showed me an ad he had clipped from that morning's New York Times. Under the heading, U.S.A. CREDIT SOUND, A. M. Lamport & Company, a bond house, gave a comparison of this nation's debt and debt service with those of Great Britain and France. On the basis of per capita wealth and income the United States was in a much stronger position than the other nations.

"Why did a Wall Street outfit run this?" the President wanted to know. "That's the last spot in the world to look for an endorsement of the New Deal. If the guy who put in this ad is not completely crazy, I'd like to meet him."

When he came to my office the next day, Arthur M. Lamport explained that he had become so tired of Wall Street's attacks on the national credit, he had had his research department prepare a comparison of the debt situations in the leading countries. Arthur was a brilliant financial analyst. Also he was a chess fan. We played regularly together until his death, in 1940. I arranged an appointment with the President, who had him at the White House several times during the campaign.

A few weeks after this ad appeared, Arthur sent me a much more comprehensive set of statistics. I called him to say, "This is great stuff. You don't have to buy an ad. We'll run it as an article and give you full credit."

"I don't want any credit," Arthur replied. "I don't want anyone to know where you got those figures. My conservative customers are still giving me hell because of the first ad. You're welcome to the material but don't reveal the source."

The Post used these statistics in a series of front-page boxes. Charlie (Charles J.) Michelson, director of publicity for the Democratic National Committee, reprinted them as campaign literature. Lamport's clear proof of the financial soundness of the government was especially important to counteract the barrage of dire warnings, by leading bankers and businessmen, that Roosevelt's spending for relief was bankrupting the nation. General Robert E. Wood, head of the Sears Roebuck & Company, and chairman of the reactionary America First Committee, was going about the country delivering speeches, all of which ended with the alarm: "When the national debt reaches twenty-five billion, the dollar will be worthless."

I kept my word to Arthur. I revealed the source of these statistics to no one except the President. When Charlie Michelson said, "Dave, you certainly are a shark at figures," I was reminded of my cub reporter days when Hank Eaton had made the same remark about my handling of freight-rate statistics prepared by a friend of my father.

Charlie Michelson was another of my chess-playing cronies. I have often wondered whether it is just coincidence that so many of my friends have been chess players—George Earle, George Backer, Arthur Garfield Hays, among others. Is there a bond between chess-minded men? Do I like the kind of man who likes chess, or do I just like to play chess? When Charlie was in New York, he spent a great deal of his time at the Post. A week before election day, we were lunching together, ostensibly to discuss last-minute campaign strategy, but really absorbed over the chessboard. We interrupted our game when a boy brought us the early editions of the evening newspapers. Hearst's Evening Journal ran the picture of a man stripped to the waist, arms stretched above his head, manacled to hooks in the wall. His social-security number hung from a chain around his neck. SOCIAL SECURITY WILL MAKE SLAVES OF US ALL was the caption. I cannot remember why this particular attack aroused our anger. All through the campaign the Republicans had been using the same line: that social security, unemployment insurance, old-age pensions, would rob a man of his independence, turn him into a robot. Perhaps the picture of the manacled slave was more graphic and potent. Charlie and I jumped into a taxi and rushed up to Democratic headquarters at the Biltmore.

"We want fifty thousand dollars to answer this canard," we told Forbes Morgan, treasurer of the campaign committee. "We've just time to wire a page ad to the cities in which this picture has appeared."

"Calm down, boys," Forbes said. "This election's in the bag."

"For God's sake, don't talk that way, Forbes." I was tense. "I'm superstitious."

"Me, too," said Charlie. "That we-got-it-in-the-bag talk is the open sesame to defeat." Forbes said he was winding up the campaign with a $500,000 deficit and, "I'm not going to make it five hundred and fifty thousand." We wore him down. Finally he gave his consent. Charlie and I prepared an answer to the Hearst attack. But for the rest of his life, whenever Forbes met Charlie or me, he kidded the veteran newspapermen who could not sense the Roosevelt landslide a week before election. As Forbes would tactfully explain, "Nobody pays any attention to what newspapers say except newspapermen."

If there had not been much truth in Forbes' jest, Roosevelt would never have been elected President once, let alone four times. From 80 to 90 per cent of the press, on the basis of circulation, was against him in all four elections. Whole sections of the country, such as New England, were without a single New Deal newspaper. Before Presidential elections, the Kansas Democratic State Committee used to take 2,000 three-month subscriptions of the Record for its County Committee members. There was not a Democratic newspaper in Kansas. In the elections of 1940 and 1944, I took steps to fill this liberal press vacuum by publishing the National Record, a weekly compilation of political news, editorials, and features from the Philadelphia Record.

Because Charlie and I, as well as a great many New Deal leaders, overrated the influence of the press as well as the reliability of the Literary Digest poll, we were running scared in 1936. Roosevelt's supporters were largely inarticulate. Their only means of self-expression was at the ballot box. The voice of the New York Post, the Philadelphia Record, and half a dozen other metropolitan New Deal newspapers, was drowned out by the roar of the conservative press. I expected Roosevelt's election by a small margin. I did not foresee his overwhelming victory.

XVII

Unexpected Competition

Back in New York after the Democratic National Convention of July, 1936, I found both Harry Saylor and Jake Omansky optimistic. Circulation had reached 250,000. In spite of the summer slump, we were carrying a fair volume of advertising. The Post's losses had been cut from $25,000 a week to $25,000 a month. Jake predicted that by the end of 1937 we would be breaking even. Everything looked so good Jill and I took a month's vacation. We spent it canoeing on the Thames and Isis. On our return I received a call from Bernie Gimbel. "I want to see you," he said. "I've important news."

"Moe Annenberg is buying the Inquirer for thirteen million," Bernie told me. "It will be announced next week."

"That *is* important news. He's tough competition."

"The toughest, Dave. In Miami Beach, I saw the way he works at close range. Jim Cox, publisher of the Miami News, can tell you. If you think you've had competition from Jack Martin, you're due for a big surprise."

"As they say in the prize ring, Bernie, the bigger they are the harder they fall." I tried to appear nonchalant. But I had a sinking feeling. This change of ownership threw a monkey wrench into my plans. The Curtis-Martin organization was soft competition. My second team could deal with them. Now the opposing team was putting a Red Grange in the line-up. I ought to be in Philadelphia to meet this threat. But here I was tied up in New York.

Moses L. Annenberg and his brother, Max, had started as newsboys in Milwaukee. Later, they went to Chicago and were employed by Hearst in his battle with the Chicago Tribune for control of the newsstands. According to the U.S. Senate committee report, both publishers hired armed gangs. Five or six men were killed in that notorious circulation war. When Hearst won, he made Moe circulation manager of the Chicago Examiner, later circulation director of all Hearst newspapers. Max went over to the other side, and became circulation director of the Tribune, later of the New York Daily News, an affiliate of the Chicago Tribune. Moe always referred to Max as "my brother who didn't make good." This "unsuccessful" brother received a salary plus bonus of more than $250,000 a year—chicken feed to Moe, who was reputed to be one of the wealthiest men in the nation, with an income of $14,000,000.

A special concession by William Randolph Hearst was the springboard for Moe's huge fortune. The tough circulation director had proved so capable that he had won his publisher's confidence. When Moe told Hearst, "I'm having trouble in Milwaukee. Do you mind if I take over that agency myself?," Hearst said, "Go ahead," thereby breaking an unwritten law of newspaperdom that a circulation director should have no financial interest in a distributing agency. There was good reason for this rule. In most cities and towns, distribution of out-of-town newspapers and magazines is handled by one distributor who is supposed to give impartial service to all publications. If a circulation director is dissatisfied, he can appoint a separate agent. But it is expensive and difficult for one newspaper to go it alone. Unless all the circulation managers in a metropolitan center get together and agree on a new distributor, a shift by one newspaper is uneconomic.

In Chicago, the circulation managers worked together. Their procedure was to notify a distributor that his services were unsatisfactory and that he was to sell his agency to a certain man for a certain figure (usually the value of his trucks and other equipment). When I was publishing the News-Record, the Springfield distributor bought the Rockford, Illinois, agency for $50,000. He paid the old agent $15,000. But before he did that, he had visited the office of an attorney in Chicago. No one was there but a girl secretary. He went into a deserted back office, placed an envelope containing $35,000 on the table, and departed. We figured that the circulation directors of the Chicago newspapers split $250,000 a year by "transferring" agencies.

With Hearst's "Go ahead," Moe bought up distribution companies in larger cities throughout the country. Growth of magazine circulation had made this business most profitable. Sale of racing publications added to these profits. Through his control of metropolitan newsstands, Moe took over the Daily Racing Form, a tip sheet, in 1922, and later the Morning Telegraph, sports daily. Then he acquired the wire services to bookmakers and horse parlors and had a monopoly of race-track information. To maintain that monopoly, it was reputed the Al Capone mob received an annual retainer of $1,000,000. Whenever a rival race-track tip sheet was started, someone broke into the printing plant and wrecked the machinery.

      *   *   *   *   *

On my return from Gimbel's office, I received a call from Irv Orner, the Record's circulation director. "There's a funny situation in Wilmington which I can't figure out," he said. "The Inquirer has just notified the agent that unless he sells out to their man they will take the Inquirer away from him. They accuse him of favoring the Record, which is nonsense."

"Have the agent in my office at nine-thirty tomorrow morning," I told Orner. "Get a drawing room on the seven o'clock train to Philadelphia," I told Frank Murphy. "Phone Fox and Rothschild I'll be in their office between ten and eleven on urgent business. Bring whatever mail you can pick up. We'll work on the train." Evidently Moe was jumping the gun.

"I can't understand what's biting the Ink [Inquirer]," Irv said when I arrived at the Record. "All they've got to go on is that Wilmington missed one drop [delivery]."

Philadelphia had been singularly free of the distribution racket which was rampant in the Middle West. In our territory, eastern Pennsylvania, South Jersey, and Delaware, a distributor's "franchise" was safe as long as he gave good service and paid his bills. I quote "franchise" because the distributors used the word to describe an agreement based on trade custom, but with no legal validity. They had no written contracts with the publishers.

"That explains it!" Orner said when I told him that Annenberg was buying the Inquirer. "The man the Ink wants to put into Wilmington is from Chicago. This is serious."

"You don't have to tell me," I interrupted Irv. "If Annenberg gets control of the distributors, he can cut our circulation overnight, or force us to the terrific expense of a separate distribution system."

The Record's lawyers—Fox, Rothschild, O'Brien and Frankel—were doubtful of what could be done. I insisted they bring some kind of court action and that Annenberg be made a party to it. I wanted Moe to know the Record was not going to take it lying down. I suggested applying for an injunction in the name of the Wilmington distributor to prevent interference with his business. Jerry Rothschild advised against such action. "We haven't a leg to stand on. We must have proof of a conspiracy to destroy this man's business."

"We'll get proof," I assured Jerry. "But that will take time. I want to apply for a preliminary injunction tomorrow, even if we know it will be refused."

Fortunately, this conservative law firm had just taken in a fighting redhead, Dan (Daniel J.) Lowenthal. He got my idea and took the case into court. Dan had trouble serving a subpoena on Moe, who kept himself incommunicado. But when he gave a reception to Philadelphia's VIPs, a well-dressed process server managed to reach the publisher's inner sanctum. As Moe described it, "A fine welcome to Philadelphia. When I get off the train, Dave Stern has me arrested."

It was a hectic hearing. Dick (Richardson) Dilworth, now Mayor of Philadelphia, represented the Inquirer. In the courtroom, Dick was still the tough Marine. (He had a distinguished combat record in World War I, which he was later to duplicate in World War II.) He interrupted Dan Lowenthal and the judge so often and so vehemently, the judge held him in contempt, fined him $100, and ordered him from the courtroom. It was the most profitable fine ever paid. Moe was so impressed by Dick's truculent tactics that he followed him out of the courtroom to retain him as general counsel for the Inquirer at an annual fee of $50,000. That retainer delayed Dick's political career. I recognized his unusual ability and offered to back him for any political post he wanted, if he would sever his connection with the Inquirer. Dick said he did not blame me for making this condition, "but I can't afford to give up that retainer." After I retired, Dick became district attorney and then mayor.

Dan won a preliminary injunction. The Inquirer dropped its attempt to change agents in Wilmington. It never again tried this tactic with other distributors.

I anticipated Moe's next move. He would send a strong-arm squad into Philadelphia to intimidate city newsstands. I hired a Chicago detective agency whose operatives knew Moe's men. I sent a reporter to Chicago to write a series on the circulation racket with special emphasis on its origin, the battle between McCormick and Hearst for control of the newsstands, in which the Annenberg brothers had played a conspicuous part. The reporter was instructed to reveal "in strict confidence" his mission to everyone he interviewed, so that Moe would be sure to get word of our inquiry.

A phone call to the White House brought FBI men to Philadelphia. Governor Earle sent a squad of State police, and Mayor Wilson ordered a special detail of detectives to guard the newsstands. Within a week the Chicago thugs departed. They complained to my detectives, "This burg is lousy with dicks." Whatever plans Moe may have had for muscling into the Philadelphia circulation system were abandoned. He did not want to give me an opening to rake up the past. He had bought the Inquirer to cover himself with a cloak of respectability. A circulation war would have torn that cloak to tatters.

The Chicago detectives came to my office with their final report, a long list of characters they had recognized on the streets of Philadelphia. They proceeded to read brief descriptions of them. "Served from 1914 to '17, three years for armed robbery; 1920, one year aggravated assault; 1922 to '28, seven years second-degree manslaughter; no police record." When this tag line "no police record," was repeated several times, I interrupted, "I don't understand. You read a list of convictions and then say 'no police record.'"

"I should have explained," the chief operative said, "in Chicago the underworld has an arrangement with the police. For two hundred and fifty dollars you can have a police folder lost. 'No record' means we know the subject has paid the two hundred and fifty."

Though Moe did not use strong-arm tactics in Philadelphia, he never pulled his punches. He bragged he was going to put the Record out of business. He boasted, "I can lose five dollars to make Dave Stern lose one." Moe spent millions on circulation promotion. An army of subscription solicitors offered lavish premiums. He increased the Inquirer's news space and added many excellent features. He issued a South Jersey edition of the Inquirer with complete news coverage in what had been the Courier-Post's exclusive territory. His Camden office was manned by more reporters and photographers than the Courier-Post had. The Record and the Courier-Post had to spend money to meet this aggressive competition, to add features, employ solicitors, offer premiums. The Post's efficient promotion department helped with puzzle contests and book distributions. We held our own.

But by squandering millions, Moe did reduce the profits of my newspapers. The steady earnings of the Courier-Post were cut in half. The Record's net was reduced a third. I had counted on these earnings to offset the Post's losses.

Although Moe kept broadcasting that he was going to "put Dave Stern out of business," he refrained from any personal attacks on me. He was more vulnerable in a mudslinging contest than I was. Instead of going after me, he pilloried my friends and supporters. At his own suggestion he lunched with Al Greenfield and Al's executives. After a pleasant meal, as he rose to leave, Moe shook hands with Al and said, "I like you, Al. But you're financing Dave Stern. I've got to destroy you to destroy Dave Stern."

Within a week, the Inquirer started a smear series which accused Al of wrecking the Bankers' Trust Company, a charge which was disproven in the final liquidation of the bank. It twisted and distorted every major transaction in which Al had had a hand.

Harold Ickes, Secretary of the Interior, came to Philadelphia to deliver a campaign speech. His theme was a description of the men who were supporting the Republican ticket. He took Moe as a conspicuous example and delivered an invective which outdid Cicero's orations on Catiline. The Record printed the Ickes speech.

This bitter newspaper war continued until Moe went to the Federal penitentiary for income tax evasion in 1940. We were surprised when he pleaded guilty. The explanation given by his lawyers was that he did so to protect members of his family. It was generally believed that a trial would have revealed the protection money which had been paid, reputedly a million dollars a year, to maintain a monopoly on race-track information. Moe had to obey the unwritten law of the underworld: "The guy who's pinched must protect the mob or be the victim of mob vengeance." He paid the government nearly ten million dollars in back taxes and interest.

When Al Greenfield heard the news of Moe's conviction he quoted an old saw, "He who digs a grave for his neighbor is apt to fall into it himself. Moe said he was going to destroy you and me. Now he's on his way to prison."

Moe's associates chose to explain that he was the victim of persecution instigated by me. I can truthfully say that I had nothing to do with it. But I know who did. When Annenberg started a newspaper in Miami Beach he incurred the bitter enmity of the Miami publishers, one of whom was James M. Cox, formerly Governor of Ohio. In 1920 the Democratic national ticket was Cox for President, Franklin D. Roosevelt for Vice President. Cox told me how he had ribbed the President: "Franklin, you ought to be proud of the way you're pulling everyone back to prosperity— including Moe Annenberg. Under your administration he's making more money than Mellon and Rockefeller combined!"

What is more to the point, Baltimore Brevities, a scandal sheet owned by Annenberg, had run a scurrilous story about J. Edgar Hoover, Director of the FBI. When the Annenberg tax evasion case came to court the FBI had gathered overwhelming evidence.

Because of illness Moe was released in June 1942. He died a month later from a tumor on the brain. This ailment probably accounts for his eccentric conduct in Philadelphia. Yet Moe had courage, executive ability, and an uncanny knack for picking the right men for every job in his many legitimate enterprises. They still prosper under the able management of his son, Walter, who has endowed the M. L. Annenberg School of Communication at the University of Pennsylvania as a memorial to his father.

I recall only one business blunder Moe made in Philadelphia, and that was a lulu! Shortly after he bought the Inquirer he was showing the Governor of Pennsylvania around the plant. He opened a door to a conference room where Charlie (Charles) Tyler, president of the Inquirer Company, was negotiating a new contract with the Newspaper Guild.

After Charlie had introduced the publisher and his distinguished visitor to the Guild committee, Moe wanted to know what all the argument was about. The chairman of the Guild committee spoke up. "We want a job-security clause which will protect an employee from being fired even if the paper is losing money and needs to economize. It will give a man a feeling of safety in his job and raise the morale of your staff."

"Charlie, why don't you give the boys what they want?" Moe was playing the benign overlord. He knew nothing of the problem he was creating. Charlie told me that he was so angry he threw up his hands and capitulated. As a result the Inquirer was saddled with the toughest job-security clause in America. A month later, when the Record negotiated a new Guild contract, it had to accept an equally unfair clause.

Moe was a strange amalgam of brilliance and baseness for which Hearst is primarily responsible. In Moe's formative years Hearst paid Moe big money to break the law. No one was ever indicted for the mob killings in the Chicago newspaper war. Small wonder that the young son of a recent immigrant should get a distorted notion of morality in this new land. The blame should be shared by all of us who drank bootleg liquor and helped to make Al Capone and the underworld rich. Our country is still suffering from the aftereffects of the Noble Experiment.

Moe's favorite expression was, "Dog eats dog." That described the world in which he was brought up. He was a casualty of the miscalled "roaring," properly called "sordid" twenties.

XVIII

Sale of the Post

Battling Annenberg was not made easier when Harry Saylor became ill. For a year and a half he was a semi-invalid. While he came to the office for a few hours a day, I had to shoulder most of his work. Again I was back in the double job of editor and publisher as in Camden. I had to give up writing myself. But I did steal the time to pound out one front-page editorial on an ideological conflict in which I was intensely interested. It brought the most immediate, adverse reaction of any piece I ever wrote. But it was a timely and useful message.

Under the heading STALIN TAKES OFF HIS MASK I came out foursquare against the united front, an alliance of communism and liberalism, for which American Communists had been clamoring. This editorial appeared on February 15, 1938. The day before, Stalin had issued a world-wide call for a united front so that Russia might have the "help of bourgeois countries . . . in case of military attack." Stalin made it crystal clear that the purpose of the united front was to strengthen communism, weaken democracy. The American Communists had been pretending to a belief in civil liberties and democratic government. Many New Dealers had been taken in by this hypocrisy. They were scared by the growing fascist propaganda in this country. Nazi bunds, with uniformed storm troopers and swastika flags, were drawing big crowds to their rallies. Only the Communists made any attempt to heckle or break up such meetings. Extremists and muddleheads, in both liberal and conservative camps, had public thinking in a fine state of confusion.

Our editorial said, "There can be no united front for democracy with the enemies of democracy. It is hard to fight an enemy disguised as a friend. . . . When the Post said that the American Communists' pretense to belief in democracy was only a deliberate tactic, the Comrades were very indignant. Are they going to be sore at Stalin for saying the same thing?"

Old stuff now but a fresh enough point of view in those befuddled days to make the fellow travelers furious. No sooner had the noon edition hit the streets than a steady stream of phone calls, wires, and letters poured into our office. What roused the pinkos even more than the editorial was a cartoon by Jerry Doyle: a smiling Stalin, shaking hands with Uncle Sam, was holding a bloody dagger behind his back.

The pleasantest parts of those strenuous days were my brief meetings with Jerry to decide on the next day's cartoon. We had a standing bet. If he used my suggestion, he gave me a cigar. If I accepted his, I gave Jerry a cigar. Over the years the score was ten to one in Jerry's favor. He was a genius at turning the gist of an editorial into a picture.

This editorial and cartoon of February 15 had many repercussions. One in particular proved how timely and much needed it was. That morning before the editorial appeared, my friend George Seldes had phoned to invite Jill and me to his home that night to meet Oliver K. Bovard, one of the best-known newspapermen in America. After thirty years as managing editor of the St. Louis Post-Dispatch, he had just resigned because of political differences with his publisher, Joseph Pulitzer, Jr. The gossips had it that both of them were against Roosevelt: Pulitzer because the President was too radical; Bovard because the President was too conservative.

George Seldes, a prolific writer, was the author of *Lords of the Press*, biographical sketches of a dozen newspaper publishers. He cut them all up into little pieces, except me whom he heaped with praise. As Jill was out of town I asked George if I might bring my older daughter. I told Little Jill she was going to meet some of my most interesting friends "who really appreciate your father."

Little Jill and I arrived late, which partially accounts for our reception. Everyone had been drinking—my host and hostess, their guest of honor, and a dozen *avant-garde* liberals. Without waiting for formal introductions, they all started to berate me for "that

abominable editorial." Fists were shaken in my face. I was glad
to get out with a whole skin. Little Jill was convulsed with laughter. "Dad, they certainly appreciate you," she said.

After nearly a quarter of a century I would doubt my memory
of this bizarre incident if I did not have my daughter to verify
my recollection. Their language was so extreme, their emotions so
overwrought I was alerted to the danger from leftist "intellec-
tuals." For the rest of my publishing days I kept hammering on
the theme that liberalism and communism were antagonistic
philosophies.

Arthur Garfield Hays was largely responsible for the emphasis
I gave this subject. As general counsel of the American Civil Liberties Union, his life was dedicated to the preservation of the
rights of the underdog. "I can't stand by and see a little fellow
pushed around," is the way Arthur expressed it. He would neglect
an important corporate case involving millions to give his time and
great ability to defend some indigent client.

Although we had known each other before, I came under Arthur's spell when I took over the Post in 1933. The Post backed the
American Civil Liberties Union on many issues. The right of
minorities to free speech and assembly was an especially difficult
problem in those days when fascists and Communists were trying
to outshout each other. Arthur had himself arrested in Jersey City
for upholding the right of free speech and assembly against the
edict of Frank Hague, whom the Post was battling.

There was a fundamental difference in our points of view.
Arthur believed the principles of civil liberties were absolute, allowing of no deviation or compromise. I insisted man was incapable of formulating an absolute rule without exceptions, that civil
liberties were means toward an end. The Right to Work laws,
which forbid the closed shop, illustrate this conflict in concept. Although he recognized their weakening effect on unionism, Arthur
felt conscience-bound to support them. A pragmatist, I was against
them, and I am glad the A.C.L.U. adopted this point of view.
Our debates usually ended by Arthur proposing, "Let's play
chess. It's so much simpler than these arguments." We were both
addicts of the game. As the years went by we found our compan-

ionship so congenial we spent more and more time together. He was my closest friend. His death, in 1955, left a great void in my life.

     ❊   ❊   ❊   ❊   ❊

In the fall of 1937 impending storm was in the air. Isolationists and conservatives predicted that government spending would ruin the nation. President Roosevelt, at heart an economic conservative, again allowed himself to be influenced by the repeated warnings of big business that he was heading for a wild inflation. Winthrop Aldrich, president of the Chase National Bank, and Marriner E. Eccles, chairman of the Board of Governors of the Federal Reserve System, persuaded him to put on the economic brakes. In the spring of 1937 business was just recovering from its 1933 tailspin. It had received an extra stimulus from the distribution of two billion dollars in soldier bonuses. Some slight stabilizing measure may have been in order. But Aldrich and Eccles talked the President into putting on all the brakes, all the way, all at once. The economic jalopy not only stopped in its uphill course, but it started to roll backward into the depression of 1938. The Post suffered a severe setback. When retail sales dwindled, stores reduced their advertising. Because the Post was the latest newspaper in which they had begun to advertise, it was the first paper they dropped. Jake Omansky had predicted the Post would be out of the red by the fall of 1937, but we could not buck the ebbing tide.

I went to see Tom (Thomas W.) Lamont, chairman of J. P. Morgan & Company. He had started his New York career as a reporter on the Post. One of Tom's assignments had been to make regular calls on J. P. Morgan. Morgan took such a liking to the young reporter that he persuaded him to come to work for him. Later, Lamont formed a syndicate which bought the Post from Oswald Garrison Villard, whose family had owned it for fifty years. After Lamont's syndicate had lost $6,500,000, it sold the Post to the Curtis-Martin Company in 1927.

"Winthrop Aldrich has persuaded President Roosevelt to throw our economy into a tailspin," I told Tom and explained why I thought so.

"I'm not an economist," was Tom's reply. "Let's see what the experts think." His partners, Russell Leffingwell, formerly Assistant Secretary of the Treasury, and Parker Gilbert, joined us. They agreed with me. They figured the government had reduced the spending of the nation by ten billion dollars. They refused to state their position publicly but they did authorize me to quote them to the President. I called the White House and arranged to see F.D.R. the next day.

As usual, the President monopolized the conversation. When Marvin McIntyre appeared to remind the President of his next appointment, I said, "I came down here to discuss the subject you always try to avoid—the monetary situation—and I haven't gotten a word in edgewise."

"If you stay over and lunch with me tomorrow," the President replied, "I promise to listen and not say a word." Needless to say, the President did not carry out his promise of complete silence but he did give me time to explain my views.

"Overnight you have taken ten billion dollars out of the spending power of the nation. That is too much of a shock for the national economy. Your Wall Street advisers may have the best intentions but they are more concerned with higher interest rates than in stabilizing the national economy."

"Where do you get that ten billion dollars stuff?" the President asked.

I pulled over a pad and wrote it out. He studied it for a few minutes. "That is an exaggeration," he said. "Eight billion would be a fairer estimate." "Ten billion is the estimate of J. P. Morgan and Company," and I told him of my discussion the day before. "But what's two billion dollars between friends?" I continued. "Whether it is ten or eight billions, you put on the brakes too hard."

"Jot down what you propose we do." He pushed the pad back to me.

I wrote, "(1) Reduce reserve requirements; (2) de-sterilize gold; (3) increase WPA payments to compensate for veterans' bonuses of last year; (4) reduce treasury balance to normal."

The President took my advice—eventually. He delayed six

months before putting the specific measures into effect. By that time the depression had gained too much momentum to be reversed by these remedies. It was not until the government increased its expenditures for defense and lend-lease, after Hitler invaded Poland in 1939, that business recovered from this artificially induced setback.

I had the small satisfaction of having correctly diagnosed the economic malady and of having recommended the proper cure. But recovery came too late to save my position on the Post.

❋   ❋   ❋   ❋   ❋

Late one Friday afternoon in December, 1938, Saylor came into my office. "My doctor has just discharged me as completely cured," he said. "No more hospitals, no more examinations. Now I can put in a full day's work."

"That's the best news since I came to New York," I told him. "We've got to celebrate. Let's have lunch together tomorrow."

The next day Jake, Harry, and I lunched in the Post penthouse. In spite of the difficult days, we were in high spirits.

"Harry and I are going to shanghai you and put you on one of those ships for a West Indies cruise," said Jake, looking down at the United Fruit Line piers twenty-five stories below. "You need a rest, if any man ever did."

"You won't have to shanghai me. I will walk aboard gladly," I assured them.

"Fine," said Jake. "If you take a rest and the three of us are hitting on all cylinders, we are going to pull through next year. We're the best newspaper team in this town or any other town. I'll follow my own advice, and lay off this Saturday afternoon for the first time in four years. After lunch I'll go home and play with my baby." Like most men who marry late in life Jake was enthralled with his first child.

Sunday morning I was awakened by a phone call from John Stevenson. Jake had died from a heart attack. They had been riding together in Central Park. Jake had slumped in his saddle. When John lifted him to the ground he was gone. This tragedy cast a pall over the whole Post staff. Jake was the most popular member of the organization and the ablest business executive with whom I have ever had the privilege of working. He was the first of my top echelon to be taken from me by death. I had come to rely on his wise counsel and courage. I am convinced that if he had lived I would not have been forced to sell the Post.

On the morning after Jake's death John Stevenson and Paul Sarazen briefed me on the promotion department, a branch of the business I had left entirely in Jake's hands. The operation had grown into a sizable business employing a large staff. It had contracts for puzzle contests with newspapers and merchandisers. To maintain this outside activity and absorb the overhead, continuing sales effort was required. Jake, with his nationwide reputation as a promoter, had been the master salesman. Also the department was carrying an $800,000 inventory of books, remainders from previous promotions, which had to be disposed of by special offers or sold at a loss. The department was a business in itself. I was depressed when I realized that I would have to learn it and shoulder this additional responsibility.

At this time I was afflicted by another run of bad luck. A few weeks later Harry Saylor's wife died. He had been devoted to Ernestine, a lovely woman, who was very dear to Jill and to me. In childhood she had had cardiac rheumatism so that a slight attack of pneumonia proved fatal. As Harry's closest friend I sat with him the three days and nights of the tragic ordeal.

Moe Annenberg started a drive against the Courier-Post with a South Jersey edition of the Inquirer. The business recession, beginning in the summer of 1937, had stopped the growth of Post advertising. To top it all, Ralph Strassburger went on the rampage with another of his proxy fights. As before, he got nowhere. But it was most humiliating because all my directors had advised me against the obvious blunder of accepting his investment in the Post. And fighting Strassburger was nasty, time-consuming business.

Shortly thereafter Ralph eliminated himself from my life by a blunder as absurd as mine in accepting his investment in the Post. To effect a tax loss Ralph had sold his stocks in my newspapers to the general manager of his Norristown newspaper. Ralph forgot this when he voted his stock, which had not been transferred to the new owner on the books of the company. A grand jury returned indictments against him and the general manager, who pleaded guilty and was given a suspended sentence. Rather than stand trial Ralph fled to France, where he lived until his death a few years ago. What a confusing bundle of contradictions he was. Our association over eighteen years had started in 1920 when I helped him to extricate himself from a newsprint gouge. He was impressed by the way I had handled the situation and went around singing my praise. Ralph was a man of sudden impulses and superlatives. He was either declaring me the smartest publisher in the United States or denouncing me, in scurrilous letters to my stockholders, as the most incompetent.

✻　　✻　　✻　　✻　　✻

By the spring of 1939 I was at the end of my rope. Because of the depression the Post's monthly loss had mounted to $75,000. Because of Annenberg's competition, assistance from my other newspapers was reduced to $25,000 a month. I had to find the other $50,000. My suppliers, especially Pop Gilman, had been more than generous in extending credit. Now they were becoming restive. To keep them quiet I personally guaranteed their accounts. I kept a record of these guarantees in my desk in the penthouse. They totaled $1,500,000.

I found it impossible to raise additional capital. In 1938 it was very different from 1928 when my friends had oversubscribed the Record stock issue. Now everyone had his own problem and wanted to keep in a strong cash position. Al Greenfield and a few other large advertisers helped out by paying for advertising in advance. It was the happy-go-lucky, harum-scarum Springfield experience blown up into a nightmare. Then I had to raise a few hundred to make the ghost walk. Now I had to meet the combined weekly payrolls in New York, Camden, and Philadelphia of $150,000.

Every Monday morning Charlie Lynch, the controller, would come to my office to tell me, "I figure we'll have to have X dollars to get through the week." Usually the sum he named was $25,000, sometimes $50,000. And every Monday morning I would answer, "I don't know where we are going to get it."

Then I would go up to the penthouse to take a drink. I would look at the list of personal guarantees. After thirty years of hard work, I was busted. I would walk over to the window and wish I had the courage to jump. Ashamed of myself for lacking the guts, I would return downstairs to the grueling grind.

One Thursday I was ready to give up. It seemed impossible to meet the Friday payroll. I had tapped every possible source of cash. I was ready to admit defeat. My unbroken record of always making the ghost walk was about to end. I was figuring how I should handle the situation, what kind of announcement I should make, when Eugene Untermyer, my lawyer, phoned. He had just received a check for $75,000 in settlement of our claim against a book printing company. We had expected this case to go to court and that it would be a year or more before we recovered any cash. This eleventh-hour windfall gave me new courage. I took it as an omen that somehow, some way, I was destined to pull through.

Among my chess-playing friends was George Backer, an ardent New Dealer. He was interested in civil liberties and had joined in talks with Arthur Garfield Hays. He shared my aversion to the United Front and Communists. Our political philosophies were in accord.

George was married to Dorothy Schiff, who had inherited a large fortune from her father, Mortimer L. Schiff, and another from her grandfather, Jacob H. Schiff. I proposed that Dorothy and George take over the Post. I offered to relinquish control on as favorable terms as had been granted me by the Curtis estate six years before, an issue of second preferred stock. Then the Post had 60,000 circulation; now 250,000. It would require an initial investment of $2,500,000 to pay the Post's indebtedness of $1,500,-000 and provide working capital. I told the Backers that they could turn the corner and get out of the red by the investment of $2,500,000 more—$5,000,000 in all. Later Dorothy told me I was not far off. She invested $6,000,000 before the Post started to break even in 1942. In the thirty-two years since Tom Lamont's syndicate bought the property from Villard, four owners had spent

$32,000,000, or an average of $1,000,000 a year, to keep the Post alive. During my six years, my associates and I lost $4,500,000.

Both Dorothy and George wanted to make the deal. But her brother, John M. Schiff, and his partners in Kuhn, Loeb & Company were opposed. To these conservative investment bankers the Post was anathema. That the estate of their founder, Jacob H. Schiff, might be used to finance a liberal (they called it "radical") newspaper was unthinkable.

Jill helped to overcome this opposition. While George and I played chess she had long talks with Dorothy. Jill described how ownership of the Post would enlarge and enrich Dorothy's life. "Owning a newspaper is more than a financial investment," Jill told her. "It's an opportunity for self-expression, a chance to become a personality, a force in community, state, and national affairs."

Dorothy is a very determined person. She was fortunate in having as her attorney Morris L. Ernst, a fighting liberal. He told her she had the right to do what she liked with her money and that the risk was not too great for a woman of her wealth. In July, 1939 Dorothy and George took control of the Post.

Most of my editorial executives insisted on coming back to the Philadelphia Record with me. I was embarrassed that I might be leaving Dorothy and George shorthanded in the top echelon. In charge was Paul A. Tierney, a most able managing editor. His backstop was Walter G. Lister, city editor, who two years later became managing editor of the Philadelphia Record and now is executive editor of the Philadelphia Bulletin. Ted (Theodore Olin) Thackrey was feature editor. When I described these men to Dorothy and George I may have overpraised them. Within three years Dorothy had divorced George and married Ted, who became editor of the Post.

I had promised Dorothy and George I would continue with the Post as director and consultant. When George left, I resigned.

XIX

Dreams of
a National Daily

"Now we can move back to our lovely home in Haddonfield and take it easier," I said to Jill, trying to put my defeat in a cheerful light. I had arrived at our Atlantic City cottage late at night after transfer of the Post to the Backers. It had been a prolonged and tiring settlement, with so many lawyers representing the Backers, the Post, the Record and the Courier-Post that they got in each other's hair.

My feelings were mixed. It was my first failure to make a property pay in the twenty-seven years during which I had built up six newspapers. On the other hand I was relieved of my $1,500,000 personal guarantees of Post debts and of the nerve-racking ordeal of meeting weekly deficits. Without the constant drain of the Post, the Record and Courier-Post were in good shape. I felt like a man who can finally take off his tight shoes and relax.

That within two months a second world war would change our lives was not in my thoughts. How indifferent the democracies on both sides of the Atlantic were to omens of an impending holocaust. The day Hitler invaded Poland, September 1, Jill and I met three Army Intelligence officers at a cocktail party. They were positive Great Britain would not declare war. Jill bet each of them ten dollars that the British would keep their commitment. On our way home I kidded Jill about knowing more than Army Intelligence. Three days later the officers came to our cottage to pay their bets. They explained that they had made their prediction because they knew how little Great Britain had done to strengthen its armed forces. Jill sent the thirty dollars to the Lord Mayor of London for his war relief fund.

When I saw President Roosevelt the following week, I found he was already planning practical measures to aid Great Britain and France. "We must help them stem the rising tide of dictatorships," he said.

"We missed a chance in Spain," I reminded him.

"In that case we were up against special conditions," was his reply, as he abruptly changed the subject, but not before I had sensed that he had been under the same kind of pressure to which I had succumbed.

"You criticized my quarantine speech," the President reminded me, referring to his courageous and prophetic statement of October 1937 that the democracies must quarantine dictators to stop the spread of totalitarianism. My editorial had said that such a startling change in our foreign policy should have been in the form of a message to Congress. But I had not given this bold new concept of national purpose the backing it deserved. So now I changed the subject.

"In this crisis you must run for a third term," I said. "Only you can put your policies into effect."

"I told you I'm retiring." He was repeating what he had said many times before. He had it all planned. He was to be editor of a national daily which I was to publish simultaneously in four or more cities, thus making possible delivery on day of publication throughout the United States—similar to the present operation of The Wall Street Journal. He had discussed it at length with Lord Beaverbrook and Joe Patterson as well as with me. He enjoyed talking over the details—proportion of local, national and international news, whether there should be local editorials, etc. Often, when I had other matters in mind, it was difficult to get him off the subject.

"Who will take your place?" I asked.

"Joe Patterson thinks we should experiment with a national weekly before launching a daily." This time the President changed the subject. I knew why he ignored my question. His white-haired boy was Bob (Robert H.) Jackson, then Solicitor General, later Attorney General and Associate Justice of the Supreme Court. But

Jim Farley insisted that *he* had earned the right of succession, and, as chairman of the Democratic National Committee, Jim controlled the party machinery. Roosevelt, himself, was the only candidate who could block Farley. In this most difficult period the President had the added burden of a bitter split in his official family.

I was up against a similar situation in Pennsylvania. It was the aftermath of the political feud which had started when I demanded that Matt McCloskey either stop taking government contracts or quit his political activities. Senator Joseph F. Guffey supported my stand. Governor Earle and Jack Kelly decided to punish Guffey, up for re-election in 1940, for having sided with me. Joe had a fine record in the Senate. He had put through the Guffey Coal Act which ended a mine slump and returned 100,000 miners to work. He had the endorsement of President Roosevelt, whose legislation he had supported. For the Democratic Party to present another candidate was political suicide, but in a vendetta neither the good of the party nor plain common sense carries any weight. George had won over Dave Lawrence, Secretary of the Commonwealth in George's cabinet. As the Pennsylvania member of the Democratic National Committee, Lawrence was the dispenser of Federal patronage. Thus George and he were in control of the State party organization. The faction which dominates the county committees usually wins the primary.

To have Dave turn against him was a blow to Joe Guffey. Dave had been his closest friend in the party. In 1938 Dave and Joe had been guests in my New York home, ostensibly to visit the World's Fair, but mainly to explore ways in which we could reunite the factions. Then their relation was that of father and son. Dave took occasion to tell me of his love and admiration for Joe. Dave's defection so depressed Joe that he wanted to withdraw his name for re-election and retire from politics. His very able sister, Emma Guffey Miller, Pennsylvania National Committeewoman, and I had a hard time persuading him to stay in the race.

Once we had convinced Joe that he owed it to President Roosevelt as well as to himself to make the fight, our next problem was to raise money for the preprimary campaign. Emma estimated that we needed a minimum of $250,000. Al Greenfield, who was partially to blame for the party split, pledged himself to raise half this amount.

"When are you going to see John [John L. Lewis, president of the United Mine Workers]?" I asked Joe. "After all you've done for his union he ought to be good for at least fifty thousand dollars."

"John has been talking strangely of late," Joe told me. "I'm not sure where I stand with him. You see him."

I had known John since Springfield days when he had a reputation as a tough, rough union leader. During the Presidential campaign of 1932 and 1936 we had met frequently. His assistant and protégé, Tom (Thomas) Kennedy—now president of the United Mine Workers—was elected lieutenant governor on the Earle ticket in 1934. Jill had never met John until we attended a reception in his honor given by Joe Guffey at his Washington home in 1937. After the reception Jill and I stayed on for supper with Joe, his sisters, John, and John's daughter, who had been graduated from Bryn Mawr. After supper Jill and John had an hour's talk.

"It looks as though John was trying to make an impression on you," I said after we left.

"He certainly did make an impression," Jill replied.

"And what was the impression?"

"He's a sinister, fascist-minded man," was Jill's answer.

"That's absurd—a woman's hunch," I scoffed. "John is a liberal labor leader and a true friend of the New Deal." It was not long before I had to eat my words!

Joe and I went together to see John. We were shown into an imposing conference room at the United Mine Workers Building in Washington. John came into the room with Phil Murray and Tom Kennedy. John had a book under his arm and I noticed he had a finger in its pages. I outlined the impending primary battle and asked for $100,000 from the U.M.W. John opened the book and proceeded to read a clause in the union bylaws which prohibited contributions to primary contests.

"This situation presents the exception when the rule should be broken," I told John. "Or avoided by an appeal to members of the union to make individual contributions. You are in a position to take either course."

Through his system of captive districts John had made himself absolute dictator of the union. The bylaws from which he had read also provided that whenever the union's national board was dissatisfied with district officers it could replace them with its own appointees. John had used this power to "capture" a majority of the districts, which insured his perpetuation in office.

"It would be a disgrace to the United Mine Workers to let down a Senator who had done so much for them," I said in closing my plea. "This issue is of international importance. President Roosevelt needs Joe in the Senate to fight the isolationists who are trying to block aid to the Allies."

"We're bound by the rules in this book," was John's curt reply as he abruptly left the room. After he was gone Phil and Tom apologized for what they realized was ingratitude and political shortsightedness.

"Dave, you made one mistake in your argument," Tom Kennedy said. "John's gone isolationist."

When I reported this meeting to the President he handed me the unpleasant assignment of bringing John back in line. I invited John to dinner. In my suite at the Mayflower, the two of us argued from 7 P.M. until 1 A.M. Finally, after a particularly long peroration in which John gave all the reasons why he was against the President and his policies, I said, "John, you have me confused. I can't make up my mind whether you talk more like a fascist or a Communist." That was the end of another friendship!

Thereafter, whenever John referred to me in a speech, it was as "that dirty Dave Stern." I found occasion to tell the public how John had destroyed democracy in the U.M.W. and made himself a labor dictator. John is an honest man who dedicated his life to improving the condition of the coal miners. He did a great job. Undoubtedly he was convinced he could not achieve his goal without dictatorial methods. In justifying his own tactics he had to deny to himself the dangers of dictatorship. That is the way I rationalize his political turnabout in 1940. Shortly after our talk he formally announced his support of Wendell Willkie, the Republican candidate for President.

I was crestfallen when I reported my failure to the President. "Don't take it so hard, Dave," he said. "The miners will obey John in union matters but I have a hunch they have more confidence in me when it comes to running their government." And so it proved in the elections of 1940 and 1944.

Despite John's turndown we raised the money for Joe's primary campaign. He won the primary by a substantial majority, was re-elected U.S. Senator, and regained control of the Democratic State organization.

I am glad to recount that before Joe Guffey died in 1957 Dave and he made peace and were friends again. Dave returned to politics to make a remarkable record as Mayor of Pittsburgh from 1945 to 1958. He accomplished the miracle of transforming that ugly duckling of a city into one of beauty. Now he is Governor of Pennsylvania and has inherited Joe Guffey's mantle as "Mr. Democrat of Pennsylvania."

After their defeat in that bitter 1940 primary, George Earle and Jack Kelly dropped out of politics. I never saw either of them again. Many of my friends ask me, "Now that you are retired don't you miss the excitement?" This explains why my answer is "No."

✻   ✻   ✻   ✻   ✻

Roosevelt's aid to the Allies was attacked from both the right and the left: by the American Firsters and fascists, who secretly admired the Hitler, Mussolini, and Franco type of dictatorship; and by the left, which took its orders from the Kremlin, Hitler's new ally. Under leadership less adroit than that of President Roosevelt, aid to the Allies would have been blocked.

The Record strenuously supported Roosevelt's foreign policy and insisted that he must carry on for a third term. The nation's newspapers were as solidly aligned against him in 1940 as they had been in 1936.

At Roosevelt's urging I undertook publication of a liberal weekly, the National Record. For its initial issue, September 25, 1940, he wrote:

A national weekly dedicated to giving a square deal to the New Deal can perform a great service in this campaign. Many sections of this great country are without a liberal newspaper. One of the bulwarks of our democracy is freedom of the press, but we cannot enjoy the full benefits of a free press if it presents only one side of the picture.

When he saw the first issue he wrote again:

DEAR DAVE: *Nothing succeeds like success and I do want to congratulate you very heartily on the splendid reception accorded the first issue of the National Record. I am glad to know that the prospects for an even larger circulation are so bright. I surely appreciate all you are doing to disseminate the truth.*

The National Record was a compilation of Philadelphia Record editorials, political articles, and cartoons. The Democratic National Committee purchased 5,000,000 copies for $50,000 to distribute through State Democratic Committees. This $50,000 defrayed the cost of newsprint. The Record donated the editorial work as a contribution to the cause.

Max Ways, later to become an editor of Time, was in charge of the project. He did a masterful job. Charlie Michelson, publicity director of the Democratic National Committee, was so enthusiastic he circularized state, county and city Democratic Committees throughout the nation urging them to purchase extra copies at a cent each. We sold 15,000,000 of the five weekly editions, an average of 3,000,000 per issue.

Most appreciative of the National Record was the Kelly-Nash machine in Chicago. It ordered 1,000,000 copies in addition to the 500,000 allotted to it by the National Committee. Instead of a check for $10,000, we received, by registered mail, a shoe box containing a thousand checks and money orders. In a letter Kelly explained that "the only way to be sure the National Record is distributed is to make each Division Captain pay for his own. If any of the checks bounce, we will make good." None of them did. It was a well-disciplined machine.

After the 1940 election President Roosevelt wanted me to continue the National Record as a permanent weekly. "It will be the nucleus of the national daily we'll start when I retire in 1945."

"I'll continue publication of the National Record if the Democratic National Committee will buy two hundred thousand subscriptions at fifty cents each for distribution through state and county Democratic Committees," was my proposition. "I'll raise a quarter of a million to develop paid circulation." The President called up Ed (Edward J.) Flynn, who had succeeded Jim Farley as chairman of the Democratic National Committee, and asked him to make such an agreement with me.

"Even the President of the United States can't draw blood from a stone," Flynn said when I saw him. "I have a deficit of five hundred thousand to meet and I don't know where I'm going to get the money. It's all right for the President to tell me to agree to pay you a hundred thousand dollars but I won't do it when I haven't got it and don't know where I'm going to get it."

Because of newsprint shortage as well as Flynn's lack of cooperation I abandoned the project. I am sorry that I did. The country needed then, as it does still, a national liberal weekly to counterbalance the conservatism of the press. In 1944 we again issued five editions of the National Record but newsprint rationing held the circulation to 5,000,000.

All I have left from much effort and high hopes are a few letters. The President signed "Subscription No. 1 to the National Record." He insisted on paying the dollar subscription price. I marked the dollar bill with his initials and the date, planning to frame it and hang it in my office. When I gave up the project, I sent the dollar back with a sour letter. The President returned it to me with the following warning on mutilating currency:

> DEAR DAVE, *I find that I cannot keep the currency because some-one has violated the law and, if this were discovered, he would go to jail. I do not want the "corpus delicti" addressed to me so I am sending the "corpus" back to you! Frame it but don't pass it!*

It was characteristic of the man to take time out for humor in the midst of the grim task of preparing for the greatest war in history. He appreciated how disappointed I felt. A letter of sympathy would only have aggravated my feelings. Instead he took the trouble to make me laugh and forget it. He was a political genius if ever there was one.

XX

Before and After
Pearl Harbor

I had promised Jill to stay home that particular Sunday, June 22, 1941. I phoned the office at noon to ask if there was anything on the wires. "Hitler has invaded Russia," was the answer. When I reached the office a few minutes later Harry Saylor was meeting with the editorial writers.

"How are you handling it?" I asked.

"The Allies welcome Russia to their side," was their position.

"But it isn't that simple," I protested. "So far this has been a war of democracy against dictatorship, free states against police states. Stalin is as ruthless a dictator as Hitler. With Russia one of the Allies, what are we fighting for? It becomes a war without principle. How can free states and slave states make common cause or lasting peace?"

"You don't mean you're not glad Russia's on our side?" Saylor barked.

"When a man is fighting a bloodthirsty tiger he welcomes any help, even from a skunk," I retorted. "But that doesn't mean he has to make a pet of the skunk."

When neither Saylor nor any other of the editorial board would buy my point of view, I said I would write the editorial. I phoned Bill (William C.) Bullitt who happened to be in Philadelphia. He came to my office and together we wrote "A Plague on Both Their Houses." As far as I know, this was the only editorial which took the position that alliance with Russia might help win the war but would destroy the peace. It advised against giving Russia lend-lease aid or any position in the council of the Allies. Its keyline was a repetition of my editorial of February 15, 1938: "There can be no united front for democracy with enemies of democracy." Under the desperate circumstances of the moment it may not have been a realistic or expedient editorial. But I am still glad that I wrote it. When I saw President Roosevelt a few days later he cut me down to size.

"Dave, your editorial does not make it any easier for me," he said. "We must help the Allies destroy Hitler before we can talk peace. I'm going to give lend-lease and every other aid I can to Russia. If Hitler takes Russia, Great Britain will be in double jeopardy. It's all right for Bill Bullitt and you to sit in your office and concoct highfalutin editorials. But the Allies have to win the war if democracy is to survive."

✻   ✻   ✻   ✻   ✻

Almost completely bald, Bill was a good-looking replica of Yul Brunner, with many of that actor's mannerisms—an abrupt, positive style of speech which was offset by his brilliance and charm. Never neutral on any issue or person, he was always enthusiastically for or against a cause or an official. He shared my admiration of Roosevelt.

The Bullitts are an old and distinguished Philadelphia family. A statue of Bill's grandfather, author of the first charter of the present Philadelphia, stands in City Hall Square. As I had, Bill deserted law for newspaper work on the Philadelphia Public Ledger. After a hitch as foreign correspondent for the Ledger, he went into the State Department. An attaché of the Commission to Negotiate Peace, he accompanied President Woodrow Wilson to Paris in 1918. He was sent on a special mission to Moscow in 1919. He returned to predict that the Lenin government would succeed, that aid to Kerensky had been too little and too late, and that all the Allies had accomplished was to convince the Russian government and Russian people the world was against them. Our only realistic course, according to Bill, was to recognize the Soviet government and try to influence it to become a co-operative member of the family of nations. When the Administration rejected Bill's advice he resigned from the State Department.

But Bill kept urging recognition of Russia. Many of his critics insinuated he was emotionally involved because he had married the widow of John Reed, an American journalist who had organized the first Communist party in America, who had fought in the Russian Revolution and who is buried in the wall of the Kremlin.

To persist in his one-man crusade for recognition of Russia required character and courage. Bill had plenty of both. Meanwhile all the European nations recognized Soviet Russia and were doing business with her. The United States and the Latin American countries were the only holdouts. Bill found an unexpected ally in Senator William E. Borah of Idaho, chairman of the Foreign Relations Committee and one of the most influential members of the Senate.

I first met Bill Bullitt when he came to my office in 1929 to ask news and editorial support for a public meeting in Philadelphia urging recognition of Soviet Russia. "President Wilson's doctrine of self-determination requires that we recognize Russia," Bill said, and paraphrased Voltaire's declaration for free speech: "I may hate your form of government but I will fight for your right to try it out."

To a distinguished audience which packed the Academy of Music, Senator Borah delivered a powerful oration. He argued that recognition was not endorsement of a form of government, otherwise the United States would be guilty of accepting fascism, absolute monarchy, theocracy and other systems abhorrent to a free nation. Through Bullitt I met Borah and Mrs. Borah, who was her husband's secretary. Whenever I was in Washington I visited them and we became friends.

Mrs. Borah had been a newspaperwoman. She read twenty-five newspapers—among them the Record—to clip stories of interest to her husband. After she had suffered a severe attack of psittacosis, or parrot fever, the Senator phoned me the news that she was out of danger. "When she came out of the coma, Dave, what do you think was the first thing she asked for? The Philadelphia Record." Whenever I called on them, Mrs. Borah used to tell me, "The Record is the best-edited paper in the United States." The two Bills, Bullitt and Borah, certainly had me convinced. I became an ardent advocate of Soviet recognition, wrote many editorials on the subject and personally urged President Roosevelt to take the historic step which he did on November 16, 1933. He named Bullitt as our first Ambassador to the Soviet Union.

With Bill Bullitt, recognition of Russia was a matter of principle. There were other elements in the situation. Some of our biggest corporations were doing business with Russia, mostly selling industrial machinery. Because the United States had not recognized the Soviet government, they had to handle these transactions through British or French agents, which was costly and cumbersome. While Borah never mentioned this in his speeches I think it was an important factor in his support of recognition.

After his first year in Moscow Bill returned to the United States for a short vacation. He was highly enthusiastic. His embassy was the social center of Moscow. All the top government officials were frequent visitors. He was developing the friendliest relations with the Kremlin, which had agreed to stop subsidizing Communist organizations in the United States and other foreign countries.

A year later a completely disenchanted Bill resigned. The Russians had broken their promises. When Bill presented indisputable proof to the Kremlin that it was sending money and agents to the Communist Party in the United States, all he got was a brush-off. His daughter, Anne, who was embassy hostess, told me that when they returned to Moscow, after their two months' vacation, the atmosphere had changed. No one came to the embassy. They tried to get in touch with their hundreds of friends. All of them had disappeared, evaporated into thin air. Stalin had begun his bloody purges. Russians were afraid to be seen talking to Americans. "If a smallpox sign had been posted on the embassy door, it would not have been more isolated," Anne told me.

"You can't do business with the Russians," Bill reported to President Roosevelt. "You can't trust them." Bill was so emotional in his disappointment and disgust with the people whose cause he had espoused, that the President discounted his advice. "If I can keep their feet under the table negotiating, patience and justice will eventually win out," he told me. President Roosevelt may be proven right but "eventually" is a long word.

When Bullitt became persona non grata in Moscow the President appointed him Ambassador to France. He served there until our declaration of war in December, 1941, when he was named Ambassador-at-Large. Between these assignments he lived in his Philadelphia home. He was there when I called him to help me write an editorial on that Sunday afternoon of June, 1941.

In 1945 I persuaded Bill to run for Mayor of Philadelphia. I believed his distinguished record, together with those of his father and grandfather, would made him a sure winner. The Republicans were committed to running Barney (Bernard) Samuels, who, as president of the City Council, had become acting mayor on the death of Bob Lamberton. Aside from being a Republican ward leader, Samuels' only other activity had been as customers' man in a brokerage office. The Republicans realized that the difference in stature between the two candidates put them at a disadvantage. They proceeded to give Bill the works, resorting to the most dishonest, underhanded smears I have ever witnessed in any campaign, and I have battled through some pretty low ones.

Bill had written, in 1926, a satirical novel, *It's Not Done*, an attack on the bigotry and snobbishness of Philadelphia society. To lampoon the characters in his novel, Bill had them express the most extreme and bitter prejudices against Catholics, Negroes, and Jews. The Republicans picked these quotes out of context as expressions of Bill's sentiments. In the columns of the Record, in paid ads in other newspapers, and in pamphlets, we explained that these quotations in context had actually the opposite meaning to what the Republicans were implying; that Bill, a true liberal, had been attacking the narrow-mindness of which these quotations were examples. The Republicans kept repeating: "Bullitt cannot deny he wrote these insults to minorities."

A week before election, the city was blanketed by a pamphlet, "Bullitt the Fascist." The frontispiece was a picture of Bill walking with Goering, Hitler's second in command. Other pictures showed Bill sitting beside Pétain, collaborationist President of France, and conferring with fascist leaders. Again we had to explain these were dirty frauds. As an official representative of the United States at the burial of Pilsudski, Poland's national hero, Ambassador Bullitt had to accept the place assigned him in the funeral procession which happened to be beside Goering. As Ambassador to France, it was his duty to call on Pétain, etc.

I sent the pamphlet by messenger to the White House and phoned for help. The President promised an immediate letter. That was the Thursday before election. When the letter had not arrived by Saturday morning I did F.D.R. a grave injustice. I thought he was letting us down. Late Sunday night I happened to notice a large envelope on my secretary's desk. It had been lying there since Saturday evening where a stupid copy boy had told the White House messenger to leave it. I stopped the presses and ran the President's letter in the third of the Monday's edition which had not already been distributed. But it was too late to get the full benefit of this important document before Tuesday's election.

The President wrote in part:

DEAR DAVE:

That pamphlet about Bill Bullitt is a mass of falsehoods.

Here, for instance, are some highlights:

Bullitt attended the funeral of Marshal Pilsudski as representative of the United States. When you or I attend an official funeral we walk into the church in the procession with anybody we are told to walk with. It is not our choice—and this campaign pamphlet is a rather unintelligent attempt to imply an untruth.

In the case of the fall of Paris . . . Bullitt did the obvious and right thing—used every effort to save Paris and its civilian population from destruction and death. This attack on Bullitt is another piece of dirty political falsification.

These and other attacks should be exposed not in a defensive way but as an offensive.

Most sincerely,
FRANKLIN D. ROOSEVELT

Of all the office snafus I endured during my thirty-five years as a publisher, this griped me the most. It was partly my fault. When the President's letter did not arrive as promised, I should have called the White House. But there was another cause for the delay of one day in delivering the letter. In a recent visit to the Roosevelt Library at Hyde Park, I found that the President had written two letters. In the first version, which was not sent, the opening sentence reads, "I think that pamphlet about Bill Bullitt is one of the dirtiest bunch of lies I have ever seen." Evidently F.D.R. was as furious as I was, but on reading it over, decided the language was too strong. As editor of Roosevelt's personal letters, Elliot Roosevelt prints the second version with a note below, "In spite of this letter Bullitt was defeated by 60,000." Elliot did not know that the letter reached less than a hundred thousand Philadelphians.

Bullitt was an excellent campaign speaker but his aristocratic appearance and Harvard accent fitted into the Republican picture of a social snob. It was a grim travesty that this fighting liberal, who had dedicated his life to government service, should have had his public image so distorted by lies. On election night, as the returns indicated defeat, the lost letter was uppermost in my mind. I kept repeating to myself from Poor Richard's proverb: "And all for the want of a horseshoe nail the battle was lost."

❖   ❖   ❖   ❖   ❖

"Sorry I can't tell you of my talk with Joe Pew," I said as Marvin MacIntyre came into the President's office to remind him I had overstayed my time and he was keeping an ambassador waiting. That was in the spring of 1941.

The President waved Marvin out of the room and motioned me to sit down again.

"Where did you have this talk?" he asked.

"In his office."

"What were you doing in Joe Pew's office?" The President could not have looked more surprised or disgusted if I had said, "In a bawdy house."

"Soliciting Sun Oil advertising."

"The Record carries Sun Oil ads?" The President was reflecting his anger at several big oil companies which were reluctant to allocate oil to the Allies.

"Mr. President, ladies must live," I replied.

F.D.R. leaned back in his chair to laugh. "Tell me about it," he said.

It was a bizarre tale of opposition to helping the Allies. J. Howard Pew, older brother of Joe and head of Sun Oil, was a liberal conservative. When we lunched together a number of times we found we held many views in common. Howard was a wise and well-balanced man on every subject but one—he was an intense Anglophobe. During the First World War he had been a member of the committee in charge of oil distribution. Against the advice of this committee, President Wilson, at the request of the British Ambassador, insisted American tankers be diverted from the Far East to the war area. When these ships arrived at European ports, they could not unload because the storage tanks were already filled. Meanwhile the British had sent their tankers to the Far East to capture that important trade.

Howard was interested in my editorials on monetary policy. He invited Joe to join us at lunch and hear my views. Joe's disagreement with everything I said was so vehement it bordered on rudeness. That was the last of my luncheons with Howard. But my newspapers continued to enjoy a fair share of Sun Oil advertising until the Record attacked Joe's activity in local politics.

Sun Oil's public relations man came to see me. He told me Howard did not like this mixing of business and politics. If I would come to the Sun Oil office and make my peace, advertising would be resumed. An appointment was made for the next day at five. I was shown into Howard's office. He explained that, while he was head of the company, advertising was one of Joe's departments and the order must come from him. He tipped me off that his brother was especially hurt by a Jerry Doyle cartoon depicting Joe as Mother Hubbard feeding hungry politicians. Howard led me into Joe's office. It was not yet five-thirty. I told Joe I was sorry if the cartoon had offended him, "But now that you are the Republican leader of Philadelphia and Pennsylvania, if not of the United States, you must expect to be the subject of public comment." Joe said he was going to resume advertising in the Record but he wanted me to understand his point of view. He launched into a ti-

rade against the New Deal and Roosevelt which lasted until 8 P.M.
I tried to interrupt with the suggestion that we adjourn to a restaurant. "Only a few minutes more," Joe persisted and continued his
monologue. He was obviously emotionally upset. He boasted that
he had his own private detective force in Washington which was
smarter than the FBI, and kept him informed on every secret move
of the Administration. He described in detail how his operatives
had broken into Tommy the Cork's (Thomas G. Corcoran) desk,
removed a preliminary draft of the Court-packing bill (to increase
membership of the U. S. Supreme Court to twelve,) photostated it,
and returned it without Tommy being any the wiser.

"I'm not surprised at what you tell me," the President said. "Joe
boasts that he has tapped the White House wires."

"Has he?" I asked.

"Wouldn't you like to know?" the President teased. "But absolutely no publicity, Dave, or I'll be in bad with the FBI and you'll
lose your Sun Oil advertising."

*   *   *   *   *

Joe (Joseph Medill) Patterson, publisher of the New York
Daily News, was another example of emotional opposition to aid-
ing the Allies. In Patterson's case it was the more striking since he
had been an ardent supporter of Roosevelt in 1932, 1936 and 1940.
As the only two New York newspaper publishers for Roosevelt, we
used to get together occasionally for lunch. Whenever I differed
with the Administration, Patterson took me to task. "So you're
wiser than the President," he would say. "Dave, how do you get
that way?"

But when Roosevelt proposed lend-lease, Joe turned on him like
a ton of bricks. From then until Pearl Harbor the News was more
vitriolic and abusive than the Chicago Tribune.

When the New York News came out against lend-lease the
President asked me, "What's biting Joe Patterson? He was purring
like a Cheshire cat when he was up to Hyde Park to see me a few
weeks ago." My several phone calls to Joe went unanswered. I had
to report, "He's off me too." I never saw Joe again. I thought I knew

what had happened. As a captain of artillery Joe had seen a lot of action in World War I. He had talked to me of the disgusting horrors of war. Inside his rather gruff exterior was a hypersensitive soul. The fear that his son might be called on to undergo the same ordeal preyed on Joe's mind.

A few days after Pearl Harbor Joe went to see the President who told me of their meeting: "Joe's first words were, 'I'm at your service, Mr. President.' I did not ask him to sit down. I said, 'Joe, your first assignment is to go back to your office and read over your editorials.' He turned on his heel and left."

Marvin McIntyre happened to be with us when F.D.R. gave this account. "Joe was crying when he came out of your office," Marvin said.

"That proves that Joe's soft inside," was my interpretation.

"Were they tears of contrition or anger?" the President asked. They were tears of anger, as Joe's renewal of his bombardment of the President proved.

I became involved in Joe's pre-Pearl Harbor attacks on the President. John P. O'Donnell, head of Joe's Washington Bureau, was constantly heckling the President at his press conferences. O'Donnell's questions and innuendoes got F.D.R.'s goat. One day the President happened to have an Iron Cross, the Nazi decoration for bravery, lying on his desk. That morning John's column had reported that the Army was issuing contraceptives to WACs. The President closed the press conference by presenting the Iron Cross to John, who, the President said, had earned it by service to the Fuehrer.

Bob (Colonel Robert S.) Allen, head of our Washington Bureau, told me that O'Donnell was an outspoken admirer of the Nazis. Both Patterson and O'Donnell had visited Germany in the spring of 1940. On their return O'Donnell said that Hitler was remaking Germany into a great country. Bob asked John how he felt about Hitler's ruthless treatment of minorities. John replied that when the Germans built a highway they went straight through and tore down everything in the way. If, in rebuilding Germany, minorities had to be eliminated, it was only an incident in the general plan.

*   *   *   *   *

In April of 1941 I took Jill on a long-promised auto trip along the Skyline Drive. We spent the first night in Washington and sat up until the small hours gossiping with Bob.

From habit, I awoke early. So as not to disturb Jill, I went to the coffee shop for breakfast. On the front page of the Washington Times-Herald was an exclusive story by John O'Donnell, to the effect that the President had broken faith with Congress and the American people by secretly ordering the Navy and Coast Guard to convoy munitions ships to Great Britain. Alongside the story was an editorial attack on the President, signed by the Times-Herald's publisher, Cissy Patterson, sister of Joe Patterson. While the two papers were under separate ownership, they shared the services of O'Donnell and the Washington Bureau of the New York Daily News.

The story was obviously a canard based on little or no evidence. My suspicion was confirmed when I picked up the Washington Post. Secretary of the Navy Knox denied that such orders had been issued.

My blood boiled. It was an outrage that the President should be subjected to such insults. I hurried to our Washington office. As I unlocked the door and switched on the United Press teletype machine, the keys began to click. They spelled out a dispatch from the White House. Stephen Early, press secretary to the President, at a special early morning press conference, announced that he had been authorized by President Roosevelt to brand the Times-Herald story as "a deliberate lie."

Just as the clatter of the teletype paused at the end of this statement, Bob Allen bustled through the door. "Bustled" describes Bob's peculiar mode of locomotion. He is short, heavy-set. In those days he was in a perpetual state of motion and emotion. He dramatized everything in which he was interested.

Drew Pearson and Bob had been representing the Baltimore Sun papers when they wrote a book, Washington Merry-Go-Round. It was too liberal and outspoken for the conservative Baltimore papers. Bob and Drew were fired. But the book had made such a hit, they started a syndicated column of Washington comment. The Record was the first subscriber. Bob became head of our

Washington Bureau while Drew devoted full time to the column.

Bob was later to serve with distinction on General Patton's staff as head of Intelligence. Shortly before V-E Day, he was severely wounded and taken prisoner. His right arm was amputated at a German field hospital. When our troops arrived, three days later, they found Colonel Allen in command. He had talked the medical staff into surrendering to him. As a token of their capitulation, the doctors had deposited their side arms in a storage room of which Bob held the key. When I heard the details of this exploit, I told Bob it only proved what I had always said: "You could talk a brass monkey into climbing a tree."

"Bob, look at this dispatch," was my greeting to him that morning in Washington. After reading it, he walked to the other side of the room without saying anything.

"What's your reaction?" I asked.

"It's just what two fighting liberals like the President and you deserve. I told you all about it. I warned you about John O'Donnell last summer. And what did you do? You let him go on adding insult to injury at press conferences."

"But, Bob, it was hard to believe because O'Donnell represented a paper which, at that time, was supporting Roosevelt." I was trying to justify my inaction.

"That's no excuse," was Bob's sharp rejoinder. "Patterson has been trying to throw Roosevelt for the past six months and you haven't called him once."

Bob worked me into such a lather I wrote an editorial denouncing both Joe and Cissy Patterson, as well as O'Donnell, and wired it to the Record. O'Donnell sued the Philadelphia Record for $50,000. The case dragged through four courts over five years. It was finally settled out of court by the Bulletin Company, after it had bought my properties, for $8,000. I had made the mistake of naming a reporter instead of confining my attack to the publishers. The juries always brought in verdicts for the employee against the employer. But I did stop John's sniping at the President at press conferences.

*　　　*　　　*　　　*　　　*

Again, just before Pearl Harbor, I encountered more of this reluctance to aid the Allies. In October, 1941, Leon Henderson, director of the Division of Civilian Suppies, proposed that automobile production be cut 50 per cent, so that more men and material could be devoted to the manufacture of armaments. William S. Knudsen, head of Army procurement, opposed this order, contending that a 25 per cent cut would be sufficient. Knudsen had just resigned the presidency of General Motors to help the government in arming the Allies and itself.

In an editorial, the Record said it did not know whether Henderson's or Knudsen's calculations were correct but, in this emergency, if there was any question, it should be decided on the side of national safety by cutting automobile output 50 per cent.

Our Detroit office phoned that because of this editorial General Motors had canceled all advertising in the Record. I blew up with righteous indignation—a not unusual phenomenon in those days. I decided to go to Detroit myself to find out how those reactionary isolationists were thinking. During a couple of hours' layover in New York I went to see Red (Paul) Garrett, vice president of General Motors in charge of public relations, who had formerly been financial editor of the New York Post.

"This country ought to know what a patriotic organization General Motors is," I thundered at Red. "How dedicated you are to freedom of the press!"

"Hold your horses," Red kept telling me. "Calm down. It's all a misunderstanding."

But I was too incensed to listen and took the train to Detroit. When I arrived there the next morning, the advertising had already been reinstated. Red had worked fast.

"As long as you're here," the head of my Detroit office said, "we want you to meet the division chiefs of General Motors. It may serve as an antidote to future misunderstanding." One of these executives had newspaper clippings spread over his desk. Pointing to them, he said, "Mr. Stern, I have here fifty editorials on the Knudsen-Henderson controversy—forty-nine for Knudsen, you alone for Henderson. Now tell me why you have to be different."

I understand how this man's mind worked, or did not work. For years his one object in life had been to make and sell more cars. That motive transcended and obliterated every other objective. He was as conditioned to make automobiles as a racehorse is to run. He was as incapable of thinking objectively of autos as King Midas was of gold.

Pearl Harbor cleansed the nation of this business-as-usual state of mind. The smog of isolationists and Naziphiles evaporated.

    ✸   ✸   ✸   ✸   ✸

Wartime publishing presented new problems. As both the Record and Courier-Post were young organizations, we were especially hard hit by the departure of many executives for war service.

It was the unwritten law that servicemen would have their old jobs waiting for them when they returned, so senior executives shouldered the work of two or three men. Jill and I closed our Haddonfield home and moved to a small apartment near the Record office. I returned to the long hours which had been my regular schedule in New Brunswick, Springfield, and Camden. My visits to the White House became less frequent. But I did happen in on the end of a session between the President and General Marshall, who was leaving as I entered.

"I need him, Dave," the President said, motioning to the General, who was already standing. "I need him here by my side and he wants to go to Europe."

Much has been written as to why Eisenhower was chosen for supreme command. In that instant I think I caught the play. President Roosevelt wanted to run the war himself. Once Marshall was in the field he would make his own decisions. The President felt that would leave him sitting on the sidelines. Loyal friend and great soldier, Marshall gave in to his Commander in Chief. He remained in Washington. But he did not relinquish direct control. Instead of placing a senior general in supreme command of the Allied forces, he selected Dwight D. Eisenhower, a younger officer who would follow the strategy formulated by the President and Marshall.

The war was a stimulus to the President. He appeared even more alert, quick-minded, and enthusiastic than ever and always in a good humor. During those war years, I would come to the White House, worn by my petty problems, to find the President exuding vim, vigor, and optimism. He usually greeted me with a gay quip. When I happened to be wearing a blue shirt and new blue suit, it was, "Here comes Dave the Hair Shirt, all dressed up like Roy Howard."

Another time I came to the White House to protest his Russian policy. To the President's cheery "How are you?" I answered, "Sick at heart, Mr. President." He sensed this was the opening for a tirade. Before I could launch it, he interrupted, "What's ailing you —indigestion?" I laughed. All the wind was taken out of my sails and the President proceeded to knock down my argument before I made it.

Often he would tell me I had the softest job in the war "writing editorials telling the President what to do, which isn't always as easy as it looks in print."

Not until after his return from Yalta, in February 1945, did I notice any weariness in the President's face or manner. At this, our last meeting, several times he asked me to repeat what I had said. Always in the past he had his answer ready before I finished a question. Now his mind was working more slowly. But I did not sense the impending tragedy. His death, six weeks later, was a terrible shock. I had come to love this valiant warrior. Now I understood how my father had felt when Lincoln died. He had cried harder, he told me, than at the death of his own beloved father.

Roosevelt's death made me realize how much his wisdom and courage had meant to me. When the fight for the New Deal was bitter and difficult, his was the stimulus which kept me talking out boldly against odds. Now that he was gone, I would continue my support of the New Deal, but the zest for the fight was no longer there.

A week after President Roosevelt's death, President Truman and I were standing in front of a portrait of Roosevelt which had just been hung in the President's office. We were reminiscing about our great friend when Sam (Samuel I.) Rosenman came in.

"Mr. President, here's final proof of your message to Congress for your O.K.," Rosenman said.

As President Truman took the document he looked up at the portrait.

"I think *he* would have approved of this." There were tears in Truman's eyes as he said it.

I knew then that Roosevelt had been wise in his choice of a successor. " 'What would Roosevelt have done?' will be my guide line," President Truman told me. He lived up to it. When support of the Fair Employment Practices Act in 1948 meant revolt of the Southern states, President Truman declared, "I'm not retreating from a single one of his [Roosevelt's] measures, even if it spells defeat." That is what won him the 1948 election. The people sensed the sincerity, dedication, and courage of the man.

Roosevelt's detractors have made much of the concessions which he and Churchill granted Stalin at Yalta to induce Russia to declare war against Japan. The same critics have attacked President Truman for ordering the atomic bomb attack on Japan. They overlook the gruesome responsibility which faced both Roosevelt and Truman. Invasion of Japan appeared the only way to end the war in the Pacific. It was estimated this operation would cost a million American casualties, 250,000 killed, 750,000 wounded—to say nothing of Japanese casualties.

In July of 1945, I toured the Pacific war area. I had hoped to see Tom, who was stationed in Honolulu as publisher of the Army newspaper Stars and Stripes of the Pacific. I missed him. He had been sent back to the States to buy equipment for two additional printing plants. Tom had drawn up specifications for machinery capable of producing 100,000 copies a day.

"That won't do at all," his commanding officer told him. "We want a million copies a day." Tom revised his plans and bought the equipment. It was crated and ready for shipment when V-J Day came and he received word to sell it. This order to produce a million copies a day indicates the magnitude of the invasion operation which was contemplated. As many as three million men would have been involved.

Admiral Nimitz impressed me as the ablest commander of the war. I lived with him for a week. He explained why the invasion of Japan was more difficult and would cost more casualties than

the invasion of Normandy. This calculating in advance what percentage of troops would be killed and wounded made my blood
run cold.

On that trip, General Douglas MacArthur told me, "Some day
there will be a bomb, the size of this desk, which will destroy a
whole city. The nature of war will change." When I left him I
told my traveling companion, Bill (William R.) Matthews, editor
and publisher of the Tucson Star, "The General talks like Buck
Rogers." We thought he was dreaming of the future. Within two
weeks an atomic bomb fell on Hiroshima.

The answer to the critics of Roosevelt and Truman is the question: "What would you do if you had to order a quarter of a
million of your fellow citizens to certain death?" Every normal
man would answer: "I would do anything and everything to
minimize the casualties." When Russia declared war, Japan would
have to divide its forces to protect its west coast as well as its
east. That would reduce American casualties.

"You gave old sourpuss (Stalin) everything but the kitchen
stove," I remarked to President Roosevelt at our last meeting a
week after he returned from Yalta.

"First things first," the President replied. "We must win the
war before we can settle the peace. I told you and Bill Bullitt that
when Russia came over to our side in 1941. It still goes. And I
told you if we are fair and patient when peace comes, the Russians will respond in kind. That still goes."

I am impatient of "breakfast table editors," the term Hank
Eaton applied to critics who dissect what the reporters and editors,
working under time pressure, wrote and put together the night before. Roosevelt and Truman acted as any patriotic American would
have acted—to win the war with the least sacrifice of lives.

❋   ❋   ❋   ❋   ❋

Shortage of manpower was only one of the difficulties of wartime publishing. Shortage of newsprint was another. The government rationed it on the basis of consumption during the three pre-
war years—1939, 1940 and 1941. These happened to be the years
when the Courier-Post's and the Record's circulations had been

reduced by Annenberg competition and the Catholic boycott. So we were harder hit than our competitors.

Pop Gilman died in 1940. I continued to buy my newsprint through the Gilman Paper Company, now headed by his son, Charles. The mill at Gilman, Vermont, had been converted from newsprint to kraft (wrapping) paper. Gilman supplied our needs through other mills. We should have dealt directly with these mills but because of the long association we continued the old arrangement. Whether through oversight or to effect some trade advantage—I have never found out which—Gilman failed to renew one of its contracts with a Canadian mill. This put us in such a tight jacket that we had to print the Record on kraft paper. Under its contract Gilman was compelled to supply us with kraft when it could not deliver newsprint.

I went to Canada and bought an old newsprint machine which had been junked. I arranged for its erection in a pulp mill with which I made a contract for pulp. This newsprint mill went into operation after I suspended publication in 1947.

Despite these difficulties, the Record prospered. In 1946 it bought WCAU, the leading radio station in Philadelphia. My associates had been urging this move for some years. The other Philadelphia newspapers had radio stations. Newspaper ownership of stations had become accepted practice. I no longer felt bound by my conversation with President Roosevelt ten years before.

The Record paid $3,000,000 for WCAU, up to that time the highest price for a radio station. Recently this station, plus television facilities, was sold for $20,000,000. To finance the purchase of WCAU, I sent for my friend Smith Davis, a newspaper broker and financial adviser. Back in 1926, he had walked into my Camden office and shown me how the Courier-Post Company could save money by borrowing $1,500,000 and calling its preferred stock. He placed the loan with the Cleveland Society for Savings, the oldest savings bank in the Middle West.

The arrangement proved so satisfactory that ten years later we made a new loan with the same bank for $2,500,000. Now I needed $5,500,000. Smith thought he could get it from the Jefferson Standard Life Insurance Company of Greensboro, North Carolina. Together we composed a three-page letter of application. I mention three pages because the answer, the insurance company's letter of commitment, prepared by its lawyers in consultation with mine, was thirty-five pages long. That was par for the course. What laymen can state clearly in one page requires ten of legal verbiage.

To see the deal through, Smith Davis, Dan Lowenthal, the Record's lawyer, and I went to Greensboro. The only important point at issue was the interest rate. We had offered four per cent. Jefferson wanted four and a half. In the tradition of Southern hospitality, after numerous cocktails we enjoyed a long and lavish lunch. Then the loan committee went into secret session. Its three members were Ralph C. Price, president of Jefferson and son of Julian Price, chairman of the Board and founder of the company; Joseph M. Bryan, vice president and son-in-law; and Julius C. Smith, general counsel.

While waiting for them to report I sat in the office of Julian Price, a distinguished white-haired gentleman who did not look his seventy-eight years. Between drinks of bourbon he told me the story of his life. He had started as a railroad telegrapher, become fed up with that noncompetitive job, helped to found a small insurance company of which he was sales manager, and built it to its present size and na'ional standing. He was proudest of its record of earning the highest return on its investments of any insurance company in America. That was the reason Jefferson took the trouble to investigate and make unusual loans such as that to the Record.

I had to respond with the story of my life. By this time we were both high. Then came the lachrymose phase. To avoid inheritance taxes Julian had given his stock and control of the company to his son and daughter. Julian assumed the role of King Lear: "What's the result? Here I am sitting on the outside, no longer a member of the loan committee, the fifth wheel on the automobile."

"Julian, we'll put those youngsters in their place," I proposed. Sentimental Tommy had to come to the rescue as he had with Ron Johnson in Colorado forty years before. "I've a hunch the committee will offer four and a quarter per cent. If they do, you tell them that you've already persuaded me to accept four and a half."

If it had been rehearsed, our plot could not have worked more smoothly. When the loan committee came to Julian's office to offer me a compromise of four and a quarter, Julian told them he had already made a better deal, and made sarcastic remarks about the business acumen of the younger generation. He was in high spirits at the dinner party that night.

On our way back to Philadelphia, Smith and Dan berated me for my "generosity." They figured the extra quarter of one per cent would cost the Record $65,000 over the twenty-year life of the loan. "More than double my fee for placing it," said Smith. "You pay Dan and me to look out for your interests and then go into a booze session with the chairman of the Board."

Announcement of the purchase of WCAU brought favorable comment, also gossip by our competitors that we had bitten off a mighty big chunk which might weaken our financial position. It was this gossip which gave the Newspaper Guild the idea we could not stand a strike and would be easy picking for a huge wage demand.

Settlement with Jefferson was set for sixty days after our visit to Greensboro. As is usual, the commitment specified that any substantial deterioration in the business of the Record during those sixty days would release Jefferson from its obligation. Suspension of publication, or even a strike, could be interpreted as a "substantial deterioration."

We had not given much thought to negotiating a new contract with the Newspaper Guild. Its contract with the Inquirer expired a month before ours. For years the Record had been forced to accept the terms of the Inquirer contract with a few minor differences. Practically, the contracts were duplicates.

This year, 1946, the Guild announced that it was going to postpone negotiations with the Inquirer and tackle the Record first. "We will stick a knife in the white underbelly of the enemy," the Guild attorney announced, paraphrasing Churchill's explanation of the Allied invasion of Italy prior to that of Normandy. To give an account of that knifing I must first review my labor relations in earlier years.

XXI

Labor Relations

Between the close of World War I in 1918 and the stock market crash in 1929, profits of industry increased 100 per cent, wages 25 per cent. In terms of a constant dollar, real wages were shrinking. At the same time, the farmers were going broke. These were the two basic causes of the devastating depression of 1930 to 1933.

I have Frank O. Lowden, who had so generously helped me buy the Springfield News in 1914, to thank for awakening me to the growing danger. After I left Springfield in 1919, we still kept in touch with each other. Whenever he came to New York I would go over to visit with him. I was active in his campaign for the Republican Presidential nomination. After his defeat in the 1920 convention he retired from public life but he still kept his interest in public affairs. He had a keen analytical mind.

"If factory workers do not have buying power they cannot consume what they make," he kept telling me. "Unions should be encouraged to raise wages at the same time that we raise crop prices. We need strong trade unions to maintain the balance between wages and profits. Otherwise we can never achieve a stable economy.

"Allowing domestic consuming power to dry up spells disaster. The conservatives are delaying this disaster by a shortsighted expedient. They are increasing foreign trade. Since Europe and South America are broke we are lending them money with which to buy our goods. But eventually we will have to pay the pied piper."

*   *   *   *   *

After I bought the Camden Post-Telegram and became a monopoly publisher, in 1926, a more personal and immediate concern with unionism was added to the economic interest which Lowden had inspired. My staff was expanding so rapidly I could not keep in touch with it, as I had on smaller operations in the past. A remark overheard in the lavatory sparked this new attitude.

"Old Pinchpenny won't allow supper money, let alone overtime pay." The bookkeeper, who was beefing to a pal, had not noticed me enter. Instead of returning to my office I went to the accounting department. Although the clock showed ten the full force was at work.

I stepped into the glass cubicle which was the office of Alfred Neef, assistant treasurer of the Courier-Post Company. He had come with me from Springfield. A loyal associate, intent on saving money and keeping down petty expenses, he was indefatigable and expected everyone to follow his example.

"Why so late, Al?" I asked.

"You know our record," Neef proudly declaimed. "Every bill in the mail by the thirty-first." He explained that increasing business made it necessary to work two or three nights at the end of each month.

"What are you paying for this overtime?" I asked.

"Nothing," Neef replied. "The boys are glad to give a little extra time to keep up our record."

"Do you allow supper money?"

Neef was nettled. "There you go again, wanting me to add to those cursed petty expense vouchers which will eat us out of house and home." He had never recovered from the worry of those hectic payroll days in Springfield, when he sat biting his nails waiting for me to bring in the cash.

I wondered how many other such petty injustices were going on in the dozen or more departments into which the Courier-Post's force of five hundred was now divided. It was a new worry. On the previous newspapers which I had owned, the forces had been small enough for me to keep in touch with what everyone was doing and getting. I called most of my employees by their first names, knew their circumstances, and helped out in case of illness or family crisis. With a larger force such a personal relationship was no longer possible. A few nights before, I had been embarrassed when the Courier-Post reporter (assigned to a meeting at which I was presiding) had to introduce himself to me.

The next day I issued a general order that all nonunion departments were to pay for overtime as the unionized departments were already doing. I went over the payroll to find many "forgotten men," most of them old, loyal workers. The older a man gets, the more fearful he becomes of losing his job, the more hesitant to assert himself and ask for a raise. It would require constant supervision to prevent injustices. The only sure protection for all employees was complete unionization.

When I bought the Record, in 1928, it was nonunion as were all the other Philadelphia newspapers. Twenty years before, the publishers had driven the unions out. I set to work unionizing the Record. I would practice what I preached. It was not as easy a task as I had anticipated.

The Typographical Union was the first I tackled. Many of my men had formerly been union members. In the big strike, they had "scabbed" and were subject to heavy fines if they ever rejoined. The local union officials were willing to cancel these fines but they had to obtain permission from international headquarters in Indianapolis. It was six months before this was forthcoming. Indianapolis was suspicious. In the union's one hundred years' history I was the first publisher to invite it in. Then I found that many of my typographers, mostly the older men, were so bitterly against the union they refused to rejoin, fine or no fine. We finally worked out a compromise that these veteran holdouts did not have to join the union. It took more than a year and endless palaver between union officials and a committee representing the anti-union faction before a contract was signed. I did not have as much trouble with the pressmen, stereotypers, mailers, and truck drivers, but three years were consumed in unionizing the mechanical departments.

Then I turned my attention to the news department. There was already talk in New York of organizing a news writers' guild. Both Harry Saylor and I urged our senior reporters to join the movement. In April, 1934, I was the first publisher to sign a contract with the American Newspaper Guild. This was for the Record. Similar contracts for the New York Post and Camden papers followed shortly thereafter. I helped to write these first contracts. At my suggestion, a provision for severance pay was included. I had picked up the idea when the publisher of a Paris newspaper showed me around his plant. In one room were a group of old men with long beards. "They are our reporters," the French publisher told me.

"Why such old men?" I asked.

"The longer a man works for us, the more we have to pay him when he leaves," he explained. "That makes us reluctant to change. Most of our employees work here until they die.

"Severance pay was fine when it started. It protected the worker from capricious firing. But over the years it has outgrown its original purpose and has become a serious handicap to maintaining an efficient staff."

I should have heeded the Paris publisher's warning. Severance pay has been distorted by the Guild. Some present contracts provide that a man who resigns to take a job on another paper can still collect severance pay. A publisher pays an employee a bonus for *going over* to a competitive newspaper.

When the first Guild contract was signed, I addressed the Record news staff of two hundred, assembled in the city room. "The Guild can raise the status of the newsman to that of a member of a learned profession," I said. "I want to live to see the newspaper editor and reporter held in equal public esteem with the doctor and lawyer. To get this program started, I suggest that senior staff members hold seminars for juniors. The Record will pay a twenty-five-dollar fee to the editor who conducts a seminar. We will also pay for courses at Penn or Temple for members of the staff recommended by the Guild. Draw up your educational plan. You can count on my co-operation."

Nothing came of my idea. Two editors started seminars but attendance was so poor they abandoned them after a few sessions. I never received an educational plan.

Our relations with the Guild were amicable. An apocryphal story went the rounds that Mac (A. McC.) Parker, chairman of the Guild negotiating committee, and I played a game of chess to decide whether a vacation clause be included in the 1935 contract. Here is what actually happened. Late one night Mac came to my office and persuaded me to accept a vacation clause which merely formalized what was already our practice. This business finished, I invited Mac to play a game of chess. He won. Mac went back to the newsroom to announce his two victories in reverse: "I beat the boss at chess and I got the vacation clause"—an example of how news can be twisted, even in a newsroom. I mention the trivial incident because it indicates my free and easy relations with the Guild those first two years.

Mac, ace reporter, and Mrs. Mac were colorful personalities in Philadelphia newspaperdom. They had twelve children. I have always suspected Mac dramatized their family problems. One story went that Mac became so incensed at his children's overuse of the phone that he persuaded the telephone company to install a pay station in his home. Mrs. Parker was sitting on the porch when the collector presented himself. "Walk right in," she said. "Only our children use that phone." The collector came out with twenty nickels and two hundred slugs. I was sorry when Mac left us to become a most successful radio news broadcaster. When the Guild struck he wrote Harry Saylor, "I want to run away and hide from the fact that I was vice-president of the Guild and partly responsible for selling that poison to the Boss, a real friend of working newspapermen."

After my recognition of the Guild in 1934 it had been my intention to organize the advertising, circulation, and financial departments in the appropriate A. F. of L. unions. Then my force would have been completely unionized. That I did not carry out this program was a costly blunder. I have a plausible excuse. In December 1933 I had bought the New York Post. This so engrossed my time and energy that I interrupted my labor relations plan. It proved a disastrous postponement.

＊　　　＊　　　＊　　　＊　　　＊

"What's the worst that has happened while I've been away?" was my flippant question to Harry Saylor. I was feeling on top of the world on my return from a month's vacation in England with Jill in September of 1936.

"It's plenty worse," was Harry's answer. "The Guild has gone CIO, changed itself from a craft to an industrial union which covers everyone not already organized, advertising solicitors, stenographers, clerks, accountants, telephone operators, even cleaning women and janitors. Editorial workers are now in the minority—two hundred in my departments to three hundred and fifty in the others."

"What made them do such a thing?" I asked.

"A new radical element has taken control," was Saylor's explanation.

I phoned Heywood Broun, national president of the Guild. During the formative days of the new union we had become close friends. A great hulk of a man, he was a fascinating many-sided character—brilliant columnist, starry-eyed idealist, race-track habitué and eccentric bohemian.

"Heywood, what in hell have you gone and done?" I asked. "What of all our fine talk about raising the status of the reporter through a craft guild?"

"Dave, the new setup gives us more power," Heywood explained.

"Power over whom and for what?"

"Power over publishers for more pay." Heywood was frank and to the point.

A few weeks later, the Guild Reporter, weekly house organ of the union, carried an editorial to the effect that there could never be friendship between labor and management. The two forces must always be in conflict. This was the straight, unadulterated Marx-Lenin line. The Commies were in control of the Guild and of its whimsical, fuzzy-minded president.

When I negotiated a new Guild contract in 1937, the atmosphere had changed. There was a concerted effort to heckle and insult me. I complained of a Guild letter to its members which made many misstatements, and demanded a correction. The negotiating committee bluntly told me, "According to the Wagner Act, management is not permitted to answer back even if a union lies about it."

After this unpleasant meeting, one of my editors overheard a Guild officer boasting, "We certainly got the boss's goat. Three of us are assigned to interrupt and annoy him so as to keep him off balance." Because of this new tactic, I was forced to give up personal meetings with the Guild. I engaged Gil (Gilbert J.) Kraus, a lawyer who specialized in labor law. We had so much work for him that he gave up his practice and became vice president of the Record Company. Union negotiations had developed into a complicated and technical business. The Guild contract was now a lengthy document listing thirty different classifications of employment.

The Guild persisted in a steady drive of encroachment on management. It demanded that more and more executives be included in its contract, assistant city editors, assistant night editors, slot men (head of the copy desk).

Since each year the Guild negotiated its contract with the Inquirer before it tackled us, we were powerless to stop this creeping invasion. By 1946, when the Guild struck, there were only six executives in the news department, out of a force of two hundred and five, who were exempt from Guild membership. Even my secretary, Ed (Edward B.) Maguire, whom I had named assistant to the publisher, was compelled to join.

Meanwhile the Guild kept up a continual personal attack. They issued bulletins to show up "the false friend of labor who wraps himself in an American flag while he connives to cheat and exploit his workers." These charges were outright lies or distorted half-truths. For instance, a girl was docked a day's pay for being absent to attend her mother's funeral. When she explained this to her department head, she received an immediate refund. But a Guild pamphlet enlarged on this evidence of the "heartlessness of management."

Grievances were another harassment. The other ten unions with whom we had contracts seldom called grievance committee meetings. In contrast, the Guild made weekly issues over trivial incidents which could have been ironed out by an employee and his department head. The Guild contract provided that employees be allowed time, at full pay, to attend to Guild business. These absurd meetings were prolonged needlessly for hours, wasting the time of our executives as well as of a dozen members of the grievance committee.

My older employees at the Courier-Post became so disgusted

with these antics, they were prepared to walk out of the Guild in a body. When I heard of the plan, I called a halt. Harry Saylor, Frank Ryan, and my son, Tom, begged me not to interfere.

"There's no living with the Guild," they kept telling me. "You might as well face the fact it's Commie-controlled. Ever since your stand against the United Front, you've been a marked man with the Communists. This needling is their way of getting back at you."

I received calls from Phil Murray, Tom Kennedy, and other CIO leaders, entreating me not to besmirch my record as the friend and champion of unionism. I fell for their blandishments and stopped the Courier-Post revolt.

"It's a young union," I explained to my executives. "We've got to wait for it to grow up. If we are patient and just, eventually they will come around." I was echoing what President Roosevelt said to me after Bullitt told him, "You can't do business with Commies." I presided at a peace meeting between the two factions. The Guild explicitly promised that there would be no reprisals against the leaders of the Courier-Post revolt. Immediately thereafter the Guild assessed fines, totaling more than $3,000. When I paid these fines, I knew that I had made a mistake.

Another mistake was my neglect of the personnel department. Other publishers were carefully screening applicants to avoid employing radicals. I could have organized an efficient personnel department, or contracted for this work to be done by an outside concern, for $25,000 a year. I was too shortsighted to take this safety measure. An assistant business manager, Merrill Lord, was supposed to handle this critical department with one extra secretary. Lord had many other duties, so his check-ups on job applicants were perfunctory. It was easy for Commies to get their converts on our payroll, especially in the departments where we employed women as stenographers, clerks, telephone ad solicitors, etc. At union meetings these girls were more vocal and extreme than the men. During the strike many of these "ladies" made a practice of spitting in the faces of the A. F. of L. union members when they came to work through the Guild's picket line. Because of America's traditional chivalry for the "weaker sex" the police did not interfere with this practice.

Looking back at my many blunders in handling the Guild, I realize that I never grew up from my small-town publishing days. On those first newspapers, in New Brunswick, Springfield, and Camden, I enjoyed complete, unstinted, loyal teamwork. I was friendly and considerate, but this had little to do with it. To command loyalty a boss must know his job and work at it. My men knew I could write news and editorials, copyread, sell advertising, lay out ads and keep books, because they saw me doing it. While I could not set type or thread a press I was well enough acquainted with the mechanical crafts to cut corners and simplify the printers' work. I raised hell when they were afflicted with time-wasting sloppy copy, or too intricate make-up. It takes the spirit out of the mechanical departments if they are slowed up by stupidities in other departments.

On these early ventures I was the first man at the office and usually the last to leave at night. My industry was infectious. I was blessed with hard-working crews. And they seemed to like the strenuous pace I set. They were always ready to pull up stakes and follow me to another newspaper. It was a democratic organization where no one hesitated "to bawl out the boss." Saylor was the severest critic of my editorials, many of which he classified as "pig iron." I abhorred yes men. I never hesitated to admit a mistake and change an order. That was why good men enjoyed working with me.

When I became the champion of unionism and urged my men to organize, I made the mistake of thinking that this had something to do with the loyalty I had come to take as a matter of course. I expected gratitude for my gift of unionization. I should have known better. I should have secretly maneuvered to let unionization be forced upon me. I am not so cynical as to say that you can find gratitude only in the dictionary. I have enjoyed gratitude from my peers, but seldom from subordinates. For gratitude is a two-faced coin with "obligation" on the obverse. Most men resent being placed under personal obligation and the degree of resentment is in ratio to the relative size of donor and donee. Senator Boies Penrose, astute political boss, expressed this most succinctly. In a battle for control of Philadelphia he was told that one of his ward leaders had deserted to the other side. "I can't understand why that fellow went back on me," Penrose said. "I never did anything for him."

When New York was threatened with a strike of elevator operators, I called up Joe Patterson, publisher of the Daily News, to ask how he was going to handle the situation. A walkout by a dozen men would seriously disrupt both the Post and News with departments scattered through high buildings.

"We have no problem," Patterson said. "We're already paying our elevator men more than the union is asking."

The next day Patterson called me back to tell me "those damned fool elevator men voted to join the union and walk out when a strike is called. If the union wins the strike, they won't get higher pay. Now they'll have to pay union dues for no more money or privileges. How do you explain it?"

"That's easy," I said. "They're willing to pay dues for a most important privilege!"

"What privilege?" Patterson asked. "We're already giving them longer vacations, better health protection, and bigger pensions than the union is asking."

"The privilege of demanding their rights instead of feeling under obligation to Sugar Daddy Patterson," was my answer.

It is about time Uncle Sam realized that no matter how generous and tactful he may be, the rich uncle is usually the most unpopular member of the family.

For thirty-five years of provocative publishing I had been on the alert against the many enemies I made. And there were plenty of them—political bosses, public officials, utility tycoons, business leaders, bankers. Using the trick my old swimming coach, George Kistler, had taught me—to think their thoughts—I had anticipated their next moves. But I had not learned that one must watch his friends as closely as his enemies. In this respect I was asleep at the switch. I felt so sure of my position I failed to organize an adequate personnel department, gave in to unreasonable Guild demands and suppressed a revolt within the Guild.

XXII

The Guild Strike

A month before its contract expired in November 1946, the Guild presented its proposal for a new contract. I had expected a stiff one, but this went beyond all reason. It raised the Guild payroll $500,000! Since we would have to grant similar increases to the other unions, the total cost would be $1,000,000 a year.

The proposed contract raised the lower echelons—unskilled workers—to almost the same pay as experienced newspapermen. The Guild asked a minimum of $100 a week for twenty telephone ad solicitors, even though this job required no previous business experience. The average pay for this class of work in Philadelphia was $35. We were paying $45. That was the pattern of their other demands. Gil Kraus declared this was not "bargaining in good faith," as the law specified. When he demanded a more realistic proposal as a basis of negotiations, the Guild replied it would consider management's statement at the next Guild meeting. In the meantime, why not discuss clauses other than the wage scale? Then the negotiating committee proceeded to stall and waste time on trivialities. The Guild asked for a change in a complicated provision that an employee earned seniority while in the armed services. At my suggestion, Gil offered a simplified clause which would give the Guild more than it asked. This ended the time-consuming argument, but it infuriated the Guild negotiators, who accused Gil of an "attempt to undermine us with our membership by granting more than we asked."

There was no pleasing the Guild in those days. It wanted a change in the pregnancy clause which provided leave of absence for a woman employee expecting a baby. Only one expectant mother had taken advantage of this clause in five years. Gil agreed. "We'll accept the change. Reword it to suit yourselves." Thereupon the negotiating committee started an argument among themselves as to just how it should be worded and persisted with these delaying tactics for two days.

By that time we knew what to expect—the Guild wanted a strike. We resolved to get out some kind of newspaper without them. To suspend publication would jeopardize my arrangement with Jefferson Standard Life Insurance Company. All the other unions— typographers, pressmen, stereotypers, photoengravers, mailers, and truck drivers—were strongly on the side of management and openly expressed their disgust with the Guild.

A few days before the Guild contract expired, I met with their committee in a final attempt to put this highly emotional situation back on a rational basis. I told the Guild that the books of the Record Company were open to it or to any reputable auditor it might select. They would show that the Record was earning $700,-000 a year. I was willing to give them half, raises totaling $350,000, and half to the other unions, in the hope that future growth of the newspaper would develop some profit for the stockholders. The one solution I would not accept was a wage scale which would throw the business into bankruptcy. My offer met with stony silence. The Guild had made up its mind to strike.

At the stroke of noon, the day the contract expired, the five hundred Guild members left the building shouting insults and threats. We had guards to prevent sabotage. One energetic young striker did manage to get into the main telephone switchboard room and foul up the lines.

After the hullabaloo was over, I walked into the newsroom. The editorial executives were already at work on the next day's newspaper—all six of them, undertaking a task which normally required two hundred. They were Harry Saylor, editor; Walter Lister, managing editor; Ace (Aubrey) Clarke, assistant managing and night editor; Bergy (Bernard A.) Bergman, assistant managing and Sunday editor; Fred Shapiro, city editor; and Bill Driscoll, sports editor. To these six were added four recruits: Gil Kraus, vice president and general counsel, who proved himself a shark at head writing and copyreading; Dick (Richard) Fishel, promotion manager, who had had experience as a reporter; and the Gold Dust Twins. Joe (Joseph) McGoldrick and Maury (Maurice) Mustin had been handling special advertising for the Courier-Post and the Record for many years. They worked on commission, and therefore were not eligible for Guild membership. A tall Irishman and a short Jew, they were inseparable at work or play—which is how they acquired the nickname Gold Dust Twins.

They were so efficient, I was always trying to promote them into executive positions. I would tempt them with salaries well above what they were earning, talk about future advancement, scold them for not using their remarkable talents to the utmost.

"We're making all we need," they would tell me, "and we like being our own bosses." I suspected that they did not want to be separated as they would have been on our regular staff. They never seemed to work very hard, but always managed to accomplish what they set out to do. A strange, detached, and relaxed pair in the tense atmosphere of a newspaper office, they have not changed in the thirty-five years I have known them and still maintain a nonchalant attitude in this go-getter world. They are wise men.

Joe and Maury proved a godsend during this emergency. For once in their lives they worked hard, eighteen hours a day, seven days a week, sleeping on cots in their office, as did the rest of the skeleton force. Their secretary, Miss Vera Billi, was loaned to me. She replaced Ed Maguire and his three assistants in my outer office. I could not have managed without her. Ed Maguire had resigned from the Guild and wanted to return to work but I was afraid this would make him the target of Guild reprisals.

To relieve Saylor, I took charge of the editorial page, but, as I had other duties, I count myself as a half-helper. Literally ten and a half men wrote and edited four daily and two Sunday editions, for eighty-seven days. Our friends told us the Record was better than ever. Whether this was true or not, circulation held. Evidently the public detected no deterioration in the product.

Eight circulation roadmen had refused to join the Guild. It was their job to call on newsdealers and agents, see that the paper was delivered regularly and properly displayed on newsstands. They lived in the territories to which they were assigned and seldom came to the office. Now Irv Orner called them in to help out. Several ran copy in the newsroom, pasted up stock tables and did other routine jobs. Irv Orner served as a copyreader when he could spare the time. Except for this assistance from the circulation department, the miniscule force produced fourteen pages of news and features six days a week, twenty-six pages on Sundays. They covered important local news by phone, wrote hundreds of headlines a day, edited reams of telegraph news pouring in over three leased wires, captioned art, made page layouts and handled the thousand and one details which go into a metropolitan daily. In all that time, there was not a single garbled story or serious mistake.

This remarkable feat was being duplicated by other departments. In advertising, George Nelson, advertising director, Sam Hill, national manager, Tom Smith, retail manager, and Walter Barkdull, classified manager, were doing the work of a hundred and fifty. Many advertisers showed their friendship for the Record by sending in their copy carefully marked for the compositors, to relieve us of this work, but how these four men managed to handle the detail of one hundred or more display ads a day, besides taking classified ads over the phone, is beyond me. They received some help from the business manager, my nephew, Dave (David Stern) Loeb, and his two assistant business managers, but most of Dave's time was occupied in the accounting department, suddenly reduced from a hundred bookkeepers, clerks, and stenographers to a force of two, the controller, Charles Lynch, and his assistant controller. While our force had been reduced by five hundred fifty, accounting still had to make up the payroll for seven hundred fifty in the mechanical and circulation departments, with deductions for social security, city wage tax, health insurance, etc., as well as bill advertisers and newsdealers.

The mechanical departments, typographers, stereotypers, pressmen, and mailers, co-operated to the limit. Unionism has established sharp boundaries between the work of the various crafts, but under the tactful leadership of Jim Toler, our mechanical superintendent, these rules were forgotten. The whole force entered into the spirit of accomplishing the impossible. Dave Loeb arranged for the best caterer in Philadelphia to supply "all they can eat twenty-four hours a day." This included three shifts of fifty policemen and detectives on strike duty, plus their friends.

"I don't know how many free-loaders we're feeding." Dave Loeb came to me in alarm. "But our food bill is running two thousand dollars a day."

"Sometimes it's smart to be a sucker, and this is certainly such a time," I reassured Dave. "Don't try to stop the free-loaders, but you might tell the caterer to cut out lobster salad and imported smoked salmon."

Besides caterers, we hired masseurs and barbers to keep the force in physical shape and their appearances neat. In contrast to the grim business on which we were engaged, there was an atmosphere of excitement and exuberance throughout the plant. Everyone appeared exhilarated in accomplishing an unusual, if not impossible task.

This miracle was being duplicated across the river, where the Guild had struck the Courier-Post at the same time as the Record. Tom, Frank Ryan, Neal Dyer, and Walter Tushingham were as shorthanded as we were, and they were issuing afternoon as well as morning editions, but no Sunday paper.

       ❋   ❋   ❋   ❋   ❋

Settlement with Jefferson Standard Life Insurance Company went through without a hitch. The representatives of that honorable company did not even mention the strike. The transaction took place in a social hall just outside the Philadelphia city limits to avoid a city tax of one tenth of one per cent which, in this case, would have been $5,500. There were one hundred and twenty documents to be signed, witnessed, and exchanged between the former owners of WCAU, the Record Company, Jefferson, and the Cleveland Society for Savings, whose loan was being paid off. As we came into the room, each of us was handed a list of these documents with the ones he was to sign plainly marked. Dan Lowenthal opened the proceedings by reminding everyone that I was a working man and had to get back to the Record to write editorials. Thanks to Dan's great ability and drive the whole complicated business was completed in less than two hours, which I think is a record for a settlement of such intricacy.

The icing I had put on the cake, the extra quarter of one per cent interest, had no bearing on Jefferson's decision to live up to its commitment. It was run by Southern gentlemen who felt bound to stand by a friend in trouble. Nevertheless, Dan admitted he was glad I had made the "blunder." After I retired, the Bulletin paid off the bonds plus a premium of $137,000 for calling them before they were due. It was one of the most profitable loans Jefferson had ever made.

The settlement completed, I hurried back to the Record office with renewed spirit and determination. A handful of us putting a newspaper together was a challenge. The product was so much better than we had expected we were all keyed up. But after the first month, the seven-day-a-week grind began to wear us down. We kept going on a diet of benzedrine and whiskey. I still wonder how we endured for eighty-seven days. Toward the end I found myself dozing off at the typewriter. We were like contestants in a marathon dance who keep moving in a daze. Most remarkable, none of the ten broke in health or nerves. No one lost his temper or blew his top. We were all too busy and too tired to talk much to one another, even when we relaxed over drinks after the last edition had been put to bed.

The police were maintaining access to the building but many of the mechanical workers preferred to sleep in the plant and avoid the barrage of spit from the women pickets. Meanwhile, the Guild was growing uglier. They recruited the longshoremen's union for mass picketing in an attempt to stop delivery. Prompt police action stopped the first attempt. When the longshoremen found that our truck drivers were still working, they refused to come back.

I tried to reach Phil Murray and Tom Kennedy, who had been so vocal in their appreciation of my championship of trade unionism. My phone calls went unanswered. Lee Pressman, general counsel for the CIO, had the situation under control and he had thumbs down on the Record. Later, under oath, Pressman admitted to a Senate committee that he had been a Communist Party member. Tom Kennedy told me that, at the time of the strike, Pressman completely dominated Phil Murray, who was in poor health. The Record was the newspaper the Communists most feared and hated.

❖   ❖   ❖   ❖   ❖

In the third month of the strike, Al Greenfield walked into my office. He brought an offer from the Bulletin to buy me out for $12,000,000. Al had figured that, after paying all debts, minority stockholders and capital gains tax, I would have enough left to make me comfortable in old age.

"Old age? Where do you get that stuff?" I snorted.

"You're sixty-one," Al replied. "At the pace you're going, drinking a quart of whiskey a day and chain smoking those Winston Churchill cigars, I don't give you many years. You nearly kicked the bucket last fall when you had pneumonia."

"I've got a job to do," I snapped. I was thinking of the editorials I had to write before press time. Al took another meaning from my words.

"Dave, you have been doing a great job, for the working man and the underdog. You were the first publisher to recognize the Guild. And what has it got you? The people you've fought for are trying to cut your throat."

"Only one crazy, Commie-controlled union. All the other unions are backing us up loyally."

"I'm sure you're going to win," Al said as he rose to leave. "The whole city is for you and your men. Maybe you can keep it up for a few more years and then Tom can take over. But when you retire, it will be with less money than the Bulletin is offering you now. Dave, you've worked hard for forty years. I know you haven't saved a cent. If anything happened to you and your newspapers, Jill would receive a little insurance money. You owe it to your wife and children to grab this chance to get out on easy street."

Al had touched my Achilles heel. I had no savings. For twenty years I had been drawing a large salary but had laid nothing aside.

My only asset was stock in my newspapers. If anything happened to them, Jill would get nothing but $100,000 in life insurance. I explained the situation to Jill and to my sister Agnes, who was the next largest stockholder. In spite of this they were both opposed to my selling. I was still undecided when a trivial incident made up my mind.

On January 15, 1947, the Courier-Post contract with the Typographical Union expired. When Tom told me the union demands I said, "They know we're in no position to argue with them. Under the circumstances, I think their demands are fair. I advise accepting them." A few days later, Tom phoned me. "Dad, we broke the record for the shortest negotiation meeting, five minutes. The contract committee will present the contract to the union meeting for ratification next Sunday." I dismissed the matter from my mind.

Tom phoned me Sunday evening. The union had turned down the recommendation of its committee and voted to demand a still greater increase in its scale. But what especially galled me, the union served notice that unless its terms were accepted within twenty-four hours it would strike.

So the Typographical Union was turning against me, the oldest union, with which I had dealt amicably for thirty-five years. What was happening in this cockeyed world? I phoned Al Greenfield, "Go ahead."

I learned later that a bitter quarrel within the union was the cause of its strange and untimely action. To embarrass their officers, who were members of the negotiating committee, the majority voted against acceptance of the recommended new contract. The officers were so furious they denounced this vote in such extreme language they brought the meeting to fever heat. It was in this atmosphere, and in further defiance of the officers, that the meeting voted its increased demands and its twenty-four-hour strike ultimatum. But when this was explained to me it was too late. I had already met with Bob (Robert) McLean, publisher of the Bulletin, and made a verbal agreement.

Dan Lowenthal worked with his usual dispatch and efficiency. Within two weeks the sale was consummated. It covered all assets of the Courier-Post and Record companies, including the recently acquired WCAU and the newsprint mill under construction in Canada. So well had the negotiations been kept under cover that no one at the Record, except Harry Saylor and Gil Kraus, had any inkling of what was happening.

I sent word to make-up to leave space for a "two-column box frontpage top." I was very tired when I brought the copy for the box to the composing room at 6 P.M. It announced suspension of the Record and Courier-Post.

After lock-up for the first edition at 6:45, the compositors left for supper. They took proofs of this suspension announcement and slapped them on the bar where the Guild strikers held out.

"Here's what you've done," the compositors told the Guild men. "Now we're all out."

At the beginning of this book is my first newspaper story, about a Mazdaznanist meeting, written as a cub reporter in June, 1908. My last piece of newspaper writing, dated February 1, 1947, read as follows:

Statement by The Record

This is the last issue of The Philadelphia Record under my management. Publication is suspended as of today.

The strike against The Record by the American Newspaper Guild has continued for nearly three months. It has been impossible to obtain a fair settlement which would enable this newspaper to discharge its obligation to the public.

This is not only because of the Guild's present excessive demands. Guild policy has been to restrict the rights of management to a degree where it has become too great a burden to operate a completely independent press.

I do not attempt to explain this strange attitude of Guild leadership. I only know that The Record, Philadelphia's liberal newspaper, has been chosen as a target for its unusual theories.

No other of the numerous unions with which The Record has had contracts for many years, has adopted such an attitude.

The assets of The Record Co. will be sold to The Evening Bulletin which is issuing an accompanying statement.

XXIII

Scar Tissue

After the strike and my retirement I was feeling very sorry for myself.

"There's nothing left of me but scar tissue" was the way I expressed it.

Scar tissue is ugly but it has advantages. It is tougher and less sensitive than the skin it replaces. Survival would be impossible were it not for this miracle of reconstruction. Under mysterious, subconscious direction, millions of cells are marshaled to patch up damage to the body.

Repair of wounds in mind and spirit is no less marvelous than the phenomenon we can watch on the surface. This inward mending must leave its scars as the process does on the outside. And no matter how sheltered or fortunate a life may be, it must suffer some of these spiritual scars. Their formation marks transition from child to adult. My early encounter with the skeleton in my uncle's closet must have left the first patch of scar tissue in my mental make-up.

I have not recalled all these inward wounds. I have tried to be objective, but, as I have already written, it is impossible for a reporter to be completely impartial—and this is especially true when the subject is himself. It is our fortunate tendency to remember the pleasant, forget the painful. Otherwise, life would be grim and the race tracks out of business. The bettor remembers and tells about the days he cleaned up at the track, forgets the time he was cleaned out.

A man who chooses an active life suffers many wounds and develops much scar tissue, which makes him tougher, less sensitive and sympathetic. The present fulminations of the angry young men leave me cold. Yet, half a century ago, I was classified as one of them. To tell the truth, many of them exasperated me then as they do now. Impatient of orderly reform, they keep demanding a man on a white horse to cure all the ills of mankind overnight.

Some of my most painful disillusionments and wounds came when extremists deserted the New Deal. Tired of marching in the middle of the road, they insisted on walking in one of the gutters, and it was usually the righthand gutter—Huey Long, Father Coughlin, Ed Flynn, Ray Moley among others. During Roosevelt's first Administration, I checked in at the Mayflower Hotel in Washington one forenoon. When I called Huey Long's room he said, "I'm still in bed but come up." I found Huey, clad in purple silk pajamas, stretched out in bed. Father Coughlin was pacing up and down the room, his head bowed, his hands clasped behind his back. He kept repeating over and over again, "I fear there will be a revolution. I fear there will be a revolution." Suddenly Huey leaped from bed to shout, "Hell, what I'm afraid of is that there won't be a revolution." Both these men had professed accord with my editorials. Huey had read many of them into the Congressional Record. Father Coughlin had quoted them in his national radio broadcasts. I left that room with the sickening sensation of a man who has just discovered that his friends are out of their minds. I never saw either of them again.

While I may have forgotten many other such painful episodes, I have tried to give a fair account of the trials and tribulations of a liberal publisher who kept to the middle of the road.

❊   ❊   ❊   ❊   ❊

Now that I have had time to think—what do I think?

I look back at my cocksureness, my faith in the nostrums I peddled to my readers—and laugh. How differently those editorial cure-alls have worked out, and with what unexpected side effects, as in the case of recently discovered wonder drugs. Why did I not foresee that organized labor, grown strong, would be just as selfish and shortsighted as management?

But I still believe in unions—to paraphrase the barroom ditty about the sailor's sweetheart. As the song goes, "She still believes in sailors," even after she has been deserted and "left brokenhearted with a dozen children." The reason for this persistent faith, "He was all she ever had," sounds like a non sequitur. I understand the grass widow's logic. If asked, she would have explained, "Soldiers and drummers are worse even than sailors." I still believe trade unions are essential to a free economy because any other method of maintaining balance between payroll and profits would be "worse even." Government regulation of pay scales is socialism, which is the soft word for slavery.

A generation ago, when unions were fighting for recognition, liberals crusaded for them and accorded them every advantage in labor laws. Unions, still struggling to organize underpaid workers, should continue to enjoy this preferred position in the eyes of the law. But strong, well-heeled unions which have achieved high wages, short hours, and liberal fringe benefits are in a different category. They must be regulated by laws as strict as those which hold private business accountable for any damage it inflicts and prohibits combinations in restraint of trade. The established union can be no more free than other forms of free enterprise.

"Freedom" is one of those sacred slogans which liberals like to worship as an absolute. There is no such state as absolute freedom. Even the anarchists have to resort to "syndicalism" as a euphemism for government control. The wisest words on freedom I ever heard were from Mrs. Sara Roosevelt, mother of the President. It was at Hyde Park in 1936. Franklin Jr. and John, the President's sons, there for the Easter vacation, came down to breakfast at 11:30 A.M.

"I'm not surprised you get up so late," their grandmother said. "Because you go to bed so late. I heard you come in. Where were you until two-thirty this morning?"

"Grandma, can't you leave us free to lead our lives?" Franklin parried the question.

"Free to lead your lives!" Grandmother snapped. "No one is free to lead his own life. Everyone is obligated to family, friends, and country. Franklin, you're grown-up enough to know that."

Unions are grown-up enough to realize their freedom is limited by obligations to others. They have graduated from those earlier years when public opinion was prejudiced in their favor, as it was for St. George against the dragon, and David against Goliath.

It was a lesson I had to learn when I became a successful monopoly publisher instead of a youngster rescuing down-and-out small-town newspapers. In New Brunswick and Springfield the crowd was for me as it is at an athletic meet watching a high jumper attempt to clear the bar. Those towns and my staffs were indulgent of my idiosyncracies. When I became successful the atmosphere changed. The public was as critical as before it had been tolerant. Dignity, diplomacy, consideration for others, were expected of me. I had to watch my step.

Many labor leaders do not appreciate their change in status. They still conduct themselves as though they were the underdogs who can count on public support no matter what they do. Unless these union tycoons learn the lesson that the price of success is obligation to the common good they will destroy free trade unionism.

⁂   ⁂   ⁂   ⁂   ⁂

While I smile at my youthful idealism it is not because I was more dogmatic than others. The idealist is usually dogmatic. Whether as editor, politician, or theologian, the reformer shouts from the rooftop, "I have the magic cure, the sure way to the millennium." This ardor for new causes has brought a peck of trouble. Because of it mankind wobbles down the ages from one extreme to the other, like a child learning to ride a bicycle. In his tense effort to keep his balance he swerves too far to the right, then too far to the left. He is not sure where he is going or whether he will fall off before he gets there. But wherever he lands, be it in flowerbed or gutter, he swears that is the spot to which he was steering.

This bluff is particularly difficult for my generation, which landed in the manure pile, composed of the bloodiest wars, massacres, and genocides in history, topped off by atomic holocausts. Nothing daunted, mankind wriggles out of the filth, remounts its bicycle and goes wobbling on it knows not where, but still pretending it does. This time our announced destination is world peace with justice, and we appear to be approaching it as surely as our ancestors did when they erected the Tower of Babel.

Man is a funny little animal who talks big. Ever since he found he could fashion stones into tools and weapons to conquer other beasts he has considered himself the dominant species, made in the image of God. But the greater his progress in toolmaking and technology, the less sure he has become of his position and purpose in the general scheme of things. Some thousands of years ago he lived in the center of the universe. Wherever he drew a map, in Athens, Alexandria, or Rome, there was the exact hub around which the sun and planets revolved. His king was a god, or a descendant of the gods, which afforded living proof of man's divine design.

Science ejected man from his vantage point, destroyed his egoistic self-deception. Reluctantly he had to admit that he was not at the center of the universe, that the earth was round and revolved about the sun. After this demotion he still clung to the belief that his sun was the center of the universe. But the scientists were not through with shrinking man's ego. They proved the sun was only a middling star amidst myriads of others in a universe vast beyond comprehension. And, as if that were not enough, modern astronomers assert the earth is only one among millions of planets capable of supporting life.

Having demoted man from the center of the universe to a remote and inconsequential corner, science attacked his self-aggrandizement from another angle. Darwin and his disciples forced man to admit, most reluctantly—with much back talk from fundamentalists at the Scopes trial—that he is not cast in a special divine mold, that he is merely a species of animal, which must some day become extinct as have billions of other forms of life.

For the dominant species it is all most embarrassing and depressing. Of course man is proud of his scientific progress, but as his knowledge has grown, his place and importance in the universe has diminished. What especially preys on his mind is the zoologist's prediction of the eventual and inevitable extinction of Homo sapiens—by population explosion if not by nuclear explosion, by the earth wobbling on its axis, as it has before, if not by the disintegration of the solar system. Subconscious dread of species-extinction reveals itself whenever man hears of the imminent end of some form of life. Be it the buffalo, the whooping crane, or the platypus which is about to disappear from the face of the earth, experts rush to the rescue. Public concern is registered by the newspapers, which herald the birth of a baby crane as prominently as that of a prince. Why such beating of drums if it were not for man's underlying fear, "Some day this will happen to me?"

The march of science has had other effects. Darwinism has jolted that self-assuring concept "made in the image of God." Man is constructed like an Addison Mizner mansion at Palm Beach. When that eccentric architect forgot some essential part of a house, such as the stairway, he slapped it on the outside. All of man's numerous organs are neatly packed in his carcass—all except his genitals, which seem to have been added as an afterthought and just at the outlet of his sewer system, with which the genitals had to be combined. The more civilized man becomes, the more embarrassed he is about himself. He wobbles from primitive phallic worship to prudery so extreme that mere mention of his bodily functions is taboo, and then to Rabelaisian jests about the droll animal he is.

Nor has the marvelous acceleration of communications bolstered man's self-esteem. In ancient times, located at the hub of the universe, he heard little of what went on outside his immediate neighborhood, and cared less. Now he is in instant touch with all the world. But the emphasis is on bad news, on his failures rather than his achievements, on meanness rather than altruism, on his weakness rather than his strength. Reading his newspaper he shudders at his iniquities, his stupidities, and his helplessness.

If two bank presidents in his town make the news on the same day, one by absconding with a million dollars, the other by donating a million to charity, the absconder gets the big headline. In this particular instance there is an obvious reason for the editor's evaluation of the news. Fortunately, more bank presidents give to charity than abscond. The unusual is an element of news. But there are other factors in this overemphasis of the negative. Man craves the melodramatic in his news as in his drama and literature. The more orderly and humdrum his life, the greater his appetite for violence and crime by proxy. Only a few newspapers refuse to pander to this craving. But most editors, who are after circulation, not only overplay crime, but smear on a little extra blood. The present popularity of Westerns on screen and television is a reaction to our exceedingly orderly existence. I have not led a particularly sheltered life but it is now fifty-five years since the one and only time I saw a gun fired in anger, in Goldfield, Nevada. I do not remember seeing a fist fight since the back street brawls in my teen-age days. Less than 10 per cent of our soldiers experienced hand-to-hand combat. The sensational newspaper supplies relief from this oppressive lack of violence. In a nation of 185,000,000 there is always someone running amok or caught with the other man's wife. If, by small chance no American has done anything dreadful within the past twelve hours, the most horrendous event in Europe, Asia, or Africa becomes the big news of the day.

This overemphasis of the negative is not confined to acts of violence. Misconduct of a government official takes precedence over his public accomplishment. The bureaucrat who accepts the gift of a rug or a mink coat is on the front page. His colleague who has arranged for the building of a dam which will make fertile 100,000 barren acres must be content with mention on an inside page. It will take five years to complete the dam, and more years before the desert turns green, a long and complicated process. The improper gifts are simple, direct, and immediate.

What if the same official who is responsible for the dam receives the mink coat? Are the two stories played in parallel columns, the good balanced against the bad? I do not remember ever seeing such treatment of the not uncommon coincidence. One or the other story takes precedence and ninety-nine times out of a hundred the negative comes out on top, with the implication that a man who would accept an improper gift has probably collected graft from a badly built dam. As I write this, the New York newspapers, for three days, have been headlining the making of a four-hundred-dollar skiff in a vocational high school for the superintendent of schools, administrative head of a half-a-billion-a-year educational operation. This lack of proportion is the cardinal sin of modern journalism, and most confusing to the public.

In his autobiography, Lincoln Steffens, arch muckraker of municipal and state governments, came to the conclusion that grafters often gave more progressive and constructive administrations than reformers. The worst deficiencies of government are lack of ideas, initiative, and plain stupidity. In Camden the Baird machine was comparatively honest, but without knowledge of or desire for up-to-date city planning. In Philadelphia it was not the 10 or 20 per cent graft contractor-bosses collected from subway construction which stymied the city's growth. It was the failure to plan the underground system. As a result many of these costly caverns remain empty and unused after half a century—and others had to be torn out and rebuilt.

Newspapers perform a public service by uncovering and reporting dishonesty. But the way in which it is blown up out of all proportion to its significance diverts public attention from vital problems. There are absolutely honest individuals. But an absolutely honest public or private organization is as unlikely as a city without a sinner. I was forever trying to stop payola on my newspapers. I kept it at a minimum, but I am not so foolish as to think I ever entirely eradicated it. Some of it I overlooked, such as the so-called swindle sheets (expense accounts) of reporters and advertising salesmen. Sometimes I got a good laugh out of the tricks which were pulled on me. The ink racket was one of my pet abominations. Because there is no scientific test of ink the publisher must depend on the report of his press foreman as to whether a brand of ink is satisfactory. The foreman is usually on the payroll of the ink company. One of the best foremen I ever had swore to me that he had never accepted a cent from any ink company. It was only after his death that I found out that for years he had had the use of an Atlantic City summer home, rent free.

Saylor sent for a wrestling promoter who was paying a hundred dollars a week to a sports reporter. The promoter could not understand Saylor's objection to what was considered standard procedure in the wrestling business. After a long lecture on the ethics of journalism the promoter said, "Mr. Saylor, I get you." The next day cases of Scotch whiskey and vintage champagne were delivered to Saylor's apartment.

Once I tried to get a paper bag contract for my friend Pop Gil-man from one of the largest companies in the world. The buyer, who received a salary of $10,000, was grafting. When I finally reached the top of the company I expressed my surprise that a man who bought a hundred million dollars of supplies received such a small salary. The most able head executive explained it to me: "If we paid him a hundred thousand a year instead of ten thousand he would still take. This way we save ninety thousand dollars."

     *   *   *   *   *

Disproportionate reporting afflicts all departments of the modern newspaper, even the financial section. As conservative a newspaper as The New York Times will headline a sudden ten-billion-dollar drop or rise in value of stocks on the New York Exchange. This figure is arrived at by applying the percentage of change in one day's trading against all the securities listed on the exchange. Such a projection is as absurd and untrue as if a village weekly headlined REAL ESTATE VALUES CUT IN HALF because one of the five hundred homes in the community had been sold at a low price.

The constant tendency to sensationalize, to dramatize, to make a mountain out of a molehill, so distorts the news that it often creates an impression which is the exact opposite of the truth. Prediction of the number of fatal accidents during a holiday weekend, Fourth of July or Labor Day, is a usual front-page feature. On Saturday and Sunday we read the death count and learn by how much it is exceeding or falling short of the estimates. Measured by millions of passenger-miles, the holiday fatalities vary little from the day-to-day average. As our highway systems and traffic controls improve there are fewer accidents per passenger-miles. But such a statistical approach is avoided. 650 TO DIE ON HIGHWAY THIS WEEKEND is a more sensational headline than PREDICT FEWER ACCIDENTS IN PROPORTION TO HOLIDAY TRAFFIC. Newspaper editors may believe they are serving the public interest by scaring auto drivers into being more careful. I think their reasoning is wrong. A report on improvement of highway safety would stimulate better driving—and it would be the truth.

Lack of proportion in modern reporting and evaluation of news is not entirely due to sensationalism. Most of our communication experts, the reporters, broadcasters, and politicians, are not number-minded. They shun figures and percentages. In prep school I noted that, with rare exceptions, the boys who had an aptitude for language were weak in mathematics. As a publisher I found the hardest jobs to fill were in the financial department—those requiring men who could write well about figures. I used to say that we did not have a top reporter on our staffs who could count above ten. It was an exaggeration with a germ of truth. The few who are endowed with both talents are usually drafted from journalism into other better-paying positions. Red Garrett and Harry Kalodner, already mentioned, are conspicuous examples.

Washington's articulates, both politicians and correspondents, thunder the horrendous warning that the national debt is approaching the stupendous sum of three hundred billion dollars. Seldom if ever do they mention that, as a percentage of gross national product, the national debt has been decreasing. With many variables, such as population, income, and value of the dollar, it is senseless to offer bare dollar figures without a frame of reference. A personal indebtedness of $30,000 has one significance for the man with a $3,000 income, another for a man with a $300,000 income.

I am reminded of a profound question put to me by my granddaughter when she was eight. "Grandaddy, how many is too many?" she asked. I explained that I could not answer unless I could read her mind. "If you are thinking of how many pieces of candy you can have after lunch, five is too many. If you are inquiring how many friends you can invite to your birthday party, I agree with your mother, twenty is too many. Numbers without a frame of reference have no meaning." When will our newsmen learn that truism? As our civilization has become more complicated the reporting of its problems demands more intelligence and technical knowledge. Modern journalism has not risen to this higher requirement. While communication has grown prodigiously in volume and facility, so that modern man is deluged with a plethora of words on paper and in the air, it has not advanced in wisdom or knowledge. As a result man is more confused and depressed than in ancient days when his only news of the world came from the occasional traveler.

*   *   *   *   *

Modern artists, dramatists, and novelists, like journalists, seem intent on shrinking man's ego. Time was when painter and sculptor glorified man's form, his religious and daily life. Today, if the artist is not concocting meaningless abstracts, he is distorting, caricaturing, and rubbing it in that "you are indeed a funny little animal." Most of our novelists and playwrights are obsessed with the same theme. The old-fashioned novel or drama offered at least one noble, courageous hero in conflict with the villain. While this romantic contrast of black and white may not have been realistic, it was at least more encouraging to man's ego than the present gray monotone which insists on the weakness and wickedness of all characters.

Belittled by the scientist, confused by the journalist, disparaged by the artist, man, in defense of his ego, must perforce turn to the theologian, who bolsters man's self-appraisal by telling him he is created in God's image, with a divine soul and mission. But at the same time the theologian insists that man is conceived in sin, is inherently wicked and dependent for his earthly happiness and future life on the mercy of an Almighty.

For a growing minority the theologian's combination of divinity and depravity offers no solace. It is not because science makes it difficult to accept the dogma and tradition with which most religions are encrusted. There are sects which minimize, if they do not entirely avoid, conflict between science and a Divine Power. What has turned many away from religion is modern history, which proves that man is still as intent on killing his fellow as was his caveman ancestor. Religion may have raised man's estimate of himself, but has it improved his character, self-control, kindliness and consideration of his neighbor? Events of the last forty years indicate that modern man, under stress, is as bloodthirsty as he was when he first heard the Sermon on the Mount.

The modern, nonreligious man is forced by science to admit that he does not know and cannot know the why and wherefore of his existence. His only fulfillment can be in his own happiness. Since we share with so many other forms of life the herd or beehive instinct, individual happiness is enhanced by working for the greatest good of the greatest number. In this concept modern man, especially the American, can find some hope and satisfaction. Never before has so large a percentage of a nation's population enjoyed so much comfort, leisure, and physical health. The marvelous progress of medicine has doubled the span of life. We can envisage the not too distant future when the average age will be one hundred, and euthanasia will be allowed to oldsters who become bored with living. The chances of an untimely death by disease will be so reduced that the dread of death will be no greater than fear of being struck by lightning in a summer storm. The work week will not be reduced below thirty hours because most men will not know what to do with more leisure. The creature comforts and conveniences of the average family will approach those of the rich, and the disrupting gap between the haves and the have-nots will disappear. The underprivileged will be cut to one per cent, an irreducible minimum of misfits. To contemplate and strive for such a millennium is inspiring.

But as we Americans advance rapidly toward that goal, we are disturbed by some of the side effects of well-being. The better off we are, the more tense and nervous we become—chain smoking billions of cigarettes, consuming tons of sedatives, and, when we have enough money, asking psychoanalysts to discover why we are not happy. It is more than a joke that the mark of success is a stomach ulcer.

If the greatest happiness of the greatest number be our goal, are we achieving it? May there not be as much or more happiness in the simpler civilizations, the so-called underprivileged and backward communities? We have no way of knowing because we have no way of measuring happiness, the most important and indefinite of all concepts.

The stress and striving to which I chose to subject myself for so many years did not make for happiness. During the short periods between newspapers when I should have been enjoying my good fortune I had worked myself into such a state that I fretted at relief from tension. Probably that is the reason I have enjoyed retirement and the leisurely writing of this accounting to myself of many blunders and a few achievements. In my active, articulate days I was very sure I knew the answers, and I put all the force of eloquence I could muster into pointing the way. That was what my readers wanted. If I had expressed my present state of mind, that mankind does not know where it is going, what it wants, or how it can achieve it, I would have been out of business.

I do not wonder that man covers his confusion and uncertainty with arrogance and dogma. Each time he finds himself up a blind alley he must bolster his courage and self-confidence by asserting he has found another way to everlasting peace and happiness. No matter how many times the new plans fail—as, recently, with prohibition, and, probably in the near future, with the United Nations —man is always ready to listen to the next huckster and buy his elixir.

I look back and laugh at the strong medicine I peddled and in which I had such complete confidence. But more important than the failure of the cure-alls is the faith which renews itself after each disappointment. We may laugh at the perplexed and pretentious little animal who talks big, but we must admire his courage and persistence.

The danger to man is not that his formulas fail to cure but that he gives up trying new ones, that he sinks into complacent acceptance of the status quo. There lies the peril of the monopoly newspaper. The competitive newspapers may have sold some bad medicine, but they did whip up interest, did make their readers care about public issues. The monopoly newspaper, presenting news which will offend no one, arouse no emotions, tread on no one's toes, offers soothing syrup as the cure for mankind's bellyache.

While local newspaper competition is about to become as extinct as the dinosaur, there may yet develop competition between national dailies, printed and distributed in all sections of the country. Great Britain has such a national competitive system. I must admit it has not raised the standards of journalism in that country, but it has counteracted the deadening effect of local monopolies.

While I laugh at my part in journalism I still have faith in the future, and enough curiosity to want to live a few years more to see how it works out. I may yet read the national liberal daily which President Roosevelt and I planned twenty years ago and which is so sorely needed to keep this country in balance. Judging by my experience, such a publication, courageously and competently edited, would develop a large and sympathetic audience.

Looking back, the most significant aspect of my newspaper experience was the more than fair hearing I was accorded. To four of the five cities where I published newspapers, I came as a stranger. I voiced new points of view in editorials which were often raucous and abrasive. I was a noncomformist, a maverick. That I won some followers was to be expected. But leaders of the opposition, who did not agree with my political philosophy, often came to my support. In Springfield, Camden, Philadelphia, and New York, conservatives invested in my enterprises. In each particular case there may have been other motives, but the recurrence of this pattern in different communities proves how strongly Americans desire fair play and a fair hearing for all sides. Also my experience indicates how tired readers are of anemic editorial policies. They hunger for bold, forceful newspapers. I am confident their hunger will be satisfied before it is too late.

Index

316